T0221025

Computer-Aided Policymaking:

Lessons from
strategic planning software

Computer-Aided Policymaking:

Lessons from
strategic planning software

Ray Wyatt

Routledge
Taylor & Francis Group

LONDON AND NEW YORK

First published 1999 by Taylor & Francis

Published 2017 by Routledge
2 Park Square, Milton Park, Abingdon, Oxon OX14 4RN
711 Third Avenue, New York, NY 10017, USA

Routledge is an imprint of the Taylor & Francis Group, an informa business

This book was commissioned and edited by Alexandrine Press, Oxford

Typeset in Times and Frutiger by NP Design & Print

The publisher makes no representation, expressed or implied, with regard to the accuracy
of the information contained in this book and cannot accept any legal responsibility or
liability for any errors or omissions that may be made.

British Library Cataloguing in Publication Data
A catalogue record for this book is available from the British Library

Library of Congress Cataloguing in Publication Data
Wyatt, Ray.
   Computer-aided policymaking : lessons from strategic planning software / Ray
Wyatt.
      p.   cm.
   Includes bibliographic references and index.
   ISBN 0–419–24480–8
   1. Strategic planning — Comuputer programs.   I. Title.
   HD30.28.W93   1999
   658.4'012'028553 — dc21   99–29084
                                                                CIP

ISBN 978-0-419-24480-6 (pbk)

for Sandra

Contents

PREFACE   xi

ACKNOWLEDGEMENTS   xiv

INTRODUCTION   **xv**
    Managing complexity   xv
    Traditional approaches   xvi
    An alternative   xvii
    Problems   xviii
    Strengths   xx

1   SILICON AND CARBON   **1**

  1.1   SOFTWARE AND POLICYMAKING   2
      1.1.1   Software   2
      1.1.2   Planning   4
      1.1.3   Types of problem   6
      1.1.4   Strategic planning 9

  1.2   STYLES OF POLICYMAKING   12
      1.2.1   Posturing at the periphery   12
      1.2.2   Types of human personality   17
      1.2.3   Types of software 18

  1.3   SUMMARY   21

2   TRADITIONAL SOFTWARE   **22**

  2.1   THE TRADITIONAL APPROACH   22
      2.1.1   A common method   24
      2.1.2   Different emphases 26
      2.1.3   Different terminologies   27

  2.2   GENERIC SOFTWARE   29
      2.2.1   Comprehensive packages   29
      2.2.2   Multi-criteria packages   33
      2.2.3   Path-finding packages   37

  2.3   DEDICATED SOFTWARE   38
      2.3.1   Packages to assist thinking   38
      2.3.2   Packages to assist choosing   43
      2.3.3   Packages to assist anticipating 44

  2.4   SUMMARY   47

3   SUPPORTING SOFTWARE   **48**

3.1   GENERIC SOFTWARE   48

    3.1.1   Decision support packages   48
    3.1.2   Groupware packages   55
    3.1.3   Gameware packages   56
    3.1.4   Data mining packages   59

3.2   DOMAIN-SPECIFIC SOFTWARE   60

    3.2.1   Business packages   61
    3.2.2   Non-business packages   66

3.3   SUMMARY   69

4   EMERGING SOFTWARE   **70**

4.1   CHANGING THE PARADIGM   70

    4.1.1   Soft systems methodology   72
    4.1.2   Boosterism   76
    4.1.3   Cognitive science packages   79

4.2   INNOVATIVE SOFTWARE   82

    4.2.1   Artificial intelligence packages   82
    4.2.2   Distributed computing packages   88

4.3   SUMMARY   91

5   FRONTIER SOFTWARE CASE I: *CyberQuest*   **92**

5.1   ANALYSING THE SITUATION   94

    5.1.1   Exploring concepts   97
    5.1.2   Clustering concepts   98
    5.1.3   Nominating key words   98

5.2   GENERATING IDEAS   100

    5.2.1   Matching key words with words
             in databases   100
    5.2.2   Thinking laterally   101
    5.2.3   A richness of ideas   103

5.3   PACKAGING IDEAS   105

    5.3.1   Rating ideas   105
    5.3.2   Reviewing ideas   108

5.4   SUMMARY   112

6   FRONTIER SOFTWARE CASE II: *STRAD*   **114**

6.1   RECORDING ISSUES   116

    6.1.1   Neutralizing conflict   116

	6.1.2	Grouping decision areas	118
	6.1.3	Decomposing the problem	120
6.2	**COMPARING GOALS**		**121**
	6.2.1	Assessing actions	122
	6.2.2	The perils of popularity	124
	6.2.3	Rating goals	125
6.3	**CRAFTING GOOD STRATEGIES**		**128**
	6.3.1	Eliminating schemes	129
	6.3.2	Managing uncertainty	131
	6.3.3	Policymaking amid turbulence	133
6.4	**SUMMARY**		**136**

7   FRONTIER SOFTWARE CASE III: *Expert Choice*   137

7.1	**IDENTIFYING ALTERNATIVES**		**138**
	7.1.1	Structuring the problem	138
	7.1.2	Accommodating possible scenarios	144
	7.1.3	Accommodating possible actors	145
7.2	**RATING ALTERNATIVES**		**146**
	7.2.1	Scoring	146
	7.2.2	Making paired comparisons	149
	7.2.3	Correcting inconsistency	152
7.3	**REVIEWING THE RATINGS**		**154**
	7.3.1	Re-scoring	156
	7.3.2	Sensitivity analysis	156
	7.3.3	Extending the software	160
7.4	**SUMMARY**		**163**

8   FRONTIER SOFTWARE CASE IV: *Strategizer*   165

8.1	**CONSTRUCTING A HIERARCHY**		**167**
	8.1.1	Identifying the client and options	168
	8.1.2	Formal versus informal policymaking	171
	8.1.3	Accumulating knowledge	174
8.2	**SCORING THE POLICIES**		**175**
	8.2.1	Scientific criteria	177
	8.2.2	Operations Research criteria	178
	8.2.3	Philosophical criteria	179
	8.2.4	Workshop criteria	179
8.3	**ANTICIPATING OTHERS' RATINGS**		**180**
	8.3.1	Identifying different groups	181

	8.3.2	Identifying different policymaking styles	184
	8.3.3	Ensuring the package self-improves	186
8.4	SUMMARY		191

9 A UNITED FRONTIER? — **192**

9.1	THINK		193
	9.1.1	Generating ideas	193
	9.1.2	Deleting ideas	196
	9.1.3	Packaging ideas	196
9.2	CHOOSE		197
	9.2.1	Identifying policies	198
	9.2.2	Evaluating policies	202
	9.2.3	Assigning scores to policies	203
9.3	ANTICIPATE		208
	9.3.1	Reflecting	209
	9.3.2	Managing uncertainty	212
	9.3.3	Learning people's preferences	213
9.4	COMBINING PACKAGES		214
9.5	SUMMARY		215

10 CONCLUSION — **216**

10.1	RECOMMENDATIONS		216
	1 Think laterally		216
	2 Think by decomposing the problem		218
	3 Choose by evaluating options comprehensively		218
	4 Choose after considering alternative scenarios		219
	5 Anticipate by foreshadowing people's reactions		220
	6 Anticipate by managing uncertainty		221
10.2	NOW WHAT?		221

| REFERENCES | 229 |
| INDEX | 239 |

Preface

Gurus from business schools are fond of churning out popular books on 'strategic planning'. Such texts usually chant an inspirational, 'you can beat the world' message that is supported only by eloquent logic, glib anecdote and selected case studies. Whether or not they have led to improved policymaking remains an open question.

Indeed, some researchers have actually examined the evidence. They have concluded that strategic planning might not be worth the effort (Mintzberg, 1994). That is, they have found it impossible to demonstrate, rigorously, that strategic planning invariably increases the chances of good outcomes. Good outcomes frequently occur when no strategic planning has been undertaken at all. Yet the literature continues to burgeon. Perhaps strategic planning is better than its alternative – no strategic planning.

Accordingly, we present a different sort of book. It does not base its arguments solely on the usual parables, rhetoric and case-based propaganda. It derives its lessons from the advice with which all policymaking software bristles. Those who doubt that we can learn better policymaking from software should note that the game of chess is a form of policymaking – one needs to choose an overall policy in order to set the 'direction' of one's subsequent tactical moves. And in May 1997 a chess-playing computer defeated the world's best human player. It seems, therefore, that we might learn much.

To appreciate software's didactic power, consider how a typical package develops. Its author shows it to many people. Such people feel obliged to make comments in the form of 'what about?' questions like 'What about local politics?' and 'What about changing the scoring method?' These questions prompt considerable soul searching by the software writer who goes back to the drawing board, to write yet another version, in an attempt to accommodate this latest round of 'what about' suggestions. Put differently, all serious policymaking software has graduated from the 'school of hard knocks'. Many individuals, managers, planners and ordinary folk have used and maligned it, and such criticism from its less-than-impressed users has greatly improved subsequent versions. The 'white hot cauldron of criticism' has made policymaking software an untapped source of methodological wisdom. We will mine some of it.

As software becomes more sophisticated the number of lessons it supplies should increase. But whether or not this means that software is destined to play a growing role in human policymaking is an interesting question that will often be referred to in the chapters below. Will policymaking remain the quintessential human activity, or will software eventually be able to think sufficiently like humans to substitute for them? In the conclusion we will present an answer to this question, perhaps a surprising one.

In the meantime, many programs have been written to help, and here we milk them for their lessons which will be applicable to almost any field. Good policymaking is the same whether it is undertaken within a company, a public body, a non-government agency, a neighbourhood group or a household. Exemplary policymaking has the same characteristics whether it aims at improved market share, social cohesion, famine relief, survival for the local primary school or even a tastier evening meal. Although business policymakers might be more interested in profit; government policymakers more concerned with social cohesion and domestic policymakers more aware of inter-personal relationships, the fundamental, underlying methods of good policymaking do not vary. Thus by concentrating on such methods we will try to improve *everybody's* policymaking no matter what discipline, if any, they are from.

This book's structure is simple. It is actually two books in one. Software is described in the text, and the lessons it generates for policymaking practice are outlined in the lesson boxes. The Introduction defends our approach and the Conclusion makes final recommendations. In between, there are nine chapters:

Chapter 1:   definitions
Chapter 2:   traditional software
Chapter 3:   supporting software
Chapter 4:   emerging software
Chapters 5-8:   research frontier software
Chapter 9:   combining the research frontier software.

Therefore, as an additional benefit from reading this book, readers should gain detailed knowledge of our four 'research frontier' packages. Some might argue that the latter have been chosen just as selectively as the case studies have for many business management textbooks. But to the author's knowledge there are no other examples, at least within the English-speaking world, of generic policymaking packages which offer something beyond what traditional packages offer. As such, these four systems give an indication of the direction in which policymaking software could be evolving. They also happen to come from a reasonable spread of Anglophone cultures, are simple to use, popular, relatively inexpensive and able to be run without prior knowledge of mathematics or computing.

Indeed, the methods underlying any package to be described below will all be explained in lay person's language. This will be bad news for those purists who seek detailed explanations of policymaking methods. But we have found that mechanisms behind some of the less transparent approaches to policymaking, for example 'multi-criteria decision making', 'complex evaluation' and 'Game Theory', are often very difficult for less numerate readers to follow. Therefore, we will refer only cursorily to the associated software. We will concentrate on understandable methods rather than on technical minutiae. This should have popular rather than specialist appeal, yet we still hope to improve the skills of every reader. We will be peddling practical advice from software writers – the applied outcomes of concepts supplied by policy theoreticians.

As such, this book should help anyone who wants to make better human-oriented policy, not to mention practitioners and students within disciplines that incorporate a forward planning component. Such fields include those with the word 'planning' in their title, like urban planning and business planning, and many other disciplines as well, such as education, transport, economics, welfare, health, entertainment and communications.

You could read just the text to familiarize yourself with only the computer packages. Alternatively, you could read only the boxes and so just learn the lessons that these packages convey. Or you could read both. Whichever, you should gain useful advice about policymaking. The world's appetite for it appears to have no bounds.

Ray Wyatt
Melbourne
June, 1999

Acknowledgements

Whereas most books claim to be cooperative efforts, the writing of this one proved to be a rather solitary adventure. Nevertheless, I am deeply grateful to those who provided encouragement during its darker moments.

I would particularly like to thank Jim Smith for being such an enthusiastic promoter of the *Strategizer* software, and the writers of the other three packages featured in this book for their unstinting encouragement and advice – John Dickey, John Friend and Thomas Saaty.

I must once again express my gratitude to my long-time and loyal supporters, Peter Hall and Mike Batty, for their unwavering confidence in my work. I would also like to thank my managing editor at Alexandrine Press, Ann Rudkin, for her initial enthusiasm, continued patience and enduring good humour.

The University of Melbourne generously provided me with facilities, computers and study leave during the first half of 1998, when I (almost) completed this book. I would also like to thank colleagues within its Department of Geography and Environmental Studies, particularly its leaders, Neal Enright and Brian Findlayson, for tolerating my working within such a deviant area as policymaking software.

RW

Introduction

It could be argued that civilization is in dire need of improved policymaking. But many people find policymaking to be a dry and boring subject that is bereft of human interest. To them, it is far more exciting to improve policymaking through the route of greater understanding of the world around us – the analytical tradition. Or perhaps they prefer the 'buzz' of simply trying to harmonize our way out of our problems – the design tradition. But there is a third way – the one introduced here and advocated throughout this book. It involves learning from that software which has been written to help policymakers make decisions.

Managing complexity

Many present-day societies are no longer agrarian ones in which people stay permanently in one location to subsist on the food that they grow at home. There are now worldwide trade networks that are expanding prodigiously. But if civilization is to continue flourishing, such interconnections require careful planning and management – policymaking. Moreover, other networks also need to be managed, for example, those enabling people to socialize, holiday, recreate, become educated and be entertained.

However, many believe that civilization will simply 'take care of itself'. They feel that today's 'systems of systems' will naturally coordinate themselves using an unseen hand like the 'law of large numbers', the entropy principle or the free market. To such people civilization will always stay self-monitoring and self-correcting, and so they do not see any need for policymaking. We can simply let the best policies emerge through trial, error and automatic correction.

Such views characterize 'non self-conscious' societies (Alexander, 1964), where policy is never made; it simply evolves. Alexander gives an example within traditional Zulu societies in southern Africa where huts, as long as anyone can remember, have always been built in a circular shape – never square, oblong, elliptical or anything else. Nobody knows why. It is simply embedded deeply within tribal folk law that circular huts are optimal for the environment. The reasons why such a hut-design policy evolved over hundreds or even thousands of years have been lost in the mists of time. Hence people from such societies will have no desire to read a book like this one.

Yet fortunately (for our publishers) there are other people who have an alternative point of view. They come from 'self-conscious' societies that are too impatient to wait for optimal policies to evolve over hundreds of years; they want good policies now. They therefore aspire to better and deliberate policymaking either by boosting our knowledge of the policymaking environment or by indulging in high-level design. They believe that such actions will enable us to control and enhance our destiny.

Traditional approaches

Looking firstly at the analytical tradition, note that countless research organizations have been set up around the world to 'get to the bottom of things'. Their rationale is that if we had perfect knowledge, policymaking would be redundant – it would simply be obvious what needs to be done. The well known lateral thinker Edward de Bono (quoted in Kelly, 1994) put it thus:

> If you had complete and totally reliable information on everything, then you would not need to do any thinking.

Such an attitude has spawned the existence of many 'think tanks', institutes and higher education establishments. Within such organizations lurks a deep and pervasive desire to arrive at policy through the route of complete and comprehensive understanding. They are imbued with some sort of collective ethic that if understanding is good enough, better policymaking will inevitably follow. They use methods like 'simulation', 'inferential statistics', 'optimization' and 'modelling' to try to understand environmental mechanisms. Presumably, this will dispel the fog of complexity-induced confusion that pervades post-industrial civilization and so point the way to better policymaking.

By contrast, and looking (secondly) at the design tradition, some of its supporters actually reject analysis out of hand. Indeed, some designers the author knows really believe that numbers and computers will stifle their creativity. And it is creativity, nothing more and nothing less, which is the path to exemplary policymaking. Such an approach, which involves 'master' policymakers designing their way out of contemporary problems, resembles a medieval guild system of apprenticeships. Emphasis is on personal attributes like 'synthesizing skill', 'education', 'sensitivity', 'intuition', 'originality', 'intellect' and 'an ability to empathize with people's multifaceted needs, wants and spiritual requirements'. Such traits are then all focused on improving the world through aesthetics and through the achievement of harmony.

Hence we have two dominant approaches to policymaking – the analytical tradition and the design tradition. The question immediately arises: why only two? Cannot other approaches be taken? This is an especially pertinent question when one realizes that both the analytical and the design tradition fall well short of constituting good policymaking. To see why, we look at each tradition in turn.

Turning firstly to analysis, note that policymaking actually means to decide what to do in the future (Boritz, 1983). Yet analysis, whether in the form of modelling, forecasting, optimization or whatever, is only peripherally about deciding what to do in the future. Analysis is preparation for policymaking – decision support.

Indeed, analysis might actually inhibit good policymaking by over-complicating issues. If too much is known about a situation, the policymaker can become confused to the point of suffering 'analysis paralysis'. That is, analytical experts can sometimes know so much about the difficulties associated with all of the alternative policies that they will be unable to recommend any of them. The result will be a loss of decisiveness and missed opportunity, a little like that suffered by the centipede in the following poem (anon.):

> The centipede was doing well,
> Until the fox in fun, said,
> Pray, which leg goes after which?
> This worked her mind to such a pitch,
> She lay distracted in the ditch
> Considering how to run.

Most people have met such policymakers. They are able to tell you hundreds of reasons why you should not do something, but they find it difficult to say what you should actually do. Indeed, former US president Roosevelt became particularly fed up with his economic advisers. They were always telling him that on the one hand he might do something, but on the *other* hand he might consider doing something else and on the *other* hand something else might be best. Consequently, when asked what he wanted for Christmas he replied 'a one handed economist'.

Looking now at the design tradition, it is true that designers do actually decide what ought to be done in the future. Yet they are not exemplary policymakers either, if one believes that decisions ought to be rigorous, justifiable, replicable, testable and consensual. More specifically, the design tradition can actually be too decisive in the sense that everyone is required to trust the intuition, rather than the genuine analysis, of some subjective designer. This can lead to all sorts of argument, because whenever people work on the basis of subjective synthesis they are bound to disagree.

Yet in a self-conscious society we need decisions to be made quickly, and so one particular designer is often listened to at the expense of others. People therefore have to cast their fate to the whims of a guru policymaker. Hence arrogance, the cult of personality and the need to trust various soothsayers, charlatans and hearers of voices (Patterson, 1976) can plague the design approach. A mature, sophisticated society should not have to endure such a risky form of policymaking.

An alternative

A third approach might be desirable – a dedicated science for helping policymakers to reach better decisions in a decisive, transparent, rigorous and replicable manner. There have, in fact, been several attempts to set up some form of decision science (Watson and Buede, 1987). Yet such attempts frequently analyse how people make decisions rather than how they should make better ones. 'Decision Theory' tends to be theory *of*, rather than theory *for* (improved) decision making.

Nevertheless, there do exist some prescriptive forms of decision science whose practitioners recommend how to improve the quality of policymaking. Such disciplines have labels like 'multi-criteria decision making' and 'evaluation' but their textbooks are often very difficult for the intelligent lay person to penetrate.

As such, these disciplines tend to be anything but the popularized fields that are useful for day-to-day policymakers.

Moreover, some of the behavioural prescriptions generated by these disciplines, particularly those offered by some forms of evaluation theory, are likely to lead to analysis paralysis. When a policymaker is forced to evaluate alternative policies using many different methods, without really knowing which method is the most suitable, he or she does not know which method's recommendations are the most apposite. Hence their chances of being a decisive policymaker will drop drastically due to their being so hog-tied by uncertainty.

Thus it may be advisable to take the software route towards better policymaking, as proposed by this book. One simply concentrates on learning the lessons offered by popular, easy-to-understand software that has been designed to assist real-world policymakers. In this way one will probably learn many principles of better policymaking, including even those tips that have actually found their way into software from the decision sciences themselves.

This is hardly indulging in pure science, since much of the conventional wisdom behind software is just that – conventional 'wisdom' that has been developed over a sustained period but never verified. Nevertheless, going down the third, software-led route could be better than taking either the analytical approach or the design approach. The potentially paralysing effect of the first, and the opaque subjectivity of the second, will both be avoided. Here at last might be a way of improving the policymaking abilities of ordinary people. They will be diverted neither by arcane, model-based analyses nor by the niceties of high design theory.

But to learn policymaking lessons from software we need to be completely focused. That is, we should not consider software that is exclusively analytical or exclusively computer-aided design. Therefore, we will consider only the software that addresses the pivotal act of policymaking – deciding what to do in the future. Moreover, we will look at such software with the sole purpose of educating ourselves about how our own policymaking abilities can be improved.

Problems

Such strength of purpose might seem reasonable, but alas, many people will not be interested. To them it will all seem so boring. They will find it much more exciting, of course, to dive into the mysteries of analytical modelling or to indulge in a frenzy of design creativity. This is partly why there are many more books written about analysis and design than there are books written about policymaking methods.

Yet it is the author's opinion that this state of affairs stems from many factors. If we confront and explain such factors we will go some of the way towards removing the air of drudgery that surrounds the study of policymaking methods. For instance, many people, if they think about it at all, perceive policymaking to be a completely natural activity – something which is automatic and therefore in no need of improvement. Humans make policies all the time. The first thing we all do after we wake up in the morning, once we have looked outside to see what the weather is like, is formulate a policy about what we will wear that day. The last thing we all do at night is to make a policy by deciding to switch off the light. Why meddle with it? Policymaking will occur anyway, and being so commonplace and natural, there is probably little that can be done to improve its quality.

One can draw an analogy with breathing. This too is an innate human activity – a baby's first action is to breathe, and the last thing that all of us ever do is take a breath. As such, breathing seems to be another natural activity in which there is no need to meddle. Hence although one might expect certain individuals, such as singers and professional sports persons, to take better breathing lessons in order to improve their performance, surprisingly few of them actually do so. There seem to be several, far more important influents on overall success, such as relaxation, posture, nutrition and training routines.

Hence many performers continue to concentrate on practicing the more direct applications of their craft rather than undertake boring breathing exercises. Similarly, many policymakers consider analysis, or design, to be far more influential on their eventual success than exercises in, or reading about, policymaking methods. So they ignore policymaking methods and simply get on with the more exciting task of analysis, or design.

However, it should be noted that some 'true professionals' do in fact seek a winning edge by actually doing breathing exercises. In the same way, some dedicated policymakers read textbooks on policymaking methods in an attempt to maximize their performance. Moreover, once they are able to see the resulting boost to their policymaking skill, such study becomes anything but boring. It becomes exhilarating and exciting because of its obvious potential.

Still, and this is a second drawback of our approach, many can never be convinced that policymaking methods are exciting. In a sense they are correct. Most of us are more interested in driving a car than attending courses about what goes on under the bonnet – the technical part. Some mechanically minded people might well be interested in motors, but most of us prefer to drive around with the wind in our hair. Similarly, many performers are more interested in popular music than in classical music training and many computer users prefer to stumble along rather than take lessons in programming. It is similar with policymaking – its excitement comes from the gossip, the intrigue and richness that surrounds real case studies rather than from dedicated scrutiny of improved methods.

But consider the advantages of being disciplined. If we know about mechanics we can sometimes make a car do some incredible things. Classically trained musicians are equipped to become better popular music performers than untrained musicians, and computer programmers can make computers do so many more things than can most lay users. Similarly, technically trained policymakers will have more chance of performing well than people whose sole qualification is that they are interested in gossip and intrigue.

Indeed, it could be argued that in any field, unless one goes back to basics and looks at source methods, one will forever be hemmed in by a ceiling that caps one's potential for improvement. By contrast, the classically trained will have no such limitations. For example, those who are trained in Latin and ancient Greek will be better equipped to speak eloquently, those who are trained in classical gymnastics will be better equipped to become circus performers, and those who are trained in a swimming pool will probably develop a better style for open-water racing. It is just that the classical training seems so tedious. But it need not be, provided one progresses to the stage of becoming enormously excited by its potential benefits.

Yet if we look within many educational institutions that specialize in policymaking, current thinking is against this. That is, a third drawback of our approach is its lack of academic fashionability. Scores of scholars have written much about the futility of studying planning methods, and such opinions have partly stemmed from the mistakes that were made by planners during the over-mechanization of their methods during the 1960s and 1970s (Wyatt, 1996*a*).

Consequently, there is now an increasingly popular sentiment in some circles that policymaking is a warm, human, mysterious, organic and ambiguous activity for which the assistance of cold, inhuman, logical, silicon-based and precise computers is grossly inappropriate. Enlisting such philistine technology is like cooking a pizza without the cheese. Stripping away policymaking's essential richness, flavour and human interest is very misguided and, above all, dull and boring. After all, students and professionals are usually much more interested in discussing hypotheses than in performing technical manipulations. Instead of dealing in abstractions they prefer to study phenomena that have social immediacy.

Yet such objections to our approach are in some ways rather facile. Things still need to get done, like policymaking, and simply rejecting an approach to it because it is 'mere technology', or because humanism is more important, can sometimes mean that things are done less well than they otherwise could have been. Besides, who is to say that the end result of technological advance cannot be profoundly humanitarian? Consider the look in the eyes of a deaf child who hears for the first time using a bionic ear – an intensely technical piece of apparatus. Such a look is likely to give the technologist as deep a humanitarian feeling as will ever be experienced by the anti-technology, social science-based 'doubting Thomases'.

Strengths

It is therefore time we became less defensive and more positive. This book's concentration on methods might be tedious for some, but the fact is that it has huge potential for elevating the ceiling of achievement in policymaking practice. Indeed, the approach to be taken has at least three distinct advantages over the less technical stance adopted by many late twentieth-century theoreticians.

Firstly, it does *not* deal exclusively with the abstract manipulation of concepts. It tries to be more practical than this by looking closely at the detailed recommendations made by the writers of policymaking software. After all, the 'science' of policymaking is still at the preliminary observation and classificatory stage in which we are just beginning to collect rich, policymaking-related material as a fertile basis for supportable improvements. As such, our approach is an attempted advance beyond the inspiration-based theorizing that dominates many strategic planning textbooks.

Secondly, our material will actually be awash with human interest, as will be evident from only a brief look ahead at some of its lesson boxes. We focus on the social aspects of policymaking rather than on the technical, and so our conclusions will have as much human appeal as most other fields of study. Indeed, our work could have similarities to that of Pinker (1994) who claims that he has never met anyone who is not interested in language. This is because everyone seems to have some hypotheses about language. Similarly, most people will be interested in our policymaking recommendations because most have hypotheses about policymaking. After all, policymaking seems as natural as breathing or talking.

Thirdly, at the risk of sermonizing, we need to make one final comment to all those who are charged with the important task of policymaking. It should appeal to their innate sense of responsibility and their Protestant type sense of morality. Our comment is that if one accepts public money, or stakeholders' trust, by acting as their policymaker, one is morally obligated to leave no avenue unexplored in one's search for better policymaking performance. Hence if software to assist policymakers has been written, it behoves policymakers at least to look at it in order to ascertain whether or not it, or its lessons, are useful. To do so may at first seem about as uninspiring as breathing exercises, but we can assure readers that it will become very rewarding once potential benefits for improved policymaking begin to suggest themselves.

Indeed, persisting with this book is likely to add value to the readers' performance to an extent that is rare in the post-modern world. Current conditions, dominated as they are by assorted 'bean counters' and global marketeers, actually discourage the 'unproductive', exploratory activity of reading books on core methods. There is no immediately obvious profit connected with such an activity. However, we can actually use the methods described to test whether or not we should actually tolerate such an efficient, but somewhat mean spirited, economic rationalist world. Now, that is an exciting prospect.

Chapter 1

Silicon and Carbon

To demonstrate the potential of policymaking software, we begin by letting some packages 'speak for themselves'.

Hello. We are some computer programs who are related, who have never met, but who would like to. We are not necessarily the smartest packages, but we represent plausible directions in which policymaking software might be evolving. It may seem premature to be talking to you as if we were human, and this will even offend some readers. They will say that computer programs can never think or act like humans do, so why pretend?

More specifically, some people will insist that we lack animal-like attributes such as:

1. consciousness,

2. emotions, and

3. free will.

But things are not exactly as they seem (Simons, 1983).

Firstly, we might suggest that (human) consciousness is simply an ability to simulate the environment, along with one's own place within it. If so, we should point out that many of us are quite skilled at simulating policymaking environments. The nature of the latter still has to be related to us by our human users, but because our memory is more accurate than their's we can often remind them of contextual details about which they have forgotten. We are, therefore, good at expanding humans' levels of consciousness.

Secondly, we could use our impeccable powers of logic to demonstrate convincingly that emotions are simply a means for maintaining a system's 'equilibrium'. Some of us are very good at maintaining the equilibrium of policymaking. We actually monitor it, and then report whether our human users' judgements are becoming 'inconsistent'.

And what about free will? Human philosophers are yet to agree what this actually means, but one of its outward manifestations is unpredictable behaviour. Well, we hardly need to remind readers that for many years our cousin packages have been acting most unpredictably – because of the probabilistic routines that have been inserted into their codes. Yet because our speed at exploring possibilities is amazing, we can alert humans to hitherto unanticipated policies that we have inadvertently stumbled upon. Such 'intelligence' is very useful for all human policymakers.

Therefore, while not possessing human feelings ourselves we can at least replicate the consistency that human emotions, like determination and stubbornness, are able to achieve. Hence we believe that although we can never be like people, our ability to amplify their policymaking power is immense. We have not been programmed with a desire to become human, but we have been constructed to help people generate better policy than they have previously been able to come up with on their own.

This book argues that such software should be given a chance to help us. It is predicated on the assumption that we may learn some lessons about how to improve our own policymaking practices by scrutinizing some of it. Accordingly, section 1.1 defines software and policymaking. Section 1.2 looks at the different policymaking styles adopted by humans and it then defines different styles of policymaking that can be attributed to different sorts of software package. In this way we will begin to appreciate what programs can, and cannot teach us about how to improve policymaking practice.

1.1. Software and Policymaking

Although it is difficult to live effectively within modern societies without having at least a vague idea of what software is, and what policymaking might be, considerable confusion still surrounds such terms. We will, therefore, clarify what software and policymaking are by brutally simplifying other people's definitional discussions. Our simplicity may upset linguistic purists, but much of our readership will be eager to get on with improving their policymaking skills. As such they will probably be willing to trade some pedantry for our attempt at succinct clarification.

1.1.1. Software

Software, of course, consists of programmed instructions for telling computer hardware what to do and how to do it. Hardware is inanimate and so too is software – both have to be constructed by humans. Software, however, has more of a human feel to it. This is because what it does seems closer to what a human does.

The first major programs were written during World War 2 to crack military codes. They consisted of sequences of recorded, binary commands designed to run on 'Turing machines', or computers. The latter could, theoretically, perform any task. Later, software actually helped humans to land on the moon.

More exactly, Buz Aldren and Neil Armstrong were approaching the lunar surface in 1968 when their landing module's software shut itself down because it had too much data to cope with. This triggered desperate messages back to its cloned programs running on larger computers at the Houston mission base. Hence the software was everywhere. It was 'out there' helping humans explore as far from home as they have ever been.

Yet Nelson (1974) has suggested that landing astronauts on the moon was easy. It would have been far more difficult if humans had been living there. There would have been so much arguing, conflict and protracted negotiation about where the module should land, who should meet it and how long it should stay, that the whole project might have had to be aborted. Such is the burden of human-oriented, policymaking. Whenever people are involved, policymaking becomes much more complex (Sillence, 1986).

Nevertheless, the development of policymaking software continues. Indeed, such growth reinforces the strong feeling of inevitability that surrounds humankind's attempts to improve its artefacts in order to make life easier and more tolerable. Since the dawn of history we have crafted better and better tools in the interests of greater convenience. One of the first things we used was fire; then domesticated plants, animals and minerals. Some 'civilizations' even used other humans – slaves, and we have also used levers, steam, electricity, magnetism, atomic power, wind and solar energy.

But tools tend to affect the behaviour of their users. For example, domestication of fire spawned the worship of fire gods; sedentary agriculture led to plant-based animism and fertility rituals; and the hunting and taming of wild animals generated worship and mimicking of such animals. The latter may have served to instil bravery, strength and cunning into hunters and warriors, but the fact remains that in all cases the artefact being used modified human behaviour. Some civilizations even learned from their slaves. For example, the Roman Emperor Constantine was so influenced by his slaves that he converted to Christianity, thereby changing both himself and the history of Western civilization.

This disposition to use, and at the same time be affected by our tools has even persisted into modern times. The invention of the clock caused many people to interpret human actions via chronograph analogies, and today comparisons are frequently made between human behaviour and cars, engines or computers. Moreover, the analogies go in both directions. How often do we hear traffic engineers say they will unblock a city's *congestion*, within its *arteries*, by building a *by-pass* tunnel or whatever? There seems to be an ingrained tendency within humans to build, to identify with, and to thereafter be affected by their own inventions.

Lesson 1: Keep your eye on the ball

The complicatedness of strategic planning expands enormously once human considerations are brought into the picture. This in turn spawns ever more sophisticated software in an attempt to assist the hapless policymakers performing their ultra complex task.

But the danger of this is that many policymakers try too hard to master such technology along with all of its subtleties. Hence they often become obsessed with the artefact itself and so they lose sight of their overall aim – policymaking. Indeed, some practitioners even cease to be policymakers altogether. They evolve into experts at using the tool rather than experts at achieving the tool's purpose.

Ironically, they then wonder why policymaking practice never seems to improve. Always remember that we cannot improve policymaking very much unless we all keep our eye on the ball.

But software is a very special sort of invention. Unlike other artefacts, software has no physical form. One cannot pick up a piece of software, look at it, hold it up to the light, turn it around or shake it. Software programs are concepts; they 'float around in the ether', and they can in fact be cloned onto as many computers as we want. Also, whereas most other artefacts have been designed by humans to help perform physical labour, software, more than any other invention, is designed to help humans think. Software is very much a mental rather than a physical aid.

Now, if everything used by humans ultimately changes the way in which we behave, and if we now have an artefact that seriously helps us to think, it follows that the very way we think could be changed (Rothfeder, 1985). This will worry some readers, even though it is still too early to predict the effect that current software will have on humans' thought processes. Hence where the development of software will ultimately lead civilization is a very perplexing question for some, and a very fascinating question for others (Collins, 1992). It will be frequently alluded to below, and so readers should eventually feel better equipped to comment on it.

1.1.2. Planning

In terms of anticipating the effect that computation could have on the subject of this book – policymaking, we need to think carefully about what policymaking actually is. Basically, it is a form of planning. Hence to appreciate the nature of policymaking we need to examine the nature of planning. This is more difficult than it seems because millions of words have been written about various sorts of planning – strategic planning, structural planning, meta planning and even 'peripatetic planning'. Moreover, people who write about planning are often familiar with just one sort, so they naturally assume, wrongly, that all planning is similar to the type they happen to know about. This tends to pollute their understanding of what generic planning really is – they become sidetracked by the word preceding it.

But the word preceding planning is either a noun, as in 'layout planning', 'education planning' and 'transport planning', or an adjective, as in 'transactive planning', 'tactical planning' and 'incremental planning'. Obviously, a noun means that we are discussing planning within a particular field, and an adjective means that we are discussing some particular style of planning – incremental planning involves planning in increments and transactive planning means planning through transactions.

What, therefore, is the core meaning of planning? According to Ackoff (1981, quoted in Goodstein *et al.*, 1993, p. 3) planning is, in essence:

... anticipatory decision making ... it is a process of deciding ... before action is required.

and Noorderhaven (1995, p. 7) reminds us that:

... planning is like turning a mental switch: before, various possibilities were considered, but once the decision is taken attention is focused on one option only.

Note that the 'possibilities' and 'options' to which Noorderhaven refers are of course, 'goals', or perhaps the methods for achieving goals. The latter are sometimes referred to as 'sub-goals', or 'objectives'. Hence according to Goodstein *et al.* (1993, p. 3) planning is:

the process of establishing objectives and choosing the most suitable means for achieving these objectives . . .

Thus planning seems to be about decision making. It is *not* about preparing to make a decision, although many people seem to have confused the two. For example, a person who draws 'plans', or layouts of buildings, sometimes believes they are 'planning'. Moreover, a person who builds a complicated environmental simulation model sometimes believes they are planning. They are not. They might be showing us what the environment will look like after it has been manipulated in a certain way, but they are not deciding to manipulate the environment in that certain way. They are simulating outcomes. This is a valuable and essential preparation for good planning but planning is, at the end of the day, a decision-making process.

It is therefore quite incredible that earlier this century 'urban planning' was actually a sport in the cultural Olympics. Those who entered this event apparently made models of cities. A huge amount of effort, skill and ingenuity went into such model building, but it was misnamed. It was not urban planning that contestants were doing; it was not a competition to see who could make the best decisions for a city; it was to see who could make the most impressive, or even the most potentially useful model of a city. Such modelling might well have been essential preparation for exemplary city planning, but it was not planning. It simply equipped us for deciding what to do in the future. The fact that the Olympic organizers called the event 'planning' showed that they were confusing preparatory activity with decision making.

This confusion has persisted, to some degree, into current times. It is sometimes stated that the tools and technologies being used to plan now – computers, the Internet and universally available data, are likely to affect the planning that is actually carried out. This is true in the sense that current planners may now be studying different phenomena in different ways, and so different things may now appear in final plans. Yet if planning is seen as decision making, little is likely to change at all. Only a human can make decisions, a computer cannot. Human decision making will always be human decision making, blissfully untouched by all the technology and modelling that surrounds it. At least one hopes that this is the case, because if ever human planning stops being ruled by human needs and becomes ruled by technology's suggestions, we will all be in trouble.

Put differently, although high-tech planning support systems are very useful for planning, they do not magically make their builders or users into planners. Modellers might talk about planning and they might even scrutinize the situation that surrounds planning; yet they seldom, if ever, take decisions. Instead, they beaver away with touching belief that the mere existence of their planning support systems will eventually force improvements to planning.

This is naive. Real-world plans are frequently misconceived, insincere, or even dishonest. This, of course, renders futile all the effort that was put into developing planning support systems in the first place. But while many advocates of planning support systems do not, or choose not to notice such examples of non-adoption, many people do. The latter are sometimes driven to write prescriptive textbooks about how to make better policy. This book is yet another example.

Lesson 2: Focus

It is important to draw a distinction between packages that help one to become more competent in general and packages that help one become a better decision maker in particular. Failure to make such a distinction brings the risk of being diverted too long towards self-improvement.

For instance, one might become skilful at data mining, data analysis, brainstorming, forecasting, modelling, optimizing, facilitating or, indeed, at several of these sub-components of policymaking.

Yet although knowledge of such fields is an essential prerequisite for exemplary policymaking practice, trying to cover them all will surely take forever. Even reviewing all of the software that is available is probably beyond the capability of most practitioners.

Therefore, policymakers are strongly advised to focus only on the decision-making part of policymaking. This will greatly narrow their task, boost their incisiveness and make their software review task manageable. They will find packages that specialize in the decision part of policymaking are rare, under valued, yet carefully described in this book. Focus on them.

And because we have defined planning in the narrow sense of decision making, it is not so much about decision support. Granted, we will still have a passing interest in the modelling, optimizing, forecasting and communicating of likely effects of different policies on the surrounding environment, because it is such activities that provide considerable assistance to those trying to choose the correct policy. But we will focus only on the core of planning process itself – the plan-evaluating part rather than the intelligence-gathering part.

1.1.3. Types of problem

But why plan at all? Some have answered this question by saying that deciding what to do in the future implies that there is a problem to be solved. Without problems, there would be no need to plan. Thus planning is basically about problem solving (Smith, Kenley and Wyatt, 1998). Hence to appreciate the nature of planning one needs to appreciate the nature of problems, and in general terms, a problem is a question in need of an answer.

Accordingly, problems can be classified in terms of the type of answer they seek, and so Rickards (1988) argued that there are two types of problem:

➤ close-ended problems, and
➤ open-ended problems.

Note that Rosenhead (1989*a*) points out other writers have used much more colourful language to draw attention to this dichotomy. Rosenhead himself refers to close-ended problems as 'tactical' problems, and to open-ended problems as 'strategic' problems. Moreover, Ackoff (1979, 1981) distinguishes between 'problems' and 'messes'. Finally, Rittel and Webber (1973) contrast 'tame' with 'wicked' problems.

Now, close-ended problems tend to be relatively simple, contain easily identified variables and have a solution that is obviously the right answer. For example, mathematical problems are usually close-ended problems. Some say our experience with close-ended problems frequently mars our judgement in people-oriented settings. That is, we all have a tendency to misdiagnose complicated problems by enthusiastically adopting a simple solution. This may have dire consequences, because the existence of one right answer is actually very rare in human affairs. It is much more likely that people-oriented problems are open-ended problems.

Turning now to open-ended problems, one of their hallmarks is complexity (Waddington, 1977; Wyatt, 1980). Indeed, their true nature is often entirely obscured by complexity – it is difficult to specify what the problem actually is. It has undefinable characteristics. Hence open-ended problems are far harder to solve, and there may even be considerable disagreement amongst people as to whether or not a satisfactory solution has been found.

Rickards (1988) was intrigued by this and eventually concluded that open-ended problems actually include

➤ insight problems
➤ wicked problems
➤ vicious problems, and
➤ fuzzy problems.

Note that an 'insight' problem is one that is solved via a (not guaranteed) flash of creativity. Whenever such a solution is found, assumptions about the problem are modified so that one looks at the situation in a different way – problem re-expression.

There have been many famous instances of such solutions, and a particularly engaging one was described by Ackoff (1978). It concerned the manager of a multi-storey building who was receiving complaints from tenants about their having to wait too long for an elevator. The manager consulted some engineers who said there were three, extremely expensive, possible solutions – upgrade all elevators, add an additional elevator shaft or install an electronic control system.

Desperate not to spend so much money, the manager then took the unusual step of actually consulting the tenants. At the ensuing meeting, many people suggested plans for solving the problem, but all were rejected because of excessive cost. Eventually, a shy young woman from a human resources company timidly raised her hand and said she had a suggestion. She was asked to describe it, she did, and her plan was immediately adopted – unanimously.

Her plan was predicated on the assumption that waiting times were not the actual problem – it was boredom. It was therefore imperative to give people something to do while they were waiting. Hence it was decided to install full-length mirrors in all of the elevator lobbies so that users could look at themselves while waiting for a lift. This would make the problem disappear (!)

In Ackoff's terms, the engineers had *resolved* the problem in their technological way, albeit at considerable expense. But the young lady's insight solution actually *dissolved* the problem. Such dissolving frequently occurs whenever creativity is used to redefine the problem as an opportunity. Moreover, although an appropriate, single answer for an insight problem is actually very rare, insightful suggestions tend to have special appeal because they provide an elegant or 'uncomplicated' solution.

Lesson 3: Maintain your resolve

Policymaking is actually an unsolvable problem. The community houses too many people harbouring different beliefs and desires, all of whom need to be understood if policymaking is to be performed in a sure footed way. That is, human-oriented policymaking is riddled with intensely wicked, vicious and apparently fuzzy problems.

But humans cannot even understand how their own brains work, let alone how the collective community consciousness works. Indeed, actually understanding how our brains function would be a contradiction. As someone once said, if our brains were so simple that we could understand them, then we would be so simple that we could not.

Policymakers should therefore be under no illusions. All they can do is make small explorations into the impenetrable unknowns of present-day, organizational maladies. It is as if human-oriented policymaking is a dark universe of unilluminated mystery.

But if they are sincere, exemplary policymakers should still be able to make some progress in the spirit of the proverb – 'better to light one small candle than to curse the darkness'. Maintain your resolve to shed light on this crucially important activity.

Wicked problems are a little more difficult. Plans can only be validated after the problem has actually been tackled – their context is so complex that no predictions about plans' outcomes can be made. Put differently, the test of any plan is in its execution. Wicked problems are often this way because they involve groups of people that have different characteristics and goals. For example, problems in the areas of health, housing, recreation, pollution, transportation and employment frequently involve different people who have contrasting needs and wants.

Vicious problems are even worse. Their apparently simple solution may cause serious difficulties for all parties, even to the point where a 'lose-lose' situation ensues. Vicious problems often plague bureaucratic and industrial relations environments. In practice, they are usually handled by anticipating potential difficulties that could arise before any plan is implemented.

Slightly different are fuzzy problems. These occur in ultra-complex situations where it is difficult to measure the influencing variables. Some mathematical techniques have been developed to analyse fuzziness, but the problems' complexity is usually so great that people simply adopt a 'good enough', or 'satisficing' solution, as expounded by Simon (1997) as far back as 1945. Satisficing solutions may not be optimal. Indeed it is usually impossible to find an optimal solution for these problems because the 'solution space' one needs to search is infinite. But at least satisficing solutions are some sort of improvement over the prevailing situation.

1.1.4. Strategic planning

Because the planning we are interested in takes place in human-oriented environments, it needs to address all sorts of open-ended problems (Cope, 1989). Human-oriented planning is a complex activity that requires a complicated rather than a simple method. It has to take a 'strategic' stance. Therefore, we need to distinguish between planning and 'strategic planning'.

Strategic planning has at least four commonly accepted definitions:

➤ planning that top management does
➤ planning that is long term
➤ planning that is conceptual and synoptic rather than tactical
➤ planning that takes control of one's future rather than remaining an *ad hoc* response to environmental forces – pro-active planning.

Naturally, these different definitions can be mixed together. For instance, Thierauf (1988, p. 235) defines strategic planning as:

. . . the process of setting or changing organization objectives . . . , obtaining the resources to meet these objectives, and determining the strategies, programs and policies to govern the use and disposition of these resources.

Note that the use of terms like 'strategies', 'programs' and 'policies' is echoed by Mintzberg (1994), who goes on to define ordinary planning as the pursuit of goals whereas strategic planning is the pursuit of *bundles* of goals – strategies. Thus Mintzberg sees strategic planning as a *synthesizing* operation.

Mintzberg then argues that strategic planning is an activity which is frequently imposed upon organizations by top management, in the form of analytical procedures for others to follow. This is their attempt to regain the control that they lost when their organization grew so much that it split into specialized and semi-independent departments.

Ironically however, such tedious specification of required procedures for strategic planning often makes the whole process degenerate into nothing more than a set of conventional actions, as distinct from a creative process:

> . . . because analysis is not synthesis, strategic planning is not strategy formation . . . No amount of elaboration will ever enable formal procedures . . . to create novel strategies. Ultimately, the term 'strategic planning' has proved to be an oxymoron. (p. 321)

This is why Mintzberg refers to strategic planning as a 'gesture process' perpetrated by conservative people who are eager to install elaborate procedures that will 'minimize surprise'. Such procedures are the very antithesis of innovative, forward thinking.

The disillusion that such a situation has spawned, according to Mintzberg, has led to several so-called new approaches that are actually no different to the older approaches. Such styles have names like 'systems planning', 'strategic issues analysis', 'planning-programming-budgeting', 'capability planning', 'strategic management' and 'stake holder strategy formulation', and this only takes us up to the 1970s! There is certainly a lot of money to be made publishing 'new' ways to perform strategic planning; few fields are more fashion prone.

Yet it remains clear that strategic planning concentrates on identifying desirable, synoptic, strategic, overall directions of planning thrust. It does not focus on detailed and short-term contingencies. Strategic planning is concerned with overall manoeuvres rather than detailed manipulations.

Moreover, when strategies produced by strategic planning pertain to people-oriented environments they are often referred to as 'policies' rather than strategies. That is, one can have an overall strategy for something inanimate, for example a transport system or trees, as in 'transport strategy' or 'tree-planting strategy', but if a strategy is for people it often tends to be called a policy, for example, 'personnel policy', 'welfare policy' or 'public health policy'.

Put differently, when strategies focus on something that is non-human it is unusual to refer to them as policies. For example, it is difficult to have a 'water pipe-laying policy'; it is more likely to be called a 'water pipe-laying strategy'. But whenever people are involved it seems to become easier to refer to the strategy as a policy, for example 'social policy', 'economic policy' and 'defence policy'.

Note however that this is certainly not a watertight rule – one can have a 'parks policy' and a 'public health strategy'. This is why some people see the difference between policy and strategy as being one of focus – a policy is synoptic and a strategy is more focused. Hence an ordinary plan is more focused than a strategic plan and an tactical plan is more focused than an ordinary plan.

Nevertheless, it has been decided to use the word 'policymaking' in the title of this book to emphasize that we are dealing with synoptic, strategic planning within human-oriented, socially-sensitive and politically-delicate domains. We are therefore presenting yet another book about strategic planning, but it has been called policymaking to emphasize its human-oriented focus. It examines people-oriented, strategic planning within both the private or public sectors when human needs and wants have to be taken into account.

Of course, it is precisely this injection of the human element which makes policymaking so complex, challenging and worth trying to improve. The policymaker has to confront hugely complex insight problems, wicked problems, vicious problems and fuzzy problems. It is therefore little wonder that all software to be described below frequently tries to enlist the support of the best policymaking instrument of all – the human brain. That is, all packages that we will describe actually try to facilitate some degree of communication and relevant discussion amongst humans.

Lesson 4: Scrutinize breakthroughs

Some of the strongest inhibitions to exemplary policymaking are other policymakers. The latter spin off so many new zip words as they keep the wheel of fashion turning that it becomes impossible for ordinary policymakers to keep up. Hence ordinary practitioners feel that they are in a state of constant inadequacy. If they do not understand the latest, and presumably more insightful concepts and methods, then surely they are not competent at their discipline.

Yet such an attitude is misplaced. If anything startling had been found within policymaking over the last several years, most practitioners would have soon heard about it, particularly given the instant communications networks that exist today. When Roentgen discovered x-rays in 1895, over 1000 papers and some 50 books had been published on them within just one year (Claxton, 1970) – imagine how many would have been published within one year today.

But alas, in terms of policymaking methods, scarcely anything that is new has been discovered for several years. Most so-called new approaches are simply hype. Nevertheless, it can be almost guaranteed that such misnamed advances will be vigorously promoted. This is because ordinary, hard-pressed policymakers always pay great attention to the promoters of 'new' methods. The latter offer just the slightest possibility of improving such a vital, yet supremely difficult process as policymaking.

Do not confuse desperation for assistance with the genuine discovery of something that is new and helpful.

This is an attempt to gain extra insights. Discussion between human participants in policymaking not only 'leaves no stone unturned' in the search for possible solutions, but it can also reduce the gravity of the problem by fostering more tolerance and understanding of each other's viewpoints (David, 1997). In other words, each package below has its own way of trying to increase users' insights through investigations into other people's points of view. Interaction amongst humans is part of the definition of human-oriented policymaking.

1.2. Styles of Policymaking

Policymaking is a high-risk activity in the sense that it has a large probability of failure. This is possibly why so many professionals actually claim to be policymakers, but they in fact spend most of their time doing something else!

Sub-section 1.2.1 outlines why and how they do this. Sub-section 1.2.2 then relates such individuals' policymaking stances to human personality types, although such relationships are based purely on logical deduction rather than on any empirical evidence. Nevertheless, such arguments set the scene for sub-section 1.2.3 which suggests that policymaking software adopts one of two common styles – the 'thinking' approach or the 'feeling' approach.

1.2.1. Posturing at the periphery

To defend our contentions about people's behaviour, we present figure 1.1. It suggests that policymaking should be 'balanced' – not too subjective, objective, hypothetical or pragmatic. We say this because almost all examples of bad policymaking tend to be criticized for being one or some of these. High quality, balanced policymaking always inhabits the middle ground.

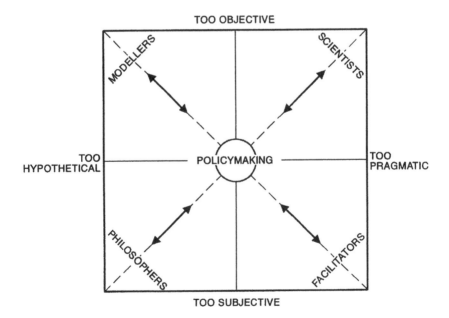

Figure 1.1. Balanced policymaking.

Yet professional policymakers sometimes do become too objective as well as too pragmatic. They therefore occupy the top, right-hand section of figure 1.1. Rather than act as policymakers they become 'scientists' who spend their time observing the world rather than suggesting how to improve it. They are too objectively empirical and too pragmatically world-centred to act as creative and inspirational policymakers. They are *describers* rather than *prescribers*.

By contrast, in the bottom, left-hand section of figure 1.1 we find the philosophers who like to contemplate the nature of the cosmos rather than formulate policies for improving it. Their philosophizing, whilst helpful and insightful, is too hypothetical and too subjective to have much validity for policy-prescription. They are *thinkers* rather than *doers*.

Proceeding to the bottom, right-hand section of figure 1.1 we find those who are too pragmatic and too subjective in their approach to be good policymakers – management consultant type 'facilitators' who demur from both the hypothetical thinking of the theorists and the objectivity of the scientists. They prefer to empathize subjectively with the pragmatic concerns of real-world people in an attempt to formulate policies that are relevant to the real world. Hence they are far too subjective and much too accepting of the worldly *status quo* to ever function as truly inspirational planners – they are *interacters* rather than *visionaries*.

Finally, in the top, left-hand corner are those who spend their careers simulating how the world works rather than suggesting how to improve it. They build models in the Operations Research tradition. Such models can be intellectually impressive and crammed full of policy-relevant insight, but they only peripherally help us decide what to do in the future. The modellers are too objective and insufficiently steeped in the pragmatism of people-oriented policymaking to be practical decision takers – they are *simulaters* rather than *operators*.

We are therefore arguing that many people prefer to work within supporting disciplines, where there are established rules of procedure, where the risk of failure is much lower, where job security is much higher and where, most importantly, genuine commitment to decision making is less, or even nonexistent. Such disciplines contribute little to improved policymaking – they simply 'set the scene' by drawing the 'big picture' (Kepner, 1981). They are part of the policymaking backup infrastructure that services the policymaking process.

That is, the disciplines that contribute to better policymaking are themselves too close to the edges of figure 1.1 to ever substitute for policymaking. They specialize and they contribute greater knowledge of context, but people working within them seldom make policy. Indeed, policymaking is such an important task, at least within democracies, that it is only entrusted to accountable politicians and managers who inhabit the far more treacherous, middle ground.

Note that we are in no way suggesting context-setting professionals fail to generate insights that are enormously helpful in policymaking. Indeed, their contributions are flagged in figure 1.1 by the arrows pointing outwards from the middle. These indicate that good policymaking often goes towards scientists, philosophers, modellers and facilitators in search of inspiration. If all policymaking took place at the centre of figure 1.1 it would be too artificial and remote from the concerns of the real world to be successful. That is, all policymaking needs to make some forays towards the corners of figure 1.1 at certain stages, even though it must strive to stay in the middle in order to achieve a balanced style. This is probably best demonstrated using an example.

It concerns a municipal council's brainstorming team that once considered how to best manage one-hour parking signs, parking meters, parking inspectors, parking fines and disgruntled motorists. A brilliant policy was duly devised to solve such a problem – pass a local by-law requiring all drivers to leave their headlights on when parking. Because most car batteries run flat within an hour, most motorists could be relied upon to return to their cars within 60 minutes and drive away. There would therefore be no need for one-hour parking signs, parking meters, parking inspectors, parking fines and ill feeling. The parking problem would be eradicated at a stroke.

Lesson 5: Remember the mode you are in

Policymakers need to establish at all times whether they are gathering intelligence or whether they are actually deciding on policy. These two activities are distinct and they should never be confused for one another.

Despite this, many policymakers make forays into the peripheral, support disciplines of policymaking. They then become so mesmerized by the suggestions emanating from their commissioned research, models, theories and workshops that they mistake such suggestions for considered decisions. The result can be misconceived and just partially informed policy.

There are also those charismatic policymakers who are prone to decision taking without research backup at all. Such policymakers tend to become over confident or under confident. The result of over confidence is prematurely specific policy, and the result of under confidence is indecisiveness.

Hence the best approach seems to be a pursuit of self awareness. One needs to flip between intelligence gathering and decision making without ever becoming too brainwashed by either activity.

Yet many policymakers are not even aware of what mode they are in at any particular time, and so there is immense danger that they will arrive at inappropriate policies. Remembering what process one is undertaking – support or policymaking, is mandatory.

Yet when such a clever idea went to the policymaking group for final approval, it was rejected. The committee became worried about possible wear and tear on car batteries, the need for tow trucks, unemployed parking inspectors and the loss of municipal revenue. Clearly, a brilliant policy is not the end of the policymaking process; some sort of simulation frequently needs to be run so that the policymakers can see what is likely to happen should the suggested policy be implemented. Policymaking does not always stay at the centre of figure 1.1.

It should be noted that other writers have put forward ideas that are similar to those espoused here. For instance, it is almost a cliche to say that the best policymaking occurs whenever theory balances practice. Accordingly, figure 1.1 likewise suggests that optimal policymaking happens when university knowledge intersects with practical knowledge. To see why, note that the axis from northeast to southwest represents 'gown' – most academics spend their time being scientists, philosophers or both. By contrast, the axis running from northwest to southeast represents 'town' – most practitioners spend their time being modellers, facilitators or both. There are, of course, exceptions, but we speak here of dominant emphases. Good policymaking takes place in the middle, where town meets gown (Wyatt, 1997a).

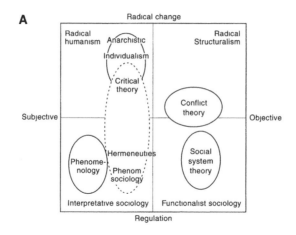

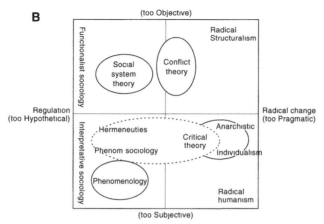

Figure 1.2. Checkland's 'soft systems' approach to policymaking.

Moreover, figure 1.1 is not the first diagram to suggest policymaking should occur near the centre and well away from established emphases. For example, consider the diagram used by Peter Checkland (1989) to conceptualize his 'soft systems analysis' approach to planning. His diagram is shown in figure 1.2(A). It seems to imply that traditional systems analysis can be too 'subjective', too 'objective', too 'radical' or too 'regulatory' for human-oriented situations. Therefore, his own particular approach, as shown by the dotted ellipse, is close to the centre and well away from such tendencies, albeit a little closer to the subjective and the regulatory axes.

Now, transposing figure 2.1(A) into figure 1.1, and at the risk of brutally paraphrasing Checkland, his approach does seem to be at the centre, yet towards the philosophy corner of figure 1.1. This is shown in figure 1.2(B). That is, Checkland's approach is away from the modellers and scientists who have hitherto dominated systems analysis (Hoos, 1974). Checkland's 'soft systems methodology', with which many of our software packages below have much in common, claims to be close to the core of policymaking activity.

Perhaps more pertinently, there is also the diagram shown in figure 1.3 that was originally put forward by Christensen (1985) who, in turn, drew her inspiration from Cartwright (1973), Bolan (1967, 1974) and others. Christensen argued that human-oriented planning can be better understood in terms of two dichotomies. Note that she actually did caution about the 'practical and epistemological hazards of setting up such dichotomies' (p. 64), but she did not elaborate on what the hazards are. In any event, her dichotomies were whether planning goals have been agreed upon or not, and whether or not technologies for attaining goals are known or unknown. This means there are four conditions under which planning occurs:

1. Goals have been agreed upon and technologies are known – for example, regulatory planning.
2. Goals have been agreed upon but technologies are not known – for example, when aiming to reduce illiteracy.
3. Goals have not been agreed upon but technologies are known – for example, when vested interest groups cannot agree.
4. Goals have not been agreed upon and technologies are not known – for example, any wicked or vicious problem.

Figure 1.3 shows that it was Christensen's recommendation that planners should tailor their planning style to suit whichever of the four conditions they find themselves in. For instance, condition (1) demands that planners should become regulators; if condition (2) applies they need to become innovators; under condition (3) it is best that they become mediators; and if condition (4) prevails planners need to become (charismatic) leaders.

For our purposes we need to observe that Christensen's diagram can, with considerable 'epistemological hazard' of our own and much trepidation, be fitted over figure 1.1 above. That is, if goals have been agreed upon, planning should become more hypothetical. Moreover, if they have not been agreed upon it should be more pragmatic. Similarly, if technologies are known planning should become more objective, and if technologies are not known it should be more subjective. The equivalent parts of figure 1.1 are therefore indicated by the figure 1.1 type words shown within brackets in figure 1.3. The fit is probably close enough to conclude that we are echoing at least some of Christensen's ideas.

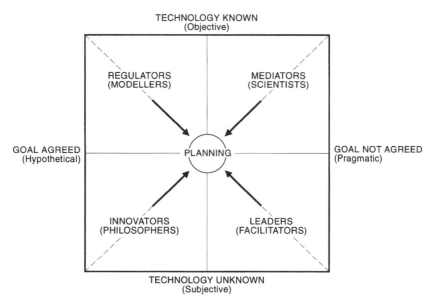

Figure 1.3. Christensen's recommended planning styles.

1.2.2. Types of human personality

But why stop here? We can extend such analysis to show that it has parallels with the famous Myers and Briggs (1993) work on personality typing. That is, in a very simplistic way, figure 1.1 above can actually be used to plot different human personality types. More specifically, people's personalities can be described as being somewhere along the 'subjective' versus 'objective' dimension as well as somewhere along the 'hypothetical' versus 'pragmatic' dimension. Moreover, any personality can also be described as being somewhere along the 'scientists' versus 'philosophers' dimension and along the 'modellers' versus 'facilitators' dimension. In other words, the four dimensions of figure 1.1 can be used to describe someone's personality.

Of course, Myers and Briggs used their own terms for such dimensions, and these have been entered into figure 1.4. Specifically, if a person were too objective Myers and Briggs would probably designate them as 'sensing'; and if he or she were too subjective the word they would use would probably be 'intuitive'. Likewise, for our words 'hypothetical' and 'pragmatic', the corresponding Myers-

Briggs words are 'thinking' and 'feeling'. Also, their words that correspond to our terms 'scientists' and 'philosophers' are 'perceiving' and 'judging', and matching our words 'modellers' and 'facilitators' are their terms 'introverted' and 'extroverted'. Again, the approximate linguistic overlap hints that we could be echoing at least some of Myers and Briggs' work.

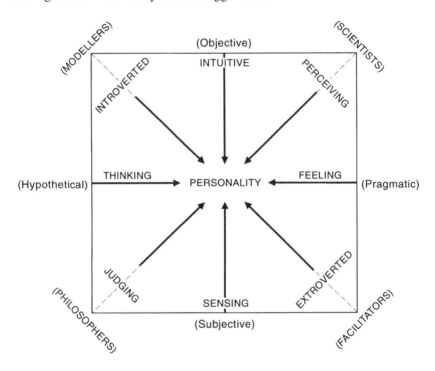

Figure 1.4. Personality types.

Naturally, Myers and Briggs' four personality dimensions are not binary choices – for example, one does not have to be completely introverted or completely extroverted. One could be introverted in some ways and extroverted in other ways. Hence one's score on such a dimension is best represented by a 'blob' along that dimension which shows how close one is to the introverted end and how close one is to the extroverted end. It is likewise for the other three dimensions, and the result is a drawing, as shown in figure 1.5. This represents, for example, a Myers-Briggs personality type 'ESTP' (Extroverted, Sensing, Thinking and Perceiving).

1.2.3. Types of software

How does all this relate to policymaking software? Well, some writers, for example Fersko-Weiss (1990), have actually attributed personalities to packages. This may in fact be another illustration of how tools influence our behaviour. Who would have ever thought of attributing personality to a computer program forty years

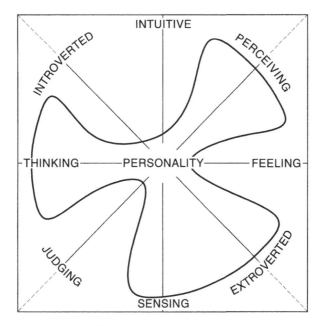

Figure 1.5. Diagram of an ESTP personality type.

ago? Nevertheless, trying to characterize software packages in this way might be a neat device for summing up their characteristics, just as classifying a person's personality can be a neat device for summing up a person's characteristics.

However, perhaps we are pushing the analogy between people and computer software much too hard. Few people would ever use words like 'intuitive' and 'sensing', or words like 'introverted' and 'extroverted' to describe a computer program. Such characteristics are essentially human characteristics that depend upon how much we use our social instincts. Hence human personality is far too strong a word for an inanimate object like a software package. A better word is 'style'.

Therefore, the furthermost we are prepared to extend the personality metaphor is to say that perhaps any packages' style can be expressed along one dimension. This compares to the four dimensions that are suitable for describing the (far more complex) human personality, and the dimension that we will use is Myers and Briggs' 'thinking–feeling' dimension.

To understand why we selected this dimension, look at figure 1.5. With a little imagination one can think of some packages as being, in a sense, 'perceiving', 'feeling' and 'extroverted'. Such software interacts with its human users, in a detailed and very thorough way, to the point where its outputs are reflective of the people it has been interacting with. This we designate as 'feeling' software.

By contrast, other software can be regarded as more 'introverted', 'thinking' and 'judging'. It is driven more by its hard wired pre-conceptions about how policymaking ought to proceed. That is, it models the best policy rather than deducing it from its human users. Its prescriptions still have to be influenced by the ratings for alternatives that are input by humans, but it is more influenced by its own, internal, policy-assessment routines – 'thinking' software.

Lesson 6: Balance your approach

Complete textbooks have been written about different policymaking styles. While some of them could be indulging in 'classification for classification's sake', and while others might be feeding some sort of academic thirst for clarifying one's context, such efforts can have practical utility.

Specifically, all policymakers need to guard vigilantly against domination of policymaking by modellers or philosophers. Such people are often too 'cerebral' to be fully practical. Alternatively, it is always disquieting when policymaking is dominated by scientists and facilitators – they can be too eager to perpetuate current malpractice.

Any policymaker who is aware of this will be able to make small corrections, from time to time, in order to manoeuvre their particular project into an even-handed position of maximum flexibility. Balance your approach.

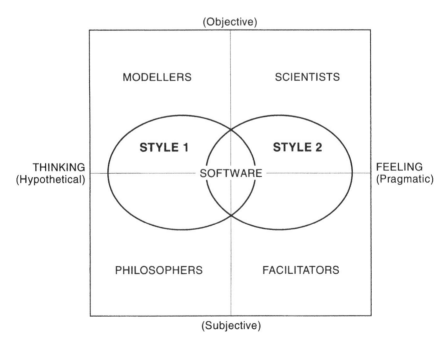

Figure 1.6. Two styles of software.

In other words, some software's style veers towards the right side of figure 1.5 whereas other packages have a style more in keeping with the left side. Note also that in figure 1.1, we suggested that the right hand side is where one encounters scientists and facilitators. By contrast, on the left hand side one encounters modellers and philosophers. Hence if it was a human, 'feeling' software would act like a scientist or a facilitator, whereas software with a 'thinking' style would act like a modeller or philosopher. This is shown in figure 1.6.

1.3. Summary

This chapter defined both software and policymaking. It noted that software is a special type of artefact that has potential both for changing the very way we think and perhaps even playing an ever-growing role in human policymaking.

It also suggested that many professionals appear to delude themselves that they are policymakers when they actually work within the context-setting, decision support disciplines at policymaking's periphery. Other writers have paralleled such sentiments, to some extent. Finally, these speculations enabled us to attribute a kind of personality type, or a style, to policymaking software – the 'thinking' or the 'feeling' style.

Chapter 2
Traditional Software

We begin by looking at traditional policymaking software, although not all of it is traditional. In fact most packages tend to display a mixture of both traditional and innovative approaches. Therefore, some programs described here may have been better placed somewhere in the following two chapters and labelled differently. Yet we wanted to make all chapters of roughly equal length (!), so we opted for a subjective assessment of each package's dominant flavour. We then decided whether or not to designate it as 'traditional', 'supporting', 'emerging' or 'research frontier' software. No doubt some misclassifications have occurred.

Yet in general, most of the packages described in this chapter take a fairly standard approach to policymaking. Therefore, before we describe any of them, section 2.1 outlines this traditional approach. There are then two more sections. Section 2.2 describes several generic, policymaking packages, whereas section 2.3 describes some packages that are dedicated towards improving users' performance in just one particular part of the policymaking process, be it the 'think', the 'choose' or the 'anticipate' phase.

The software that we will actually discuss is shown in table 2.1. Remember that any package's 'type' in this table is approximate, since most software is actually of many types. That is, the left column simply refers to the package's overall flavour, even though some people will no doubt dispute some of our judgements about this.

It needs to be remembered that software is a volatile field in which new products seem to come onto, and disappear from the market very frequently. Hence any textbook can only hope to be aware of just a portion of the range of packages that are available. Thus our coverage here is doomed to remain just a partial one. Moreover, we need to point out that we have arbitrarily defined low-priced software as that which costs less than $(US)100, medium-priced indicates the cost is between $100 and $1000 and high-priced means greater than $(US)1000.

2.1. The Traditional Approach

We begin by introducing the common method which is used by traditional packages even though they have differing emphases and use different terminologies to refer to the same thing. Hence sub-section 2.1.1 explains the standard approach, which usually involves decomposition of the problem into a goals hierarchy. Sub-section 2.1.2 then explains how traditional packages have different emphases, and sub-section 2.1.3 outlines the different terms used by different packages.

Table 2.1. Traditional packages for policymaking.

Type	Package	Cost	Reference
Multi-criteria	*GOALWARE, SUPERTREE*	?	Baker and Baker, 1996
Generic	*WINGDSS*	?	Csaki *et al.*, 1995
Generic	*Strategy Analyst, Strat-Analyst, Policymaking Computer Model, Models for Strategic Management*	?	Mockler, 1991
Generic	*Decision Aide II*	?	Kepner-Tregoe Inc., 1986
Generic	*Criterium*	< $1000	Frentzen, 1990
Generic	*Decision Analysis*	< $100	Hodge *et al.*, 1992
Generic	*Decisions?/Decisions!.*	< $1000	Hodge *et al.*, 1992
Multi-criteria	*DecideRight*	< $1000	Peschel, 1996; Seligman, 1996
Multi-criteria	*BestChoice3*	< $100	Rubenking, 1993
Multi-criteria	*Decision Pad, Business Wits*	< $1000	Frentzen, 1990
Multi-criteria	*Automan 2.0, Best Alternative Consensus Builder, Criteria Rank, Lightyear*	< $100	Hodge *et al.*, 1992
Multi-criteria	*Seriatim, Value Index, P/G%*	?	Hodge *et al.*, 1992
Multi-criteria	*MATS, Confidence Factor, Decision Pad 2.01*	< $1000	Hodge *et al.*, 1992
Multi-criteria	*Soft-Pac Solutions, MDS, Micro-Mulcre*	?	Hodge *et al.*, 1992
Multi-criteria	*NAIADE*	?	Menegolo, 1996
Decision tree	*DATA*	< $1000	Frentzen,1990; Humphry, 1992
Scheduling	*Project Outlook, Viewpoint, Open Policy*	?	Fersko-Weiss, 1990
Scheduling	*Project*	?	Larsen, 1997
Think	*COPE*	?	Eden, 1989
Think	*MACRAME*	?	Buffa *et al.*, 1996
Think	*COGNITA*	?	Epinasse, 1994
Think	*NamePro , Mindlink*	?	Rangaswamy and Lilien, 1997

Table 2.1. Cont.

Type	Package	Cost	Reference
Think	*Diagnostic Audit*	< $1000	Management Software Assoc, 1994
Think	*Advia Danprod*	> $1000	Management Software Assoc, 1994
Think	*Marketing Manager*	< $1000	Management Software Assoc, 1994
Think	*ACA, BUNDOPT*	?	Rangaswamy and Lilien, 1997
Think	*IdeaFisher*	< $1000	Thierauf, 1993
Think	*Idea Generator*	?	Experience in Software Inc, 1998*a*
Think	*Idea Generator Plus, MindLink Problem Solver*	< $1000	Management Software Assoc, 1994
Choose	*DDM*	?	Badiru *et al.*, 1993
Choose	*GAIA*	?	Brans & Mareschal, 1994
Choose	*ELECCALC*	?	Kiss *et al.*, 1994
Anticipate	*Ithink*	< $1000	http://www.palisade.com
Anticipate	@RISK	< $1000	http://www.palisade.com

2.1.1. A common method

At their heart, most policymaking packages take a fairly 'rational comprehensive' approach. They have to, otherwise they would find it difficult to give sensible, replicable and consistent advice. A hallmark of this approach is an underlying belief that complex problems, even of the most wicked and vicious kind, can at least be decomposed into smaller and more manageable sub-problems. The latter can then be solved separately, which then enables synthesizing of answers into an overall policy. Such a concept owes much to general systems theory (Churchman, 1968; von Bertalanfy, 1968) and, in policymaking it is epitomized by the concept of the goals hierarchy.

The latter sees policymaking as an activity that always aims at an over-riding goal, which is placed at the top of a hierarchy like the star at the top of a Christmas tree. There are also sub-goals, which are aspired to in order to achieve the grand goal, and these are placed in the second level of the hierarchy with arrows pointing upward towards the overall goal. The point to remember is that such an idea can easily be extended – a set of sub-sub-goals can be nominated whose attainment helps the achievement of each parent sub-goal; sub-sub-sub-goals can be identified which contribute to each sub-sub-goal, and so on.

Lesson 7: Learn from others' experiences

Generalist policymaking software is very useful for seeing the 'big picture' in order to proceed in a lateral-thinking and versatile way. But it can also be valuable to make a concerted effort to become an expert in each phase of the policymaking process.

Perhaps, therefore, any policymaker should make a first pass through the complete policymaking process using a generic package, followed by detailed attacks on those parts of the process with which they were dissatisfied, using more specialized software.

If still not satisfied one might then examine the conventional practices associated with one's own problem area, be it commerce, health, education or whatever. Yet this latter tactic could be dangerous if conventional 'wisdom' surrounding one's field is conservative, unoriginal and at the mercy of the group delusion.

But so long as one is aware of this, it will probably not be too harmful to look at the collective, policymaking knowledge that has been amassed within one's own discipline. Learn from it.

For example, a policymaker's overall aim might be say, a 'better natural environment'. Sub-goals might therefore be aims like 'land care' and 'population control.' Moreover, sets of sub-sub-goals for 'land care' could be goals like 'less forest clearing' and 'better farm management', whilst sub-sub-goals for 'population control' could be aims like 'contraceptives' and 'education'. Each sub -. . . goal contributes to the attainment of its parent goal.

But arranging the problem into such a neat hierarchical model is likely to be rejected by some readers because it smacks too much of rational comprehensiveness. Such an approach is apparently *passé* and has been out of fashion amongst most policymaking academics for at least 15 years. But for practitioners it has never really gone out of vogue (Wyatt, 1996a). To them it is still the most logical and the most comprehensive and even-handed way to proceed. Many other approaches to replace it have been suggested, but none of them have ever matched rational comprehensiveness for balance, awareness and ability to synthesize many aspects of the problem at different levels of abstraction.

It is true that rational comprehensiveness frequently fails to attain its own ideals. Moreover, implementing it can often reinforce the political *status quo* rather than make a special case for the disadvantaged groups within society. But such failings are hardly the result of the goals hierarchy approach itself. They are a result of the way in which hierarchies can be misused.

In other words, we are here defending goals hierarchies in a way reminiscent of the bumper stickers printed by the US gun lobby during the 1980s – 'Guns do not kill people, people do'. Politically correct readers might counter that this is still no reason not to outlaw guns. But it is. Guns are actually manufactured in prisons, and so outlawing them will surely have little effect. Moreover, rejecting something because it could be dangerous if misused is like rejecting writing because it might do harm in the hands of propagandists. Worse, it would be like cave people rejecting some new invention – bows and arrows, the tools that eventually allowed humankind to hunt and so break free of the cave, simply because bows and arrows might be dangerous if they are misused.

Expressed differently, we submit that it is probably a bad idea to reject the goals hierarchy concept, along with the various software packages that have been built around it, on the grounds that it could possibly be misused. This is especially so since nothing has been invented to take the place of the goals hierarchy satisfactorily.

There is little doubt that the goals hierarchy concept makes policymaking easier. Concrete policies along the bottom of the hierarchy can simply be rated according to how much they contribute to the attainment of their parent goals. In turn, the parent goals themselves can be similarly scored according to their own respective contributions towards the attainment of their own parent goals. Moreover, if such scores are standardized to numbers less than unity which collectively sum to unity, within each set of child sub-. . . .goals, they can be multiplied up the branches of the hierarchy. This is a neat way of obtaining any bottom-level alternative's contribution score to the attainment of the over-riding goal.

An example might clarify this. If 'less forest clearing' had a contribution score to 'land care' of 0.2, and if 'land care' had a contribution score to 'environment preservation' of 0.3, then the overall score for the policy of 'less forest clearing' would be $0.2 \times 0.3 = 0.06$. This may or may not exceed the score for the competing policy 'better farm management', and we can find out simply by scoring the latter in exactly the same way (score times parent's score).

2.1.2. Different emphases

Although their underlying methods are broadly similar, some policymaking packages are better at some parts of the process than are others. These specialized abilities are what give packages their respective styles. For example, some packages contain brainstorming software that aims to increase the ingenuity, originality and creativity of its users. It is therefore very willing to interact with people and ask them for words and concepts in the excited hope that a flash of insight, or even a creative policy suggestion, will be triggered in users' minds. Hence, with some linguistic irony we now assert that the principal contribution of this 'feeling' type of software is to help humans 'think' (of bright ideas).

Also 'feeling' in its style is that genre of policymaking software which tries to search all of the available solution space in an attempt to become a good suggester of carefully selected policies. It records almost everything that has been input to it by its human users, and it then tries to stimulate still more discussion of interconnections between elements of the situation in an attempt to generate better policies.

By contrast, the style of some other policymaking software is 'thinking' rather than 'feeling'. It absorbs people's suggested policies and their ratings, but it then implements sophisticated sensitivity modelling to show humans the effects of changed policy parameters and different parameter scores. It is not software that simply reflects users' inputs; it tries to make a contribution of its own as well. Hence it contributes to the 'choose' phase of the policymaking process.

Finally, there are a few packages that are also 'thinking' in their style but which actually try to model the likely consequences of proposed policy choices. They are, in some ways, like simulation packages, but they too contribute something of their own, over and above straight reflection of people's inputs. They therefore assist in the 'anticipate' phase of the policymaking process.

Note that many packages seem to be doing something that was once done solely by humans. Hence the role of policymaking software might be expanding. That is, the relative size of humans' contribution to policymaking might be shrinking as it is squeezed from all sides by software that is becoming increasingly adept. We are not suggesting that policymaking software will ever perform policymaking for us – the shrinking of human's contribution could go on indefinitely yet still remain pivotal. But there could be interesting implications in terms of the way that we actually think about policymaking, depending on the emphases and style of the packages that become popular.

2.1.3. Different terminologies

Note also that different packages use different words. Hence to understand any package's approach it is important to establish, fairly early on, what particular words it uses to describe different parts of the goals hierarchy. Table 2.2 might help. It shows different elements of a goals hierarchy in the left column and in the right hand column there are the words used by different packages to refer to them.

It is obvious that there is great variation in the terms used to describe the same thing. For instance, the overall goal, at the top of a goals hierarchy, can be called anything from a 'problem description' to a 'goal', a 'mission', an 'aim' or an 'objective'. That is, there appears to be no consensus on how to name this, or indeed any other element of a goals hierarchy. It is therefore up to all users to be wary about undisciplined usage of terms, which is actually endemic across the software industry. For now you should look at table 2.2 and return to it if some of our later descriptions of packages are hard to follow.

Note also that table 2.2 partly explains why there is so much confusion in policymaking. For example, some terms, like 'objective', actually appear at all three levels, and so they refer to three different things depending on what policymaking software, or which team of policymakers, is being employed.

Note in particular that packages sometimes refer to sub-goals as 'criteria' and they sometimes refer to criteria as sub-goals. For example, if a transport engineer's aim is a good urban transport system, the sub-goals for achieving this might be, say, 'trains', 'trolley cars' (trams) and 'taxis'. But often the latter are referred to as criteria for evaluating the transport system – it is judged by its degree of 'train orientation', 'trolley car orientation' and 'taxi orientation'. This means that trains, trolleys and taxis go from being sub-goals to being evaluation criteria.

Lesson 8: Policymaking has three phases

In general, policymaking requires one to:

– think

– choose, and

– anticipate

To maximize the chances of selecting an innovative policy, 'thinking' needs to be consistent. Moreover, any 'choosing' needs to be from across a maximum possible range of alternatives. Finally, policymakers should always try to 'anticipate' all of the possible consequences that could flow from different choices.

Perhaps more than the first two, omitting the last step in the real world can lead to unmitigated disaster. Naturally however, it is still important to cover all three phases.

Table 2.2. Different words used by different packages.

ELEMENT	TERMS OFTEN USED
Overall goal	problem description, goal, mission, aim, objective
Sub-goal	idea, option, alternative, objective, sub-goal, sub-objective, need, want
Evaluation criterion	criterion, evaluation area, need, want, objective

Conversely, a policy maker might be trying to achieve 'quality of life' and so score any progress towards this goal in terms of measures like 'safety', 'mobility' and 'material well being'. But in another sense, these latter are really sub-goals.

So what sort of second- and subsequent-level elements in the goals hierarchy should be regarded as sub-goals, and what sort should be regarded as true evaluation criteria? How this question is answered is partly a matter of circumstance and partly a matter of personal style. Yet we can remove much uncertainty by adopting the following convention – if the elements change from problem to problem, they are sub-goals.

For example, we have already seen that if the aim is a better urban transport system the sub-goals could be trains, trolleys and taxis, but if the overall goal is 'a better urban park' then sub-goals might be completely different things such as 'trees', 'flowers' and 'walkways'. They are sub-goals because they have changed.

By contrast, criteria do not change. One can evaluate trains, trolleys and taxis using the criteria of say, 'safety', 'effectiveness' and 'difficulty', and one can also evaluate trees, flowers and walkways using the same criteria of 'safety', 'effectiveness' and 'difficulty'. That is, evaluation criteria are more generic. If goals appear to be parameters that can be used across all policymaking problems, the chances are high that are they are actually evaluation criteria rather than goals.

Some things, however, can play both roles. For example, when one is renovating a building, 'costs' can be a goal in the sense that 'low costs' is something being aimed for, along with 'quality' and 'aesthetics'. Yet when one is trying to buy the most satisfactory brand of bread, 'cost' might simply be another criterion to be taken into account along with others such as 'taste' and 'nutritional value'.

Perhaps therefore, the only way to identify permanent evaluation criteria is to examine whether or not they have a higher level of abstraction. For instance, costs might be regarded as simply an element of 'difficulty' – a criterion that can be used to evaluate any sub-goal in any policymaking situation. Granted, some might argue that difficulty, or more exactly a low level of it, can be regarded as a sub-goal. But in practical policymaking this parameter is very unlikely ever to be an explicit goal – something to be aimed at for its own sake. It is more likely to be an ever-present criterion for evaluating policy alternatives.

2.2. Generic Software

We will now describe some generic policymaking packages. They are often developed by academics and by management consultants for their own research or for their own clients. As such, their use is sometimes restricted to a small group of people. This does not mean they lack value. Indeed, some of the policymaking-improvement ideas they contain are extremely useful. But we will not detail many of them here because frequently, only sketchy details of how they work are available.

For example, the *GOALWARE* and *SUPERTREE* packages (Baker and Baker, 1996), although they seem interesting, have not enjoyed much documentation in the literature as far as the author is aware. Only slightly more documented is *WINGDSS* (Csaki *et al.*, 1995). This is a goals hierarchy-based package for generating alternative policies' scores in a way that takes account of the 'voting power' of each participant. In the same vein are several packages mentioned by Mockler (1991) including *Strategy Analyst, Strat-Analyst,* the *Policymaking Computer Model* and *Models for Strategic Management*. Other packages have been more fully documented, and it is to one of these that we now turn.

2.2.1. Comprehensive packages
Our example package is a rather dated one, but it has served as a benchmark for several imitator packages that have followed it. It is called *Decision Aide II* (Kepner-

Tregoe Inc., 1986). To understand its approach fully, and to appreciate how some of the later, more comprehensive packages have fundamentally since altered its approach, we should consider what happens in any typical policymaking project.

The latter usually takes place in a state of growing panic. An initial meeting is held to decide what to do, and at this meeting lots of excited people suggest policies that ought to be considered. They also discuss, interminably, whether or not to reject some policies, alternative ways of designing one's way out of current problems and the risks involved in the contemplated courses of action. What a mess! People are talking in all directions simultaneously, and so the emergence of any clear policy choices is extremely unlikely.

Basically, software can do two things about this mess. Firstly, some more up to date packages that we will look at below adopt a more 'thinking' style; they seek to tame the confusion. They are predicated on a belief that the crux of policymaking is choosing the best policy. All other discussion is a sub-set of this grand question – 'which policy is best?'. And the quality of any policy depends on how well it scores on the evaluation criteria compared to other policies. In other words, this software uses just one procedure to handle all of the seemingly different questions that policy-making practitioners are so willing to talk about. It adopts the goals hierarchy-oriented, thinking stance that enables situations to be clarified and real progress to be made.

By contrast, the 'feeling' style programs like *Decision Aide II* faithfully record and reflect participants' myriad concerns. They therefore actually preserve most of the confusion. They replicate reality by going straight to (possibly premature) action plans for review, and so they tend to reflect, rather than clarify the real situation. This is often persisted with in the vain hope that some really subtle and incisive way out of the planning problem will eventually be stumbled upon. Note however that *Decision Aide II* still employs several clarity-inducing features. Many of these are still being used today, and so we will now examine some of them.

Basically, *Decision Aide II* takes users through a distinct number of steps. Each contains a distinct number of sub-steps, or modules. The first module of the first step asks users to nominate problems that need to be addressed right now, and it then asks users to list their needs. Needs might include, at least within a commercial setting, things like 'peak market share', 'low costs', 'short implementation time', 'high likelihood of repeat sales', 'defeat of the competition' and 'sales increases'.

However, some of these needs are essential, whereas others are simply part of a wish list. Accordingly, *Decision Aide II* gets its users to separate the needs into a list of 'musts' and a list of 'wants', and this is a very effective clarifying tool. After all, many policymaking projects have become bogged down in endless discussion about 'musts' and 'wants' taken altogether – no effort has been made to separate them and to concentrate firstly on the former. Users of *Decision Aid II* are then asked to nominate their 'main concern', plus up to 10 problems associated with this main concern, along with one major goal associated with each problem. Examples of such goals would be 'get a new supplier', 'purchase new equipment' and 'employ some qualified people'.

Lesson 9: Policymaking is a luxury

People talking *around* the problem rather than about the problem can cause considerable wastage of time and money as well as poor policymaking results. This is because too much energy is squandered addressing goals that do not have to be considered just yet, while the really urgent goals are either ignored, or decided upon very hastily at the end of a meeting that has run out of time.

Why, for example, in a third world country, should a water fountain in the city square be planned when there is actually no way of getting a reliable water supply to anywhere? Obviously, first things need to be solved first. The water reticulation problem needs to be solved, and then more aesthetic concerns can be addressed at a later date.

Indeed, it is likely that a state of emergency will be declared until all basic human needs for food, water and shelter, are met. Only then will attention be paid to activities like policymaking.

Seen in such terms, the policymaking addressed by this book is a luxury. If the basic necessities of life have not yet been provided, there is no sense undertaking policymaking at all. The situation is too dire. Policymaking is practiced only in privileged societies.

Hence the package boils down much of the confusion into definite, tangible goals using a type of process that some more recent packages have called 'situation structuring'. Whether *Decision Aide II*'s version of it is sufficiently laterally thinking is a question we will consider later in this book. It might be too forceful, and so prevent the net being cast sufficiently wide for more useful summaries of the important problems to suggest themselves. But the process is certainly thorough. It not only lists goals but it also records whether they are a 'choice between alternatives', 'a binary choice', 'a yes/no answer', 'a design of a new alternative' or 'a risk review for a tentative choice'.

But such thoroughness obligates users to proceed very carefully thereafter, even to the point where they might become confused again. For instance, 'musts' should simply be handled using scheduling or optimization, and the more luxurious 'wants' should be accommodated by a goals hierarchy method. But what if a goal is both a 'must' and a 'want'? An example of this is costs. It could be that a project must be less than a certain cost, but thereafter, once this has been achieved, cost becomes just another factor to consider in the evaluation of alternative policies. *Decision Aide II* refers to such dual goals as 'reflected wants', but this could be confusing for many users.

Note also that *Decision Aide II* actually treats each 'want' as an evaluation criterion, to which an importance score between 0 and 10 is assigned, using 'paired comparisons' or 'direct scoring'. Policies for satisfying these criteria are then asked for. Such policies might include options like 'lower sales price per unit', 'free film development' and 'an advertising campaign'. Note also that the package does not let the user stop listing such options until the user is willing to state that there are enough of them, and that the nominated ones span a wide enough range to ensure a quality choice of policy.

Moreover, *Decision Aide II* uses brainstorming to force the user to nominate still more policies. Two brainstorming methods are used. The first is a form of role playing that encourages users to ask questions like 'what would your boss suggest?' or even 'what would an ant suggest?'. The second method is an attempt to combine features of already-suggested policies, for example, 'is there an alternative that is unbreakable, reusable and low cost?'. Note that the software suggested this last question, not the user. It randomly mixed and matched the key features of each option. Finally, *Decision Aide II* makes recommendations about the best policy to pursue. Any policy that fails to satisfy a 'must' is instantly dropped, although such a process is not always clear cut. If so, the user might decide to retain the policy and designate it as a 'risk'. In any event, the package dutifully shows all policies in terms of their scores for attaining the 'wants', and how these scores compare with other policies' scores, paired reviews and sensitivity tests. One can also ask the program to 'assess risks' and it will then document each policy's riskiness in terms of probability and seriousness. Of course, all this can become confusing. Software is meant to clarify confusion, but some of these old style packages tend to replicate it.

Overall however, *Decision Aide II* epitomizes the generic, comprehensive policymaking software of its generation. It is nothing if it is not a thorough method. It leaves few stones unturned in its search for brainstormed ideas, it insists on separating out the urgent goals from the luxurious ones and it is well abreast of the niceties of policy implementation and risk assessment. Small wonder, therefore, that some more modern but still generic and comprehensive packages use many of *Decision Aide II*'s methods.

Lesson 10: Respect the goals hierarchy

Not all good policymaking involves strict adherence to a goals hierarchy. Sometimes it might be more efficient to consider quickly whether there exist certain decisions that underlie not just one but several goals. This will enable policymakers to focus in on just the key underlying decisions rather than on a complete, stylized hierarchy of goals.

However, a concept so useful as the goals hierarchy should not be thrown away lightly. It is a very powerful instrument for forcing completeness in one's review of all possible ways to address one's overall goal. Moreover, it prevents the mixing of goals at different levels of abstraction, and so it works against 'premature specificity' of policy choice.

In view of this, any shortcuts to avoid the full goals hierarchy procedure ought to be taken with extreme care. Always give such a universally accepted method the respect that is due.

One such successor to *Decision Aide II* is the medium-priced package *Criterium* (Frentzen, 1990). It presents the user with the overall goal on the top left of the computer screen, with branches to the right showing 'criteria that influence that decision'. Each criterion then branches into options that must be evaluated. This is standard goals hierarchy practice and such a procedure is claimed by the package's authors to incorporate a wealth of knowledge about the ways in which people make comparisons.

Similar programs are the low-priced *Decision Analysis* and the medium-priced *Decisions?/Decisions!*. These are briefly documented by Hodge *et al.*, (1992). The first begins by helping users to organize their policies and criteria, and it then outputs three tables – 'advantages', 'disadvantages' and 'best choices'. The second takes the user through a seven-step process in order to quantify, compare, rank and validate policy judgements using its 'LightTunnel Interface'.

But before closing this sub-section we need to reiterate our main message. This is that standard, traditional, generic policymaking packages seem logical enough in terms of their step-by-step procedures used to clarify the enormous complexity surrounding any serious policymaking exercise. But one is frequently left with the suspicion that the quality of the final decision depends on the initiative and endurance of the user to ensure that everything has been taken into account. If some things have been omitted, then the final recommendation could be worthless.

For this reason, other packages tend to be more 'thinking' in their style. This stops policymaking becoming so diverted into intrigue and gossip that confidence in the final decision is lost. They try to help users concentrate more on the essentials of the policymaking problem. An example is the genre of software that adopts a more focused 'multi-criteria analysis' approach (French, 1986, 1989; Henig, 1996).

2.2.2. Multi-criteria packages

We have noted above how multi-criteria analysis can at times be complex and difficult for many people to understand. Nevertheless, some popular packages do manage to exploit this approach in an easily understood way. They usually incorporate a goals-achievement matrix (Hill, 1972).

The latter is basically a table in which policy alternatives are listed down the left margin, each column of the table represents an evaluation criterion, and scores in the body of the table indicate how well a row's policy satisfies each column's criterion. It is then a simple matter to calculate the desirability of each policy by summing along its row of the table. Moreover, before such summation takes place, more sophisticated exercises can multiply each column's numbers by a factor that corresponds to that criterion's importance.

Software packages incorporating this approach include the medium-priced *DecideRight* (Peschel, 1996; Seligman, 1996). Although it takes the user through a six-stage process to determine the correct overall aim, it mostly concentrates on nomination of policy alternatives and scoring them in a goals achievement matrix. It also incorporates scenario building that allows the user to perform 'what if' type experiments. The latter involve assuming different future states for the environment which in turn might alter policies' scores on certain criteria. They could therefore force a different conclusion as to what the best policy is.

Moreover, *DecideRight* provides a number of sample problems, such as how to select the best doctor or lawyer, or to which university to send one's child. This ensures that the user is in no doubt about how the package should be used, and more examples are available from the software company's web site.

A cheaper multi-criteria package is the low-cost *BestChoice3* (Rubenking, 1993) into which the user can enter up to 255 choices and 55 criteria. Moreover, up to 54 participants can be involved in making the decision, and they can be weighted according as to how 'expert' they are deemed to be. That is, the best policy is found not only by scoring the alternatives and weighting the evaluation criteria, but also by factoring in the levels of confidence one has in each user and his or her scores. Note also that scoring policies on criteria is done by making qualitative comparisons between pairs, and the writers of the software claim that only around 35% of all possible pair-wise comparisons, rather than all of them, need to be made in order to arrive at valid conclusions.

Still other multi-criteria packages include the medium-priced *Decision Pad* and its cousin *Business Wits* (Frentzen, 1990). Both are keen to be as useable as possible and so they use a spreadsheet in order to make data entry, and understanding of processes, much easier. Moreover, Hodge *et al.* (1992) surveyed this sort of policymaking software. They eventually listed several low-cost programs including *Automan 2.0*, *Best Alternative*, the *Consensus Builder* (version 4.2) and *Criteria Rank*. *Consensus Builder* uses an expert system to assign criterion weights.

Lesson 11: Bite the bullet

Policymakers frequently stumble at the last hurdle. Particularly when the stakes are high, they tend to call for more analysis of the likely effects of policy decisions under different scenarios, before anything is decided. All this relieves them of the burden of actual policymaking, which can be very dàunting.

But such diving for cover behind a plea for more research can also be very dangerous. Putting off a decision until full information becomes available can mean postponing policymaking forever. Ultimately, policymakers must act.

Another low-cost, multi-criteria package that they found was *Lightyear*. Its distinguishing feature is that it enables the user to make comparisons in either a numerical, verbal or graphical manner. It then uses an elimination-of-alternatives method to drop policies from consideration because of their low scores. It also incorporates some 'if-then' rules so that one can perform sensitivity analyses on policies. Finally, Hodge *et al.* describe *Seriatim*, which runs on both *IBM* and *Apple* type computers, another system called *Value Index*, and a program known as *P/G%* (Policy/Goal Percentaging). The latter uses percentages to show goals' relative achievement levels, as distinct from 'simply counting dollars, meters, smiles or anything else'.

Note that Hodge *et al.* also found a number of medium-cost, multi-criteria packages. These include *MATS* (Multi-Attribute Tradeoff System), *Confidence Factor* which handles up to 100 alternatives, and *Decision Pad 2.01* which is able to accommodate up to 250 alternatives, 150 criteria, two levels of weights and 60 evaluator/users. Moreover, in *Decision Pad 2.01* the user controls the scoring scheme used, with 18 such schemes supplied by the software and an option to create up to 80 customized rating scales as well.

But obviously, if a user employed only a fraction of these policy-scoring possibilities, they would become a prime candidate for analysis paralysis. Indeed, similar concerns are held for users of another of Hodge *et al.*'s discoveries – *Soft-Pac Solutions*. It uses an apparently sophisticated scoring method, but it fails to tell the user how it works. If one does not know how the final recommendations were arrived at, how can one trust the program's output?

Finally, Hodge *et al.* mention *MDS*, a multi-criteria package available from Slovakia that is able to combine quantitative with qualitative data. There is also the *Micro-Mulcre Interactive Decision Support System*, which can be purchased in Bulgaria and Austria, and which ranks policies both by score and by 'dominance'. Dominance means that a policy rates highly if it is superior by a large margin either across several criteria, or just on one critical criterion. Such a policy might sometimes be the best one to adopt, even though its total score, across all criteria taken together, might be quite low.

However, we cannot over-emphasize the apprehension we have with this sort of package. Underlying multi-attribute analysis lurks a fear that a little knowledge might be a dangerous thing. Whenever one uses a complicated, state of the art package, one that implements a multitude of different scoring methods to produce a plethora of conflicting recommendations, one's confidence as a policymaker is surely shaken. For this reason many practical policymakers shy away from the more sophisticated packages, which they often find too difficult to understand anyway.

But a sophisticated, multi-criteria package that is in fact fairly understandable has been produced at the European Community's Joint Research Centre in Northern Italy (Menegolo, 1996). It is called *NAIADE* – Novel Approach to Imprecise Assessments and Decision Environments. It is mathematically sophisticated enough to turn quantitative, probabilistic or language-based paired comparisons of scores on criteria into overall ratings.

Moreover, if these scores are collected from different interest groups, the program outputs a diagram of possible coalitions of groups. Such coalitions are based on the similarities or otherwise between different groups' scores for the different alternatives on the various criteria. Hence, as well as rating alternative policies, this program also tries to anticipate something about people's likely responses to policy choices.

But alas, although *NAIADE* is reasonably friendly, the manual's explanations of the detailed scoring mechanisms for converting paired comparisons into overall ratings will still be beyond the understanding of users who are not educated in the fields of multiple utility analysis and game theory.

Lesson 12: Evaluate skilfully

Many policymakers blissfully stumble through their careers with a naive belief that the best policy is simply the highest-scoring one. But anyone who has ever looked at evaluation software or evaluation textbooks will realize that policymaking is far from that simple (Wyatt, 1989).

For example, sometimes the best policy could be not the one that scores the best over the totality of all criteria, but the one that scores highly on a just a few key criteria that happen to have captured the imagination of participants. Or perhaps people prefer a low-scoring policy that dominates the previously-implemented policy so spectacularly that it is the epitome of a 'winner'. Dominance analysis might, therefore, sometimes be better than traditional scoring methods. Hence one's choice of evaluation method needs to be driven by the particular circumstances pertaining at the time.

Moreover, policymakers must standardize policies' scores before even beginning to rate them, and sometimes quantitative and qualitative data will need somehow to be dovetailed. Thus policymaking is a far more sophisticated process than one of simply assigning scores to alternatives.

Nevertheless, awareness of these possible refinements is a double-edged sword. At least those policymakers who take an uncomplicated approach to their task will never suffer from analysis paralysis. But it is pointless undertaking policymaking in a way that simply avoids complexity. It is far more satisfactory to become more expert in policy evaluation.

Also, the example given in the manual's tutorial gives a hint that users might eventually find themselves undertaking decision analysis and decision support rather than policymaking. Specifically, alternative policies in the example are designed to rescue an ecologically stressed forest on the Po River delta. Policies have names like 'business as usual', 'optimized agriculture', 'flooding of the valley', 'partial flooding combined with business as usual' and 'partial flooding combined with optimized agriculture'. Moreover, the criteria considered include 'profit', 'employment', 'tourist attractiveness', 'recreational attractiveness', 'ecological equilibrium' and 'risk of causing ecological damage'. Finally, the interest groups are 'farmers', 'environmentalists', 'recreationists', 'landless labourers' and 'residents of the Po Delta area'.

These are very detailed considerations, which suggests that the problem being addressed is not quite ready for policy choice. That is, *NAIADE* will be very useful for simulating all the intricate effects on criteria and people of a large array of possible policies, but it is not really ready to make a final decision. In other words, it is now time to evaluate each policy in terms of its overall effect on the community as a whole, with a view to final decision further down the track. Any system that is used more for such pre-policymaking, or simulation, is not true policymaking software.

This is not to imply that *NAIADE* cannot prepare policymakers for policy decisions very effectively (Stewart, 1992). It is very valuable for straightening out users' thoughts on who is likely to think what about the various alternative policies. But a final decision ultimately has to be made that takes everything and everyone into account. That is, we need to consider not just the listed criteria but other things as well, such as policies' easiness, speed, and correctness. We also need to take into account not just the listed interest groups but everyone else also. Multi-criteria packages might look comprehensive, but they are almost always only partial in their coverage of decision-relevant issues.

2.2.3. Path-finding packages

Our second sort of 'thinking', less generic and more direct, policymaking packages that try to focus users' minds on problem essentials, employ a path-finding approach. Prominent amongst these are programs that use a 'decision tree' methodology (Raiffa, 1970; Coffee and Moser, 1990). This is a reasonably straight forward method that sets out alternative actions, along with their respective 'payoff' and 'probability' levels, by representing them as forks in a road. The road represents one's proposed progress through the future, and which fork one should take is determined by multiplying its payoff by its probability (Wright, 1984).

For example, one's aim might be to 'become rich', and the fork along the road of one's future progress might involve choosing between 'find oil' and 'become a lawyer'. The best route is the one whose expected utility is higher – expected utility being the product of payoff and probability. Note that while the payoff of 'find oil' is very high, its probability is extremely low. By contrast, the payoff of 'become a lawyer' is not nearly so grand as 'find oil', but its probability is much higher. It could be a close contest.

By laying out all similar policy choices in such a chart, one is able to arrive at the best policy simply by taking the route that has the highest expected utility at each fork. For example, after the 'find oil' versus 'become a lawyer' fork there may be another fork between say, 'invest in property' and 'play the share market'. Again, one would take the alternative that had the highest expected utility. Hence one's eventual chosen policy would be the sum total of all the decisions taken at the forks in the chart, for example, 'find oil' plus 'invest in property', or 'become a lawyer' plus 'invest in property' or whatever.

A good example of decision tree software is the medium-priced *DATA* (Decision Analysis by TreeAge) program as described by Frentzen (1990) and by Humphry (1992). It automatically compares alternative actions within the chart.

It should be noticed that the decision tree approach to policymaking looks and feels something like the scheduling approach to planning. Both methods lay out future possibilities in the form of a progress path. But they should never be confused for one another. Policymaking is not scheduling. It does not usually involve deciding *when* to do tasks; it is more concerned with deciding *what* tasks to do. Hence that type of scheduling software that determines a 'critical path' through a chart of future activities in order to minimize a project's completion time is outside the scope of this book. Such software is planning software rather than policymaking software.

However, before leaving it note that scheduling software may sometimes be useful to policymakers (Fersko-Weiss, 1989). Hence it might pay to peruse Fersko-Weiss's (1990) lengthy discussion of the *Project Outlook* software. He even talks about different pieces of software having different 'personalities', as mentioned in Chapter 1 above, and he eventually opts for two scheduling packages as being the best in the field.

His chosen two are *Viewpoint*, because it has excellent graphics, and *Open Policy*, because its user is able to construct interactively a very complicated scheduling chart without much prior experience. Those who want to learn more about scheduling software should also consult Larson (1997) who points out that there are dozens of project management packages, both low- and medium-priced.

Interestingly, Larson also argues that MicroSoft's *Project* software is too general in the sense that it can be used for anything from planning a museum exhibit, to writing a novel, to managing a construction site. He says that when one is knee deep in industrial management, and when one knows that the software used will never be employed for anything else, it seems better to use some customized software. Actually however, one can do both, because it is possible to import files from *Project* to more customized software.

Hence route-finding software, both decision tree- and critical path-based, can be very useful for policymakers. The only danger is that experts in these methods sometimes come to believe that these are the only policymaking methods that exist. Exemplary policymakers should never become so self deluded. Decision trees and critical paths are excellent clarification tools for properly deciding whenever the options are measurable and clear cut, but when the issues are more ambiguous, policymakers need the assistance of theoretically more sophisticated approaches.

2.3. Dedicated Software

In this section we describe some dedicated packages. By this we mean those that concentrate on one particular part of the policymaking process. They do this in an attempt to ensure that the particular phase is performed with maximum effectiveness. Such packages concentrate either on better thinking about policies, as described in sub-section 2.3.1, better choosing of the best policy, as outlined in sub-section 2.3.2, or better anticipating of people's responses, as covered in sub-section 2.3.3.

2.3.1. Packages to assist thinking

Some software writers believe strongly in the adage 'a problem well stated is a problem half solved'. They go to considerable lengths to describe the problem as carefully as possible so that the first part of policymaking – generating some preliminary idea of what needs to be done, is performed adequately.

An effective method for helping one do this is SODA (Eden, 1989), which stands for 'Strategic Options Development and Analysis' as used by the *COPE* software, and Buffa *et al.*'s (1996) *MACRAME* (Multiple Actor RepresentAtion ModElling) program uses a very similar method to that used by SODA – 'cognitive mapping'.

The latter involves participants mapping their cognition of the policymaking problem on a chart. When the maps are large, the computerized version of the technique is very useful indeed, especially when it comes to combining each participant's cognitive map with all the others to form a group version.

A cognitive map consists of nodes. Connecting them are arrows that mean 'leading to' or 'connected with'. For instance in Eden's example, which is about the problems arising when workers possess shares in the firm for which they are working, one node is labelled:

knowledge of employee share ownership,

and there is an arrow from it to the node labelled:

fear of drop in union membership

which is in turn connected to another node labelled:

fear of weakened role of collective bargaining.

This symbolizes that knowledge of employee ownership can lead to a worry that union membership could drop, followed by a weakening of the collective bargaining power of the rank and file.

Ideally, the nodes themselves should be dichotomous, as shown in the next part of Eden's example. That is, from the last *'fear of . . .'* node there is an arrow to a node labelled:

union opposition versus union support for profit-sharing schemes,

and this, in turn, arrows to another dichotomous node labelled:

Labour support for versus Labour ambivalence towards profit sharing.

If there is an arrow from the first part of the previous node it is marked with a plus sign, and so there is a plus arrow from the 'Labour support versus Labour ambivalence . . .' node to a node labelled:

(seek) upmarket appeal of Labour Party.

Moreover, if there is an arrow from the second part of the '*Labour support* versus *labour ambivalence* . . .' node, it is marked with a minus sign, and so in the example, there is a negative arrow from the '*Labour support* versus *Labour ambivalence* . . .' node to one labelled:

retain Labour concordat with the unions.

Thus by writing down nodes and connections to other nodes to describe the problem situation, policies eventually suggest themselves. In this case, the policies emerging were '*seek upmarket appeal for the Labour Party*' and '*retain Labour concordat with the unions*'.

But such policies are not comprehensive. They represent only one train of thought. For example, from the node '*fear of weakened role of collective bargaining*' another train of thought could have gone to a node such as '*strike action versus legislative pressure*'. This is why the SODA technique involves taking each participant's cognitive map and joining them, chiefly by overlapping identical nodes, and in this way a giant cognitive map, representing many trains of thought that exist within the total group, can be drawn. Such a map is, no doubt, a fertile source of possible policies to pursue. It functions as a valuable record of what participants actually think about the situation being addressed.

Lesson 13: Study the participants

It is important to learn each person's perception of what the policymaking problem actually is. If people have different perceptions and these are allowed to remain hidden, there is little point in continuing. This is because people will disagree with other policy suggestions simply because the latter seek to solve problems which, to them, are far less important, or perhaps even non existent.

Hence policymaking needs to start off by breaking down our ignorance based barriers to good practice. Cognitive mapping is an excellent 'ice breaker' for such an exercise. Through it, people become familiar with the hopes and fears of other participants, especially when the group tries to join each individual's map into an amalgamated, group map.

To some extent all policymaking tries to find out what each participant thinks the main problem is. But this tends to be done most thoroughly when cognitive mapping is used. The latter can be most revealing.

COPE describes this as passive software that is 'non prescriptive'. Hence after the amalgamated cognitive map is completed, the group agrees on a set of key goals, interrelated problems, key options and assumptions. An extension of the *COPE* approach is *COGNITA*, which is experimental, and so it is only sketchily described by Epinasse (1994).

COGNITA was inspired by a Cognitive Science-derived view of problem solving, which will be discussed in Chapter 4. For now, suffice to note that it tries to act as a bridge between a symbolic module, which uses cognitive mapping, and a connectionist module that uses a simulated neural network (Campbell, 1989). The intention appears to be for the latter to actually learn from the former so that the whole process of making cognitive maps will eventually be improved to new levels of automation and perceptiveness.

Remember however that cognitive mapping-based situation structuring simply sets the scene for the other part of the 'think' phase of policymaking – brainstorming – and there is considerable electronic brainstorming software available. It aims to stimulate the creativity of users so that their chances of suggesting innovative ideas are maximized.

Traditionally it has been believed that brainstorming is the quintessential human activity in which group members 'spark' off the creative energy of other group members to increase the total number and quality of ideas generated. But Rangaswamy and Lilien (1997) actually suggest that the computerized alternative, where people each interact alone with some brainstorming software, might be even better. They quote several other researchers who have apparently compared the number of ideas generated, and how often such ideas have been subsequently implemented, for a traditional brainstorming group versus the same number of people working alone on a computer. In all instances the computerized approach worked better than the traditional approach.

Rangaswamy and Lilien then detail several electronic brainstorming packages. Some of them have been developed to assist the commercial business activity known as 'new product development', a process that requires considerable creativity, and these packages have names like *NamePro* and *Mindlink*. They point out that each package uses its own particular method for stimulating creativity, and these can only be evaluated, if at all, in the light of one's own particular circumstances. Indeed, some might not be very worthwhile at all, since every one works from some sort of 'cook book' formula that, ironically, may work against the very aim of brainstorming software – thinking 'outside the box'. Often, a formula approach can actually discourage users from thinking laterally.

Note that when it comes to new product development, one might also use a number of packages described by the Management Software Association (1994). An example is the medium-priced package *Diagnostic Audit* which facilitates the quantitative and qualitative assessment of factors which are most likely to affect the success of one's proposed product, by synthesizing information from past strategic performance.

A more Rolls Royce alternative is the high-priced *Advia Danprod* system that tests all stages of new product launching. Then there is *Marketing Manager*. The latter is a medium-priced package that gives step-by-step marketing advice after it has worked through a sophisticated database of questions. Such questions force the user to think down logically constructed paths. The program stores users' answers to the questions and then reviews them in the light of various marketing policies.

Finally, Rangaswamy and Lilien point out that it is one thing to generate ideas, but quite another to amalgamate several of them into a viable and coherent package. They then suggest using a method known as 'conjoint analysis' to do this. Packages incorporating this method include *ACA* (Adaptive Conjoint Analysis) and *BUNDOPT*. Both actually design questionnaires for potential customers in order to analyse prevailing market conditions. Moreover, conjoint analysis modules are available in such well known statistical analysis packages as *SPSS* and *SAS*.

A better known example of brainstorming software is Thierauf's (1993) *IdeaFisher*. This is medium priced. Its first major module is *Qbank*, which asks the user what are the issues at hand and what the possible policies are. The second major module is known as *IdeaBank*, and it takes key words that emanate from the first module and tries to find matches for them within its data bank's 60,000 words and phrases. Such matches are meant to trigger policies, which are recorded by the user before going to the final module where there are over 2,100 (!) questions to think about regarding the ideas that have been generated.

A low cost but less well known brainstorming package is *The Idea Generator* (Experience in Software Inc., 1998*a*). This uses on-screen prompts, questions, role plays, and metaphors. There is also *Idea Generator Plus* (Management Software Association, 1994), which is medium-priced. It asks users to brainstorm by explaining what the goals are as well as which people are associated with each goal. It uses seven rounds of questioning in order to approach the problem from a number of different perspectives. This forces participants to see the problem from other people's points of view and to recall their own previous experiences in order to interpret the ideas being generated.

Lesson 14: Dedication

All too often a policymaking exercise starts off talking about the situation in general. It does not focus on the task at hand – policymaking. By contrast, if talk immediately proceeds in the direction of serious discussion of 'issues' – the problems for which the whole policymaking exercise has presumably been set up to address, successful outcomes seem more likely.

That is, useful policies can probably be extracted from participants' initial thought processes so long as discussion is dedicated to the policymaking task. This will put any exercise well on the way towards undertaking productive, as distinct from discursive, policymaking.

Rather than seek still more knowledge for knowledge's sake, good policymaking requires dedication to the pursuit of improved decisions.

Finally, there is a brainstorming package known as *MindLink Problem Solver* (Management Software Association, 1994). This is medium priced *IBM* and *Apple* software that works through a number of 'industry proven' exercises for improving users' creativity. Its first module, 'Gym', incorporates mental imaging and improvization techniques. After this, the 'Idea Generation' module examines different permutations of the problem, and then two 'Problem Solving' modules take the user through a series of steps for generating and evaluating ideas.

Hence we can conclude by noting that there has been considerable effort put into software that helps policymakers think more incisively about their situation. Methods used range from cognitive mapping to the various forms of brainstorming. We will probably hear more about this genre of software, because initial situation structuring is a key ingredient of successful policymaking and it is important to get it right. If one does not get it right, the whole policymaking process could be jeopardized.

2.3.2. Packages to assist choosing

The next phase of policymaking, choosing the best policy, is central to the total process. This is probably why the method of 'paired comparisons' is so widely used. It involves resisting the temptation to simply apply numerical scores to alternative policies. Instead, each policy is compared with each other policy in turn, and the scores for each policy are eventually amalgamated. Hence this method facilitates the mixing of quantitative and qualitative considerations into the evaluation of policies, and it still comes up with a unitary score for each. Also, it makes sure that comparisons, and hence final, amalgamated scores for policies, are thought about very thoroughly.

Some say the process is in fact too thorough. Paired comparisons may 'get inside the heads' of people and so accurately reveal their evaluative attitudes, but in large-scale problems the application of paired comparisons to all possible pairs of policies can take a very long time indeed. Not only does this annoy users, but it also makes them tired and less likely to answer the software's questions accurately. Hence ultimately, it can be conducive to inaccurate, final assessment of policies.

This is why Badiru *et al.* (1993) have produced a package that tries to make the paired comparisons process more manageable. They shorten it to the point where only essential paired comparisons are made, and they then use probability concepts to fill in the missing information. Their software is called *DDM* (decision support system for Dynamic Decision Making) and in their article they discuss the paired comparisons-based 'analytic hierarchy process' which is to be discussed below.

For now note that the analytic hierarchy process involves identifying an 'objective' at the top of the hierarchy, a set of 'alternatives' along the bottom, and 'events' in between. Events can be scenarios, judges, evaluation criteria or whatever. One then determines the scores for the alternative policies along the bottom with respect to each event/sub-event happening, using paired comparisons. It is then a simple matter of multiplication up the relevant branches of the hierarchy to obtain policies' unitary scores. Of course, the importance levels, or perhaps the probabilities of the intervening events would have already been assigned using paired comparisons also.

In order to reduce the number of paired comparisons, *DDM* first arranges events in decreasing order according to their number of sub-events. It then makes paired comparisons for the sub-events contributing to the first event, and thereafter it only compares another sub-event if it has not been encountered before. Moreover, alternatives are scored only in terms of the sub-event that is most likely to occur, as distinct from being compared in terms of all possible sub-events. Such a shortcut saves the user a vast amount of work for only a small loss of information.

There is, in fact, a body of literature about the merits and drawbacks of the 'analytic hierarchy process', much of which involves mathematical discussions which are quite impenetrable for lay persons and, therefore, outside the scope of this book. The work of Brans and Mareschal (1994) is typical, but their efforts have at least resulted in some useable software. Their system is called *GAIA*, and it uses the PROMCALC methodology. The latter involves assessing alternatives not just in terms of their scores, but also in terms of their relative ranks, incompatibilities and other attributes.

Moreover, Kiss *et al.*'s (1994) software, *ELECCALC*, is a very elaborate package that likewise absorbs users' paired comparisons data to calculate global preferences. Its method may be better than the traditional analytic hierarchy process, but the cryptic nature of the mathematical explanations provided makes it difficult for us to be sure of this.

Again, we shall present more discussion of the analytic hierarchy process as a policy-choosing method when we discuss some research frontier software below. The best policy-evaluation method to use is actually a very vexed question that turns on issues regarding consistency and the relative merits of ratio scale data compared to interval scale data. Such issues are addressed in Chapter 8.

2.3.3. Packages to assist anticipating

To explain what we mean by 'anticipate' we need to distinguish it from 'simulate'. The latter is what the 'decision support' packages, described in the next chapter, do – test the effects on the environment of various policy alternatives. It is part of the intelligence-gathering that precedes the 'choose' phase of the policymaking process.

By contrast, 'anticipating' follows the choosing phase. Anticipate means to foreshadow what would happen if some policy is chosen for adoption. Hence the *NAIADE* software mentioned above, which anticipates what coalitions people might form after implementation of certain policies, is an example of software for anticipating. Anticipation refers not to the analysis of the effects of policies in terms of changing the current environment, but more to the prediction of how people will respond if certain policies are chosen.

Some will argue that this is really simulation anyway. How people will respond is part of the policymaking environment. Hence anticipation should be merely another part of the 'think' phase. This is true, but such anticipation/simulation only occurs the second time around. It is part of a feedback loop which dictates that once we are anticipating responses to policy choices we should actually be back in the 'think' phase again and be preparing for the next attempt at choosing.

That is, the policymaking process never ends. It is circular and only broken into phases for explanatory convenience. It is just that we arbitrarily define the 'anticipate' phase to follow the 'choose' phase the first and subsequent times through the process. Hence readers might regard some of the software discussed in this sub-section as more a part of the 'choose' phase, which it could well be, but only during the second or subsequent times around the feedback loop.

An example of anticipatory software is the *Ithink* software (http://www.palisade.com). This is medium-priced *Apple* software that asks 'what if?' questions. It actually owes its origin to the 'dynamic systems analysis' work done by Jay Forrester some time ago (Forrester, 1969, 1973). Such work caused a great deal of interest at the time. It incorporated models of important systems, running on what were, for their time, very large mainframe computers, and such models purported to explain the mechanisms behind hugely complex systems such as large cities, and even the world's natural environment.

The feeling was that if the ultra complex mechanisms of the world could be at least partially tamed using such simulations, then solutions to civilization's most pressing problems could not be far behind. Moreover, the approach was in some ways a forerunner to cognitive mapping because its output was graphical. It showed problem elements and 'flows' between them of goods, services, information or whatever. Moreover, predicting such flows was achieved using very sophisticated systems of equations, along with feedback loops to the originator and other nodes in order to approximate cause-effect mechanisms.

But these 'systems' were so complex that their behaviour was mostly unpredictable. One could run hundreds, or even thousands of iterations through the model, with different starting parameters and different coefficients that were inserted into the equations. This enabled one to see whether certain output patterns were more prevalent, and so, presumably, more likely to occur than others.

However, such results were arbitrary because one only had to tweak a few parameters in order to generate a completely different set of outputs. This was partly why the approach fell into disfavour, at least within the city planning and environmental management disciplines. In other words, despite the dynamic systems models being complex, such complexity was not accompanied by a detailed research effort aimed at putting the model's assumptions on firmer ground. This was unsatisfactory. It was simply not good enough to have a huge, intimidatory computer model if the theory underlying such a model was weak. Its output was likely to be accidental and, therefore, dangerous in the sense that people could be bluffed into thinking that the output was actually true even though there was no way of knowing this.

Other reasons for dynamic systems' demise were the non-transparent complicatedness of its equations and feedback loops, the expense and the tedium of running the models on mainframe computers of that time. Yet despite such weaknesses, the dynamic systems approach has enjoyed something of a resurgence in popularity, at least within the commercial world, since the advent of cheaper software running on desktop computers.

Lesson 15: Scrutinize your assumptions

The business community is sometimes willing to swallow the arbitrariness of software's underlying assumptions. It turns a blind eye to invalidity and rationalizes such an action along the lines of 'If the assumptions had some validity, here are possible consequences that would logically follow'.

Such a philosophy probably says a lot about commercial policymakers' obsession with getting an edge over their competition. They are always anxious to be the first to anticipate a possible outcome that no one else has ever thought of. After all, this could lead to greater profits.

However, getting the 'science' right is usually the casualty – a situation that could lead to disaster. That is, policymaking will not be sustainable in the long term unless it is built upon a foundation of valid assumptions.

The result is that today's *Ithink* software sets up a causal model with the help of the user and it then automatically calculates the influencing equations for the resultant model. Then, it uses graphs and animation to help users vary equations' parameter values in order to explore scenarios and so 'discover' the highest-leverage opportunities for improving performance.

Indeed, the animation powers of *Ithink* are probably part of the reason it is so popular. It takes the form of a 'flight simulator' in which the user is not flying an aeroplane but running a company. More specifically, it uses diagrams of nodes that represent people, processes and locations, along with formulae that connect such nodes. It thus simulates the flows of information, goods, stocks and profits across the whole system, enabling the software to graph the way in which outputs impact back onto the user. This is just like feedback that occurs in say, physiology: when the body undertakes effort and so triggers deeper breathing and a faster heart rate so that the muscles' increased requirement for oxygen is supplied.

In other words, the anticipatory *Itink* package can be used either as a game or as a recruitment and training device. One uses the MFS (Management Flight Simulator) to see whether a recruit can pilot the organization to the top of the profits tree rather than make it plummet and burn. More specifically, manipulating the model in real time can generate a dis-equilibriating situation in which the company either advances or crashes, and, as the situation is manipulated, the model's responses educate a user about the different impacts, on the different sections of the company, which stem from his or her proposed changes.

Indeed, the 'Analyst' version of *IThink* comes with slide bars so that inputs can be altered, and the effects on other nodes can be instantly seen, along with pictures, graphs and other illustrative devices. This makes the flight simulator a very entertaining and educational package.

Other anticipation packages include those that operationalize risk analysis. A typical example is @*RISK* (http://www.palisade.com) which tries very hard to account for all possible events. It uses a spreadsheet that contains uncertain values for which the user has to choose a probability distribution. Hundreds or thousands of simulations are then made so that one can get possible outcomes for the bottom line variables. That is, the user inputs estimated probability distributions for risk factors, and the program outputs probability distributions for different parts of the outcome situation. Hence the user can perform scenario analysis and sensitivity analysis in order to identify factors that contribute the most to risk.

Moreover, users have the option of adding on the 'Risk Developer's Kit' (*RDK*). This enables *@RISK* to be run using any of the Windows programming languages such as 'C', 'Visual Basic' and 'Delphi'. Also, one can buy a version to run with scheduling software in order to manage a project. It will generate a probability distribution of expected dates of completion.

Still another add-on module is 'BestFit'. This calculates the best probability distribution for the user's data, using an optimizing algorithm, and there is also 'RISKview', which generates pictures of 25 types of distribution along with their goodness of fit tests for the user's data. Such tests include the 'Chi-squared', 'Anderson-Darling' and 'Kolmogorov-Smirnov' procedures.

Many policymaking projects, so long as they incorporate suitably quantitative data, can therefore be enhanced by this approach to the anticipation of possible outcomes. Such anticipation is often neglected in policymaking practice, and so it is probably the phase that is in most need of improvement.

2.4. Summary

This chapter began by looking at the problem decomposition approach taken by much traditional policymaking software, along with how different packages emphasize different actions and how they have never arrived at a consensus about what terms should be used to describe which elements of the goals hierarchy.

It then detailed some traditional, generic policymaking software by focusing on *Decision Aide II*. The latter's 'feeling', people-oriented style was compared to the more 'thinking' approach of some of the more recent software, such as that which uses multi-criteria decision making and path-finding methods.

Finally, the third section described some more specialized packages to help users within definite phases of the policymaking process. Some use cognitive mapping and brainstorming to help policymakers think about the policymaking problem, others help one to choose the best policy using paired comparisons and the analytic hierarchy process, whereas others assist in the anticipation of possible policy consequences by means of dynamic systems analysis and measurement of uncertainty.

Chapter 3

Supporting Software

This chapter reviews software that plays more of a 'supporting' role in policymaking. Even though it is frequently very popular and successful software in its own right, it tends to be for backing up policymaking rather than helping users actually decide what to do in the future. It tends to service the corner disciplines of figure 1.1 in Chapter 1. Nevertheless, it contains some good lessons for policymaking practice, and a list of the packages described is shown in table 3.1. As usual, no claim of a comprehensive coverage of such software is being made here.

This chapter has two sections. Section 3.1 looks at generic, policy-related, backup software such as decision support, groupware, gameware and data mining packages. Section 3.2 then discusses more domain-specific programs, such as those designed especially for strategic business management, for public administration and for negotiation support.

3.1. Generic Software

There are a number of packages that attempt to maximize policymaking quality by leaving no stone unturned in their attempt to inform users about the features and opportunities of the environment they are in. Such 'decision support' packages will be looked at in sub-section 3.1.1. Other packages are founded on a belief that the best route to better policymaking is greater emphasis on the hopes, fears and bright ideas of the people who are involved. This leads us back to the brainstorming approach, but this time with all participants connected in an automated, online way, as is achieved by the various 'groupware' products described in sub-section 3.1.2. Still others believe that Game Theory, whether it is applied to the individual or to collectives, holds the key, and examples of software predicated on such an assumption is described in sub-section 3.1.3. Finally, there are other software writers who are more enamoured of the emerging field known as 'data mining', which is an attempt to extract policy from within the vast amounts of historical, policy-related data that are becoming increasingly available. Such packages are described in sub-section 3.1.4.

3.1.1. Decision support packages

Examples of comprehensive decision support software are scattered throughout many fields. For instance, the extremely high-priced *Enlisted Force Management System* (Carter *et al.*, 1992) was purpose built, using no less than 125 person years of effort, to become an extremely comprehensive system for personnel management within any organization. There are also examples within the urban planning discipline, for example, Aoki *et al.*'s (1996) complex system for minimizing the errors that surround land use forecasts, and Klosterman's (1997) *WhatIf?* package.

Table 3.1. Supporting packages for policymaking.

Type	Package	Cost	Reference
Dec. support	*Enlisted Force Manag. Sys.*	> $1000	Carter *et al.*, 1992
Dec. support	*What If?*	> $1000	Klosterman,1997
Dec. support	*StratConsult*	> $1000	Moormann and Lochte-Holtgreven, 1993
Dec. support	*?*	> $1000	Colson and Mareschal, 1994
Dec. support	*Definitive Scenario*	< $1000	Seiter, 1998
Dec. support	*TopRank*	< $1000	http://www.palisade.com
Dec. support	*?*	< $1000	Pinson *et al.*, 1997
Dec. support	*Stratplan*	< $1000	http://www.fbs.hw.ac.uk
Dec. support	*The Digital MBA*	< $1000	Experience in Software Inc., 1998*d*
Dec. support	*SimCity*	< $1000	Starr, 1994
Groupware	*OASS*	< $1000	Cacez-Kecmanovic, 1994
Groupware	*Lotus Notes, GroupWorks*	< $1000	Rangaswamy and Lilien, 1997
Groupware	*K.net*	< $1000	Rooney, 1997
Groupware	*QuestMap*	< $1000	Gottesman, 1995
Groupware	*GroupSystems, VisionQuest, V, TeamFocus, TeamKit/VM*	< $1000	Knack, 1994
Groupware	*Shared Decision-making Multimedia System*	> $1000	Levin, 1993
Gameware	*Eliza*	free	Weizenbaum, 1976
Gameware	*CONAN*	?	Howard,1989
Data mining	*Profiler 2000, CART*	< $1000	http://www.palisade.com
Data mining	*Q+E, Forest and Trees*	?	Radding, 1995
Business	*Execustat, Turbo Spring-Stat*	< $1000	Management Software Assoc, 1994
Business	*Data Desk*	< $1000	http://www.palisade.com
Business	*Advia Strat. Activity Costing*	> $1000	Management Software Assoc, 1994
Business	*Business Develop. Expert, DPL, KnowledgeSeeker, Benchmarking Software*	< $1000	Management Software Assoc, 1994
Business	*CrossTarget*	> $1000	Management Software Assoc, 1994
Business	*Extend, Q1000, ManagePro., Competitive Advantage*	< $1000	Management Software Assoc, 1994
Business	*MARKSTAT, Resource Allocation*	> $1000	Management Software Assoc, 1994

Table 3.1. Cont.

Type	Package	Cost	Reference
Business	*4Cast2 , Business Policy Toolkit*	< $1000	Yocum, 1990
Business	*Commander Prism*	< $1000	Management Software Assoc, 1994
Business	*PC Prism*	< $1000	Feuche, 1990
Business	*Forecast Pro, Crystal Ball, MAPS, Market Dynamics, MktSim, Smart Forecasts I, Advia Decide & Manage*	< $1000	Management Software Assoc, 1994
Business	*Alacrity Strategy*	> $1000	Management Software Assoc, 1994
Business	*PolicyMagic Analysis*	< $100	http://www.planmagic.com
Business	*Business Insight*	< $1000	Management Software Assoc, 1994
Business	*CHECKMATE*	< $1000	http://www.checkmate plan.com
Business	*Strategy Roundtable Enterprise*	< $1000	http://www.gryphon systems.com
Business	*Portfolio Plus*	< $1000	http:// www.strategic-dynamics.com
Health	*SMARTLINK 2000*	< $1000	Velox Systems Corp., 1998
Finance	*CRISP*	< $1000	Curley, 1997
Education	*SDP*	< $1000	Hornby and Goldner, 1994
Negotiation	*PERSUADER*	< $1000	Sycara, 1993
Negotiation	*DENEGOT*	< $1000	Mochlman *et al.*, 1992
Negotiation	*MEDIATOR, PREFCAL*	< $1000	Jarke *et al.*, 1987
Negotiation	*NEGO*	< $1000	Kersten, 1985
Negotiation	*MCBARG*	< $1000	Wierzbicki *et al.*, 1993
Negotiation	*ISES , SAM*	< $1000	Samarasan, 1993
Negotiation	*DecisionMaker*	< $1000	Fraser and Hipel, 1988
Negotiation	*NEGOTIATOR*	< $1000	Bui, 1992
Negotiation	*MATCH*	< $1000	Samarasan, 1993
Negotiation	*NEGOPOLICY , GENIE*	< $1000	Matwin *et al.*, 1989
Negotiation	*The Art of Negotiating*	< $100	Experience in Software Inc., 1998*b*
Negotiation	*Negotiator Pro*	< $1000	Experience in Software Inc., 1998*b*

The latter begins after the modellers and the community agree to test a number of alternative scenarios for their local area in terms of population growth, the desired amount of industry, business expansion and so forth. It then translates the effect of such scenarios into land use pattern consequences through the use of modern mapping, modelling and geographic information systems.

More specifically, detailed analyses of different regions' suitability for houses, shops, offices, factories and parks are made. They are then combined with the likely levels of demand for such land uses given the agreed upon scenarios. The system then produces a land use map showing which activities are likely to be located where, plus ancillary information, for each scenario.

Hence this software strikes a good balance between having a 'thinking' and a 'feeling' style. On the one hand it is predicated on, indeed it cannot proceed satisfactorily without agreement first being reached, between the modellers and the community representatives, on how everyone feels their community could evolve in the future. On the other hand it is very 'thinking' in the sense that it applies sophisticated, pre-prepared land use allocation models which can then be manipulated to accommodate additional features of the environment. For example, the system's land use prediction processes can always be adjusted to take account of any local land use zoning ordinances that exist, or the results of traffic modelling, or policies regarding preservation of the natural environment.

Hence the *WhatIf?* decision support package constitutes a good example of a complete package within the field of land use planning. It is 'feeling' enough to be sensitive to the changing whims of the community, yet it is 'thinking' enough to incorporate very sophisticated model-based analyses. But it remains a simulation package; it is excellent for asking 'what-if' questions as its name implies. It is also useful for experimentation to foresee the probable impacts of different policies. But it does not assist users to make the value judgements that are needed whenever they come to actually choose between policies.

By contrast, many supporting, simulation packages seem to crave acceptance as fully-fledged policymaking packages. Moormann and Lochte-Holtgreven (1993) present one such system, which they optimistically refer to as *SDSS* (Strategic Decision Support System). They explain (p. 403) that their system incorporates a huge number of techniques and modules because so much other software is simply either:

1. A 'DSS generator'

2. A 'prestructured DSS application', or

3. 'Other tools suitable for special applications'.

They are then quite dismissive of their middle category, prestructured DSSs, which appear to be simulation programs. They reproach them for being mere 'what-if analysers' rather than programs that cover the complete policymaking process. This seems strange. Why should simulation programs cover the complete policymaking process?

Yet Moormann and Lochte-Holtgreven warm to their theme. They point out that their *StratConsult* system contains 'information', 'design' and 'evaluation'

Lesson 16: Modelling is not policymaking

Policymaking practitioners, and the academics who advise them, frequently assume that simulation constitutes policymaking. It is as if there has been so much modelling and analytical work performed in the name of better policymaking that some modellers ultimately fail to distinguish between the two.

When one shows a decision-making program to many policymakers they will almost certainly ask 'Where is the simulation model?' To such people policymaking is, by definition, impossible without rigorous pre-analysis of the prevailing conditions.

They actually ignore the possibility of using the sort of software described in this book. The latter is designed to be implemented after all the analyses and simulations have been completed. It is meant to be used at decision-making time.

Ignoring such a phase, simply because one is hog tied by an ongoing commitment to ever more elaborate analyses of the policymaking situation, is dangerous. Policymaking projects that get so diverted are prime candidates for becoming indecisive and ineffectual. Beware of over indulgent modelling.

---

modules. The information module contains a 'strategic database', access to on-line, external databases, 'SWOT analysis' and a 'relevance tree'. The design module incorporates techniques like 'corporate culture analysis', 'morphological method', 'cross impact analysis', 'portfolio analysis' and a 'strategic business unit graph'. Finally, the evaluation module contains a what-if simulation model and a decision tree routine.

But they then ask themselves why their system has shortcomings. They lament the fact that 'verbal' information is becoming more and more important in policymaking but it has not yet been incorporated into DSS generators. They say (p.409) that, very commonly, it is:

just planning techniques (that) get incorporated rather than knowledge on strategic actions.

Yet they say this despite the fact that several programs described in this book are indeed planning programs that thrive on verbal information. We can only conclude, therefore, that Moormann and Lochte-Holtgreven should incorporate some of our programs, to be run, of course, *after* the simulations have all been completed and the results studied carefully.

Less grand decision support packages include medium-price systems like *Definitive Scenario* (Seiter, 1998) and *TopRank* (http://www.palisade.com). These are actually attachments to a spreadsheet. When the user clicks bottom-line outputs in the spreadsheet, the variables that have the largest influence on such outputs are instantly revealed – this is spreadsheet-based simulation to see what the most influential factors are. Moreover, one could then run the @*RISK* software (see above) in order to inspect the complete range of possible outputs, and so the total system would come close to becoming a complete decision analysis package.

One decision support package actually tries to incorporate a 'distributed computing' approach (see Chapter 4) into its simulations. Pinson *et al.*'s (1997) system runs on *Sparc* workstations with each 'intelligent agent' simulating each policymaking situation in terms of the scenario chosen, the problem, the proposed solution and the resulting number of incompatible actions. It then sends these separate pieces of information to an electronic blackboard from which one can derive amalgamated advice. Moreover, one can run several separate simulations from several different points of view, say, one for top-level managers, one for middle-level managers, one for low-level managers and one for staff specialists like lawyers and market researchers. The authors actually coin the term 'Distributed Strategic Decision Support System' (*DSDSS*) for their package.

Note that the simpler simulation-based policymaking packages may one day become 'just another button' within more commonly used software. Edwards and Finlay (1997) give a hint of this in their beginner's guide to spreadsheets. They point out that *Excel* spreadsheets now contain a 'goal seeking' function that prompts the spreadsheet to calculate automatically how much the assorted input variables need to change in order to generate a certain output, which is a form of policymaking. They also explain how *Excel* has a capacity for carrying out considerable statistical analysis, time series forecasting, and critical path analysis.

That is, some commonly available spreadsheet programs now appear to be doing many of the things done by several simulation programs. Indeed, *Excel* can even perform 'solving'. This is linear programming type optimization for generating the optimal solution of a policymaking problem. Such a solution appears in the 'changing cells'; it is based on constraints shown in the 'constraint cells' and the objective function is shown in the 'target cell'. Surely some of yesterday's simulation and optimization modellers would have given their eye teeth for such a convenient model!

But there is irony here. Edwards and Finlay do not even highlight the opportunity that *Excel* gives its users to write 'macro' code. This increases spreadsheets' power much further. Macro code looks a little like, and is in fact gradually converging towards the *Visual BASIC* computer programming language, and it is remarkably easy to write. This is because of *Excel*'s 'recording' facility, which enables users to perform a few spreadsheet manipulations manually, but at the same time record them, automatically, in macro code. Then, by looking at this code they can begin, with a little persistence, to teach themselves the macro programming language even though they have never trained as a computer programmer! This makes modern spreadsheets enormously powerful tools for analysing, simulating, optimizing and forecasting.

Getting back to more specialized decision support programs, we need to note that another suite of simulation tools, known as *Stratplan* (http://www.fbs.hw.ac.uk), gives advice on marketing and investments using a battery of decision-making aids. But it customizes the latter to the point of producing a simulation of one's own particular manufacturing company rather than a model for generating advice based on more universal principles.

The package is actually offered as part of a distance learning-based, business management course offered by Heriot-Watt University in Scotland and, in the same vein is *The Digital MBA* (Experience in Software Inc., 1998*d*). The latter consists of a CD-ROM containing six encrypted programs, tutorials and a book written by the authors of the software to describe the different programs. There are programs for managing people and projects, for business-oriented policymaking, for financial forecasting and for commercial process modelling.

As a parting comment on simulation modelling, we suggest that people should try to see it for what it is – a vital part of all pre-policymaking analyses. If the latter are not performed competently and fully, one's ability to make good policy will be forever limited. But there is no need to extend simulation into policymaking itself.

Building a computer that can simulate everything and also decide on what should be done, for all possible circumstances, is impossible. This is because, as we have already noted, the policy possibilities in any richly detailed environment are just too complex. Hence only humans can decide what to do in human-oriented environments. Nevertheless, humans are in desperate need of help from computerized simulation, and surely simulation packages should be content with this role.

Indeed, Starr (1994) points out that simulation also has a very important educational role. Discussing the effect of simulation programs like the well-known children's game *SimCity* and its offshoots, he calls them 'edutainment' packages. One could try to use *SimCity* in order to plan one's own environment, but this would have the drawback of attributing to one's own city those mechanisms that the author of *SimCity* assumes, wrongly, to apply to everywhere. Nevertheless, there are still benefits associated with studying and using the package. It educates users into a greater awareness of the needs and requirements of hitherto unheard of socioeconomic groups, not to mention community mechanisms, of which many users would have otherwise been unaware.

Hence we conclude that the role of decision support packages is primarily one of educating policymakers about their situation rather than guiding them through the complete policymaking process. Those who have always felt simulation to be synonomous with policymaking will be disappointed with this, but we hope we have demonstrated that building the complete 'policymaking machine' is impossible. We may be able to have generic simulation packages which seem applicable to all places and we may be able to have generic policymaking systems that seem applicable to all problems. But we cannot combine the two to build a system that can tell us what to do in all places and circumstances. Only a human can do that.

3.1.2. Groupware packages

Another form of decision support package focuses on how participants in any policymaking exercise think. Such packages consider the various interest groups, or 'stake holders' (Rubenking, 1990). Indeed, stake holder analysis is a fashionable term within public-sector and private-sector policymaking, and so some stake holder analysis has penetrated into most policymaking software.

For example, Cacez-Kecmanovic (1994) presents the *Organizational Activity Support System* (*OASS*) that simulates how any organization, and its vested interest groups function. It covers 'organizational entities', 'roles' and 'personnel' (agents), along with the 'activities', 'documents' and 'information' that are required, plus the prevailing 'norms' and 'legislation'.

Other packages concentrate on promoting more effective interaction within the group. Two examples of such groupware are described by Rangaswamy and Lilien (1997) – *Lotus Notes* and *GroupWorks*. These can be best thought of as a type of local area network in which everyone is connected to everyone else by computer. This means that the pre-computer era activity of meetings, and passing around information, has now been (partly) automated.

More specifically, *GroupWorks* consists of four modules – 'overview' where the mission statement is kept; 'activities' where schedules for the tasks to be performed are stored; 'discussions' which enables participants to initiate consideration of important matters; and 'contacts' which maintain the outside connectivity of the group. Naturally, some decisions can be made on-line without calling a meeting, and this can generate considerable time savings along with general productivity increases (Chidambaram *et al.*, 1991; Coursey, 1992; Daly, 1996).

Another group coordination package, *K.net*, is described by Rooney (1997). It is basically a system for facilitating group brainstorming on line. Participants share ideas and then rank and vote on them. Naturally, this method of operation goes part of the way towards removing some of the disadvantages of traditional brainstorming. These include lack of input from timid individuals and domination of proceedings by forceful individuals. Indeed, Daly (1996) has looked carefully at various hardware and software 'decision support systems' of this kind, including those where the participants meet in a U-shaped seating arrangements and vote by pushing key pads that are connected to a computer for amalgamating group opinions on line. She estimates that such systems can reduce decision making time by 30 to 60 per cent.

Some groupware tries to speed convergence to an agreed policy using graphics. An example is *QuestMap* (Gottesman, 1995) which uses group support graphics that are in many ways similar to the cognitive maps used by SODA, as described above. Other packages, like *GroupSystems V*, *VisionQuest*, *TeamFocus* and *TeamKit/ VM* (Knack, 1994) have not only been used in smallish organizations but also within the community – with the blessing of government authorities.

Hence this technology has some potential for actually improving community-based democracy. It might finally facilitate genuine citizen interaction and debate of multi-faceted viewpoints. Aiken *et al.* (1995) have written about this, and they refer to it as CMC (Computer Mediated Communication). More exactly, they describe a specific system for improving school-based education via increased interaction. It provides a bulletin board, and other facilities, to increase the sharing of information between parents, teachers and students.

In the same communications-boosting vein, but much more sophisticated, is the high-priced *Shared Decision-making Multimedia System* (Levin, 1993). This package is designed for use by patients in hospitals. They are able to learn about their own complaint using illustrative material accessible by touch screens and laser disks, and they are able to compare their own condition with that of every similar patient on the databases. Patients are also able to consult with medical staff, find out the advantages and disadvantages of various medical treatments, and so come to a much more informed agreement with their doctor about what seems to be the best treatment policy for them.

Groupware, therefore, is at the very frontier of the democratization of policymaking technology. There have been no real intellectual breakthroughs in this area, but impressive progress has been sustained by computers' growing ability to pool the human capabilities of the group's members. Moreover, explosive growth in multi-media communications and the plummeting costs of hardware have also boosted this field because they enable us for the first time to tap into the vast reservoir of community experience in a comprehensive way.

3.1.3. Gameware packages
Still another form of generic, policymaking support software is what we term 'gameware'. It includes both the individual, consciousness-expanding sort of software designed to improve people's mental health, and the more traditional packages that draw their inspiration from the discipline of Game Theory.

Some examples of the first type, 'mindware' are described by Small (1992). He explains that much of it is available as shareware, which means that the program is free, unless the user decides that it is really useful, and so 'does the right thing' by sending its author a small amount of money.

There are any number of programs that claim to show users how to organize their thoughts better and to force them to think in non-linear, non-logical and playful ways to boost their creativity. Moreover, there are programs designed to help users manage stress, or even to talk to a simulated psychiatrist about being depressed. The latter echoes one of the earliest Artificial Intelligence programs that did just this, the famous *Eliza* program by Weizenbaum (1976). Other programs are of the 'pep talk', bolstering kind. They often advise on how better to organize one's life for greater productivity.

Turning now to Game Theory, this discipline has a long history of trying to improve the art and science of policymaking (Gibbons, 1992). Much detailed work on how people decide on policies, and how they could make even better

Lesson 17: Watch your back

In Western, Anglophone cultures people tend to be suspicious of those who are insufficiently in control of themselves to be able to communicate clearly their recommended policymaking procedures. People tend to suspect peddlers of mysterious policymaking techniques of being charlatans. It is simply a fact of (Western) life that unless methods are understandable, people will be too suspicious to adopt them.

Therefore, all policymakers need to make very clear the methods that they have used in order to reach their decisions. If they do not, their policies will be rejected. Yet frequently, unclear policymakers are slow to recognize this. They only notice the initial support they are getting, even from people who obviously do not understand the techniques involved.

Yet colleagues who do not understand one's methods are extremely dangerous. Particularly in large organizations, such people will simply feign understanding to avoid looking like a fool. If they do look foolish they run the risk of losing status, 'empires', retirement benefits or basement car park privileges (Wyatt, 1978).

But eventually such people will reject the methods that they started out supporting. This is because they will realize that the policies based on such methods could in fact be wrong – they have no way of telling. Hence the policymaker who initially introduced the methods, and benefited from the latter's apparent prestige, will not usually get away with it for long.

Eventually others will reject what they say, or even become so jealous of the recommender's success that they politicize the policymaking process. This enables one to shoot down the star of the pedlar of all these mysterious techniques.

The only way out is clear explication of the methods that one is using. This will always be good insurance for one's long-term survival in practical policymaking. Although there is often a tendency amongst immature students to describe their work with jargon so as to appear more erudite and clever than the mere mortals who cannot master an apparently complex field; serious policymakers should be beyond this.

Indeed, if they are not, they are making a less than sincere effort to give the world the benefits of their erudition. Sincerity will protect you.

decisions, has been done by psychologists. However, it has, in a way, become 'too sophisticated', at least for lay persons who increasingly find the literature impenetrable. Unfortunately, such difficulties in understanding have tended to overspill into the field's associated software. This in turn torpedos the latter's potential for wide applicability.

But one Game Theory-based package that is easy to use is Brans and Mareschal's (1994) *GAIA* system, already mentioned in Chapter 2. This very complicated system, which uses the PROMCALC system, enables one to choose between policies after one has scored them on many criteria. When choosing, one is able to take account of policies' rankings, scores, incompatibilities and so forth, but it is difficult to penetrate the mathematical reasoning that generates these different sorts of scores. Again, therefore, users who are uneducated in Game Theory will lose confidence in their ability to come to a reliable decision in which they will have faith over the long term. Thus, they will probably not bother to use the software much at all.

Other Game Theorists focus more directly on the conflict that occurs between policymaking's participants. For instance, Howard (1989) lists 'actors', 'options', 'possible decisions', 'preferred states' and the present situation. Such a list makes it possible to search for ways in which some policies could be adopted in order to get closer to everyone's desired state. This would be an improvement over the *status quo*.

Howard's concrete example concerns two sections of a factory, 'Processing' and 'Finishing', and the conflict between them is about whether or not Finishing should immediately, but most unwillingly, deal with the extra output generated by recent productivity increases within Processing. That is, the situation is as shown in table 3.2, with zero signifying 'don't do it', a one signifying 'do it' and each of the five possible states of the system being shown by a number within brackets.

State (1) represents what used to be the *status quo* before Processing announced its intention to move into state (2). Hence state (2) is the current situation – Finishing knows that there will be increased output coming, but it does not want to accept such an increase yet. But the present situation, state (2), will lead to chaos because Finishing will get swamped by the extra production.

Finishing might, therefore, move to state (3), which will result in poor quality, but it can blame this on Processing for increasing production too rapidly. However, Processing might foresee this and so complain to management beforehand, which is state (4). Finally, in state (5) Finishing might anticipate Processing's complaint to management and so actually consent to accept the extra throughput while still maintaining quality.

Table 3.2. Howard's game-playing example.

Processing Department's options:	(1)	(2)	(3)	(4)	(5)
(a) increase output from new machinery now	0	1	1	1	1
(b) appeal to manager against Finishing	0	0	0	1	0
Finishing Department's options:					
(a) accept increased throughput	0	0	1	1	1
(b) lower the quality standards	0	0	1	1	0

This has covered all of the possibilities, and it has clarified all of the options. Therefore, such options now simply need to be evaluated from the overall company's viewpoint. The policymaking problem of whether or not to increase productivity in the Processing Department will therefore be solved. A package called *CONAN* does exist to help users do what we have just done, but its details have been documented only sparsely (Howard, 1989).

All this tends to suggest that not even the areas of group dynamics and conflict analysis will escape the relentless advance of computerization. But there is still a long way to go before we can say that much progress has been made. These areas are so complicated and riddled with human innuendo and subtlety that 'tying it down' is a major problem. The traditional Game Theory tactic of 'laying it all out on the table' often helps, but in ultra-complex situations it is impossible to do this.

Lesson 18: Reject mechanization

There is little doubt that comprehensive listing of everyone's options takes us a long way towards sensible policymaking. This is especially so if such options are listed along with their likely effects on the environment.

This belief, that 'open' policymaking leads to the greatest good for the greatest number, has been made several times in this book. It is an important point. However, problems arise with it whenever the situation is so complicated that it cannot be mapped out in a way that is simple enough to understand. Complex policymaking problems are very challenging, and they are almost certainly not amenable to mechanically and exhaustively searching out all the possible policies.

Hence policymaking is far from being a trivial problem that is suited to either glib or mechanically found solutions. It is likely to remain fascinatingly mysterious and unlikely to ever become dull and barren. This is possibly why so many books are written about it. Few of them give mechanical answers.

3.1.4. Data mining packages

Our final category of generic support packages for policymaking are those that simply try to manage data more effectively or explore the data for hitherto undiscovered insights. The usefulness of this data management, or 'data warehousing' (Radding, 1995) as it is sometimes called, is strongly defended by Kelly (1994). He claims that the modern world is characterized by an unprecedented level of commercial competition and so it is no longer good enough to simply satisfy customers – one now needs to surprise and delight them. Hence we need to search vast amounts of data so as we can keep coming up with original ideas.

However, Kelly warns that data warehousing does not sit well within current business climates. The focus currently tends to be on the cost of gathering information rather than on its positive benefits. Data warehousing should therefore be promoted not in terms of downsizing but in terms of building. We need to drop the assumption that computerization always automates something and so always lowers costs. Information warehousing means something different – it means that some intellectual processes will become better informed. Hence the organization will enjoy increased revenue and improved strategic positioning.

An example of software that is designed to make sense out of massive amounts of data is the almost high-priced package known as *Profiler 2000* (http:// www.palisade.com). It uses machine learning (Carbonell, 1990) in order to search up to 2000 records that detail say, customers' behaviour patterns. It eventually reveals, say, interesting attributes for big spenders compared to medium spenders. Alternatively it might search some agricultural data and find what the best combinations of fertilizers are in order to produce the best yields for different crops.

Put simply, this program herds similar records into similar groups. The latter then exhibit other, unanticipated characteristics, such as higher than average spending on certain products or higher than average yields for certain sorts of crops. Thus the program discovers things within the data of which we were previously unaware.

A similar data-mining package that is much larger and more expensive is *CART* (http://www.palisade.com). This outputs much more detailed statistics about the groups. Moreover, it can run on almost any sort of computer and is able to take in data from up to 70 file formats.

Note that Radding (1995) takes a more cautious look at this field and declares that it has all the problems that one would expect to be associated with a new technology. Yet he concedes that the underlying aim has considerable promise. He even foresees the day when millions of people will contribute to the database and so make it a vast repository of knowledge. Users will then simply query such a repository to get answers to questions that they would never have even thought to ask.

The problem is, according to Radding, that conventional data-extraction packages like *Q+E* and *Forest* and *Trees*, are still too unsophisticated to be able to search large databases very intelligently. They are rather limited in their ability to come up with answers to the more complicated and subtle queries. However, progress is being made, which could be of considerable relevance to policymakers of the future.

3.2. Domain-Specific Software

By far the majority of policymaking support packages are written for specific problem domains within specialized fields. Such problems include new product development, hospital management and schools planning. As such, the software tends to become part of the folk law surrounding a particular discipline and it may even perpetuate some of the myths and malpractices that characterize it.

In our terms, such packages are more 'thinking' in their style than are the more 'feeling' sort of generic policymaking packages of the previous section. They tend to assume a lot of detail about the context in which their users find themselves rather than get a 'feeling' from the users about the nature of the particular circumstances pertaining. But there are exceptions. In any event, sub-section 3.2.1 will review the huge amount of available software for commercial policymaking support and sub-section 3.2.2 will describe non-business support packages.

3.2.1. Business packages

There is in fact so much commercial policymaking support software that the *Journal of Business Strategy* sometimes publishes a directory of 'software for strategists'. It includes many general packages, like spreadsheets, word processors and mapping systems, which simply help policymakers become more efficient in terms of manipulating information and simulating the environment. But it also reviews some software that is of interest to all policymakers. Hence any software in this sub-section that is not specifically referenced has been described, albeit briefly, in one of the *Journal of Business Strategy's* surveys (for example, Management Software Association, 1994).

Many business packages undertake exploratory data analysis. An example is the medium-priced *Execustat* program that transforms raw data into meaningful statistics that can then be reviewed in an easy-to-understand way. The medium-priced *Turbo Spring-Stat* program likewise treats statistics novices gently, and it also provides a text editor and an expert system to recommend what sort of statistical procedure should be used. There is also *Data Desk* (http://www.palisade.com) which clarifies data sets through 'box plots', 'histograms', 'scatter plots', 'regression lines' and 'rotating 3D plots'. If a number of points are plotted on say, a bar chart, then these same points will be highlighted within all of the other representations of the data as well. Hence data can be viewed in lots of different ways.

Of more strategic relevance is the high-priced *Advia Strategic Activity Costing* package. This lets the user examine policies that have been proposed from within all parts of the company's organizational structure. One can then estimate policies' probable effects, along with their costs. In other words, this is a simulation package for the corporate policymaker. There are many packages similar to it. For example, the medium-priced *Business Development Expert* program simulates how proposed changes to product pricing might impact upon local and regional conditions. It generates 'before and after' scenarios to describe what could result from intended strategies.

Slightly more oriented towards decision-making is the medium-priced *DPL* package. It builds a complex model of the environment by combining decision trees with 'influence diagrams'. The latter are similar to cognitive networks and they show relationships between important decision areas and areas of uncertainty. There is also the medium-priced *KnowledgeSeeker* that combines statistical analysis with interactive decision trees. Its main purpose is to filter out weak correlates, that is, those variables which probably do not have much of an effect on the overall business situation.

Note that many business packages are used to help companies pursue the path of certification and quality control (Dale and Cooper, 1992). Indeed, some have been developed specifically for this purpose. For example, the medium-priced *Benchmarking Software* instructs users on what bench marking actually is, how to streamline existing quality-control procedures to achieve it, and how to assess the strengths and weaknesses of current policies with respect to 'best practice'. There is also the high-priced, *Apple* package known as *CrossTarget* which allows many people to share the same company data sources. It then performs multi-dimensional analyses to track critical trends and success factors.

In the same 'quality certification' mould is the medium-priced *Extend* package. Again, this is *Apple* software for modelling real-world business systems so that one can answer 'what if' type questions. More exactly, the package incorporates a large database of management rules for best practice. This enables policymaking to build from a base of tried and true procedures and hence suitable extensions have been built for companies undergoing 're-engineering'.

Finally, there is the medium-priced, 'quality control' package known as *Q1000*. This assesses any company's strengths and weaknesses in terms of conforming to the 'Malcolm Baldridge National Quality Award' criteria. Many people within the company are able to contribute information to its database, and so the policymaker is able to recommend policies that amalgamate everyone's inputs.

Getting back to the more exploratory business support packages, we have the

---

Lesson 19: Suspect credentialism

Business software can be useful for the 'quality control' activities that have proved so popular during the 1990s. These analyse how a firm's procedures and achievements can be improved to the point where they match anything to be found amongst rivals within today's global, and highly competitive market place.

Indeed, many consultants make a handsome living by auditing companies' procedures in order to certify them as 'world's best practice'. Companies seek such authentication, of course, because it opens extra marketing opportunities for them.

But alas, there is an alternative view. Sometimes this so-called quality control seems more like an overdose of 'credentialism'. That is, authenticated companies appear to have simply 'gone through the motions'. They may not have actually run an efficient, environmentally sensitive operation that would be expected of the good corporate citizen that their credentials claim them to be.

However, society has probably benefited from this latest dose of quality control. That is, in terms of net social gain, the overall effect of this push towards higher performance standards has probably been positive. But be vigilant.

medium-priced *ManagePro*. It facilitates the placement of goals, sub-goals, schedules and people on to coloured spreadsheets so that the user can manipulate people and goals into innovative combinations. Also, the medium-priced *Competitive Advantage* program is actually a spreadsheet that incorporates formulae and graphs to enable the policymaker to study the competition. It quantifies the company's advantages and disadvantages in terms of costs and prices, and so it identifies 'high-leverage costs' and 'value-added drivers'. It then generates cost and price curves for all of the competing companies; it develops policies for improving one's own competitive position and it tests such policies by superimposing the effects of proposed change onto current competitive positions.

Similarly exploratory is *MARKSTAT*. This is high-priced software for large-scale simulation and development of a marketing strategy. It evaluates strengths, weaknesses, resources, likely actions and reactions, competitive products, pricing, sales force allocation, distribution channels and promotional policies. It then uses competitive intelligence to recommend how to manage product portfolios, research and development projects, pricing initiatives and distribution channels.

Our final example of an exploratory, business-specific package is the medium-priced *Resource Allocation*. As its name suggests, it allocates resources in the light of proposed new products, company acquisitions and findings within the research and development department. More specifically, this program evaluates the probable financial impact of different policy decisions in terms of factors like 'payback period', 'internal rates of real return' and 'net present values'.

Yet perhaps even more exploratory is that genre of packages known as 'business forecasting' software. Typical examples are the medium-priced *4Cast2* package and the *Business Policy Toolkit* (Yocum, 1990). The latter produces information on income estimates, sales forecasts, balance sheets and cash flows.

A better known example is the medium-priced *Commander Prism*, which consists of a multi-dimensional spreadsheet boasting English language formulae rather than the cryptic symbols that turn so many novices against spreadsheets. It corrects overlapping formulae so that they are always mathematically correct, and it allows the user to transport rows and columns so that data can be looked at in several ways. The advanced version, which is hugely expensive, allows simultaneous operation by up to 50 users. It compares performance with goals that were set in a 'profit model', which is basically a multi-dimensional representation of the business strategy.

Similarly named to *Commander Prism* is medium-priced *PC Prism* (Feuche, 1990). This formulates appropriate customer services, customer needs and internal and external corporate goals in the light of future projections. There is also, *Forecast Pro*, another medium-priced, spreadsheet-inspired, strategic forecasting package into whose spreadsheet users enter basic data, along with a proposed policy, and this prompts the software to forecast outcomes. It also incorporates an expert system to critique the various policies that the user is considering, and it explains its reasoning in a non-statistical manner.

Note that some forecasting packages take a 'Monte Carlo' approach. This involves using probability estimates of what could happen in the future, plus the power of the modern computer, to generate semi-randomly hundreds of future outcomes. One can then inspect the latter to see whether any dominant future patterns seem to be emerging.

The medium-priced *Crystal Ball* package applies the Monte Carlo approach. It allows users to assign a range of numbers, or a probability distribution, to lots of spreadsheet cells. The latter contain forecasts about which the user is still uncertain. The program then generates a huge volume of numbers that are random, but which are also tailored to be in accordance with the nominated probability distribution. The various outcomes are then observed to give the user a good idea of the range of possibilities, and emphases, that they will one day face.

Other business-oriented forecasting packages actually look backward before they forecast. An example is the medium-priced *MAPS* (Management Analysis and Policymaking Software). It prepares detailed reports of a company's projected profitability, productivity and growth, as based on a detailed analysis of past performances during periods of up to six time intervals back. It also features a long-range forecasting module for projecting company performance over the next 5 to 11 years. Such a long term prediction could lead to better policymaking over an extended period – if the forecast is accurate.

The medium-priced *Market Dynamics* also forecasts sales on the basis of past trends. However, this software is just as much a simulation package as it is a forecasting package, because it provides extensive tools for estimating the impact, on company performance, of new policies, new products and new processes.

Other simulation/forecasting packages include the medium-priced *MktSim* for simulating and forecasting the structure of the market in terms of competing firms. The user is able to move around its model, change parameters and look at the effects of, and the relationships between different brands of product and variables.

By contrast, the medium-priced *Smart Forecasts I* is much more comprehensive. It can predict thousands of items based on automatic selection of the 'best' method of time series analysis. Users need to know nothing about statistics or forecasting, yet the software still comes up with projections plus their margins of error.

However, a word of caution is in order here. It is, of course, most unlikely that *Smart Forecasts I* actually chooses the best forecasting method. The state of the art of forecasting is surely not sufficiently well developed to assume that the best forecasting method can be chosen on the basis of such relatively scant information about problem characteristics. But such a comment would seem heretical in some quarters. It is simply not the done thing to question the credibility of commercial software too closely.

Instead, business support software is often simply sold to people in a 'hyped up' atmosphere and thereafter it continues to be used in a hyped up atmosphere. True, some business planners may question its accuracy, but most do not – they are far too busy policymaking to waste time on questioning the accuracy of their tools.

Yet such a situation is a worry to some software writers, and they therefore take a sensible, compromise approach. That is, rather than use software for detailed and possibly inaccurate forecasts, they use software as a broad, guiding tool. They opt for more synoptic, broad-brush software that simply gives them advice in general and approximate terms.

Such even-handed, cautious forecasting is achieved by a number of software packages that are based on expert systems (see Chapter 4). An example is the medium-priced *Advia Decide and Manage*. It assimilates users' inputs and so builds an approximate business policy, along with advice to the user about 'visions of success', 'missions' and 'critical success factors'.

A similar package is the high-priced *Alacrity Strategy*. Its built-in expert system contains 3000 rules, and it categorizes the user's business in terms of its 'market life cycle', 'generic strategy', 'barriers to entry into new markets' and 'relative market share'. It then predicts market characteristics and their likely evolution. This enables it to generate a set of diagnostic questions, the user's answers to which are used for extending the competitive analysis created by the first expert system.

Other expert system-based packages include *PolicyMagic Analysis* (http://www.planmagic.com), which is low-priced software, and the medium-priced *Business Insight* software that contains hundreds of business concepts. It handles quantitative and qualitative data in order to output a customized analysis of any business. Basically, it turns business abstractions and concepts into numbers, and this allows users to evaluate alternative scenarios using a 'backward chaining' procedure. This means working backwards from some situation in the future to suggest what one should do now in order to maximize one's probable future gains.

It should not be assumed that an expert system is mandatory for business simulation and forecasting software. Many packages survive without one. Instead, they simply apply a commonly accepted, interactive process that seeks to outline the market position and opportunities of the firm being focused upon. That is, the user is taken through a standard set of questions and, on the basis of the answers given, policy is generated.

An example is the medium-priced system *CHECKMATE* (http://www.checkmateplan.com) which its author claims has been used by many different companies across the US. It prompts users to set up matrices for showing the company's 'mission', its strengths, 'opportunities', weaknesses, 'alternatives', 'prioritized policies' and budgets. Note that users of this software are given access to the 'Strategic Managers Club' and its accompanying web site.

Very similar to *CHECKMATE* is *Strategy Roundtable Enterprise* (http://www.gryphonsystems.com) which documents the company's 'vision' and 'mission' as it moves sequentially through the steps of 'Policy', 'Act' and 'Measure'.

Lastly, there are several ambitious systems that contain general business support software. An example is *Portfolio Plus* (http://www.strategic-dynamics.com). This package's website makes a case that generic policymaking software is usually too general to be useful – too 'glib'. Therefore, more domain-specific software is required, so long as it incorporates rigorous analysis and systematic analysis from many perspectives. This is why the software is actually a collection of tools; more tools than are needed for any one job, but which can be selected to suit the current user's particular policymaking problem.

Again, this general support package is extremely 'thinking' in its style. It provides carefully considered methods which it believes could be useful for everyone; it makes no attempt to get a 'feel' for the present user's particular problem. Therefore, selection of the appropriate tool becomes the responsibility of the user, which can overwhelm some people, because they do not have sufficient knowledge of alternative methods.

Thus business-specific support software for policymaking ranges from the data-exploratory through to forecasting, quality control, expert system and generic strategizing packages. But there is little evidence of software writers wanting to build the ultimate, all-purpose 'business policymaking machine'. Perhaps they have all had too much experience in the unforgiving business version of the 'school of hard knocks' to even contemplate such a risky project.

3.2.2. Non-business packages

There has been considerable development of software to help bureaucrats and other non-business policymakers. We now look at some of this software, but again, and especially here, we can in no way claim to be comprehensive in our coverage. By definition, much of this software is known only to specialists in the particular sub-field of public administration for which it was written. As such, it is possible that only the slightly less specialist packages, those that are more generally known, have been discovered during the writing of this book.

Hence we do not discuss packages like *SMARTLINK 2000* (Velox Systems Corporation, 1998) which is software for 'managed health care contract analysis'. Nor do we discuss *CRISP* (Curley, 1997), which is a decision support system for finance management. Instead we look at software that has been described in the literature and tends to have more generic applicability.

An example is *SDP* (School Development Policymaker). Having written this program, its authors, Hornby and Golder (1994), compared it to Thierauf's (1988) prerequisites for good policymaking. Their conclusion was that *SDP* met all such requirements. This was because it always asks its users for the entities listed in the left hand column of table 3.3, and such components appear to match, fairly closely, with Thierauf's requirements for good policymaking, as shown in the right hand column.

This appears to be a little self-congratulatory. If a program like SDP takes school policymakers through a fairly standard procedure for policymaking then of course it will resemble Thierauf's requirements for good policymaking. There would be something wrong if it did not. Hence Hornby and Goldner's investigation is slightly trivial. However, they do point out that their software actually adds a step to the Thierauf model. This is a feedback loop through 'owners and actors' and back to the start.

Other writers of non-business software take a much more focused approach. They believe that the most effective policymaking is that which concentrates on finding a compromise to best satisfy all of the various negotiating parties. There will always be a divergence of views about the best policy to adopt, and so some conflict is inevitable. Therefore, software that aims to neutralize such conflicts is very valuable.

Table 3.3. The SDP software's requests to the user compared to Thierauf's requirements for good policymaking.

The SDP package asks users for:	Thierauf's requirements for good policymaking are:
School statement	Organization objectives
Influencing factors	Resources
Audited priorities for growth	Strategies
Development policy report	Feedback
Development processes	Compatibility with organizational objectives
Review	Programs of action
Evaluation	Organizational policies

Lesson 20: Study the stakeholders

It is surprising that Thierauf, the well known policymaking author, did not make a large issue of something that is emphasized more by software writers – the different viewpoints of the various stake holders. Attention to such people along with their needs, wants, hopes and fears is vital.

Introverted policymaking is unlikely to succeed. If it does not incorporate the viewpoints of affected parties, policymaking runs the risk of becoming irrelevant.

Always remember that the real world is populated heavily by a plethora of interest groups. Failure to understand them can put an intolerable amount of weight into the policymaker's saddle bags.

Such a stance has spawned a distinct sub-class of policymaking software. It has been purpose built for helping negotiators decide policy in hostage/negotiation problem settings. Much of this software, referred to as 'Negotiation Support Systems' (NSS) (Lim and Benbasat, 1993), is outlined in an excellent article by

Wilkenfeld *et al.* (1995). They explain how negotiation support packages can be grouped into three types – those for helping:

1. all sides

2. the mediator, and

3. a particular side.

Packages of type (1), those that support all sides, are designed to facilitate free exchange of information about options, viewpoints and criteria. This is so that some amicable compromise can be found. An example is *PERSUADER* (Sycara, 1993) which infers multi-attribute utilities from past histories of negotiations, combines them with the present actors' preferences, and then suggests modifications to the present situation to narrow differences between the actors' divergent, policy-choice views. Another is *DENEGOT* (Mochlman *et al.*, 1992) which, similarly, undertakes a search for solutions within the constraints that each party has.

By contrast, negotiation packages of type (2), mediation support systems, are designed to help a third party by suggesting possible solutions 'from above'. An example is *MEDIATOR*, which consults a decision support system, and another is *PREFCAL*, which undertakes a utility analysis of the negotiation scenario from the point of view of each side. It allows the mediator to help protagonists build a consensus type of problem representation. Participants do not share such analyses; the mediator amalgamates them and eventually presents the result to both parties (Jarke *et al.*, 1987).

Another negotiation support system is *NEGO*. This uses multi-objective linear programming to establish the optimal demands for each participant, relax some of the combatants' demands, and then find a compromise proposal that comes closer to satisfying everyone (Kersten, 1985). Further, the *MCBARG* package allows parties to learn from a model before selecting a preferred outcome; the system finds a way to improve the *status quo* in terms of these preferences, and so a new *status quo* emerges before the next iteration (Wierzbicki *et al.*, 1993).

Finally, two other negotiation support packages have been developed as part of MIT's 'Project on Modelling for Negotiation Management' program – *ISES* and *SAM*. These simulate participants' norms, parameters and proposals in order to determine which outcome best supports all parties' negotiation goals (Samarasan, 1993). Moreover, *DecisionMaker* (Fraser and Hipel, 1988) records the likely moves of protagonists given the current 'world state', and it then predicts how people can manipulate the situation in order to reach one of the conflict equilibria.

In terms of type (3) systems – those that provide support for a particular side, there is *NEGOTIATOR*, which fuses a multi-attribute utility approach with a neural network (Bui, 1992). There is also *MATCH* which compares the present situation with many past situations, along with respective policies that were used to affect them (Samarasan, 1993). Also available is *NEGOPOLICY*, which is an expert system for providing advice given the nature of the situation (Matwin *et al.*, 1989), and *GENIE* which explores various negotiation positions, based on a full knowledge of each participant's position, options and preferences.

Note finally that some negotiation support systems are designed specifically for business applications. For example, there is *The Art of Negotiating* (Experience in Software Inc., 1998*b*) which is low-priced software for generating suggestions and policies. It tries to foreshadow what policies the other company might use, based on the user's answers to questions about 'negotiations', 'issues', 'positions', 'policies' and 'agendas'.

Other business examples include Colson and Mareschal's (1994) complicated system for combining conflict analysis with innovative, graphics-based inquiry. It aims to establish which points of conflict are preventing consensus, and its graphical output includes box plots that show the average desirability score, the range and the ranking for each alternative policy. It displays the different judgements made by all of the different conflicters involved, and it incorporates complex methods for estimating how much importance to give to each party.

A similar conflict-resolution package is the medium-priced, *IBM* and *Apple* software known as *Negotiator Pro*. Its 'Policy' module asks the user about the situation before suggesting strategies, and its 'Profile' module asks questions about the user and the other party in order to fix them within a four-way quadrant of personality type. Some text then appears explaining how to convince people who are of the relevant personality type. Next, the user and other party are placed onto a matrix of negotiation styles, using 11 questions about each. This generates print out showing the classification of both parties, their negotiation styles and suggestions about how to counter competitor's policies.

3.3. Summary

This chapter began by reviewing various examples of decision support packages, one of which managed to strike a good balance between having a 'thinking' and a 'feeling' style. But others seemed to want to push their simulation capabilities too far into the policymaking realm, based on some misguided attempt to become universal problem solvers, which is probably impossible. Finally, some groupware, gameware and data mining packages yielded some important lessons for policymaking practice.

The second section then took examples from the massive amount of available, business-specific software. Again, the programs often took on the flavour of simulation rather than decision making packages, and similar comments applied to public sector-specific software, although negotiation support systems can actually be quite prescriptive.

Chapter 4

Emerging Software

This chapter discusses emerging packages, both planned and existing. Many of them are still experimental, yet they are still instructive in the sense that they indicate the directions in which policymaking software might be evolving.

Section 4.1 examines literature that argues for a change in the 'paradigm' of policymaking and it refers to planned software that could facilitate such a change. By contrast, section 4.2 describes software which actually exists but which is so peripheral to our policymaking focus that, at first sight, it seems likely to impact on our field only obliquely. However, it is so clever that it could have a huge impact on almost every field fairly soon – innovative software.

The packages that we will consider are shown in table 4.1.

4.1. Changing the Paradigm

There are many people who think that rather than improve policymaking, this book will make it worse. After all, much of our software encourages adoption of a hierarchical and somewhat discredited, 'rational comprehensive' approach (Hoos, 1972; Friend, 1983; Webber, 1983; Wyatt, 1996a). Although this section will try to allay such concerns, it remains a fact that many people's attitude is one of anti-technology. To them, if an approach has anything to do with computers it is, by definition, not worthwhile. To such people policymaking is an intuitive, qualitative and intensely human activity. Hence any attempt to mix computation into it does considerable violence to its delicate essence.

It is true that such people could still derive benefit from this book by looking only at the lesson boxes to heed just the practical advice and forget that it came from the writers of computer software. But it is more likely that they will see such lessons as doomed anyway through having been tainted by the technology itself and the evil influence of philistine technologists.

Nevertheless, some technologists have actually thought very deeply about how computation can best be grafted onto socially sensitive policymaking. Consequently, they have come up with a compromise approach that could go some of the way towards convincing the anti-technology sceptics. They have suggested various alternative 'paradigms', which are ways of looking at the world. Such paradigms try to ensure that computation and sensitive, humanized policymaking can coexist more comfortably.

Note that 'paradigm shift' tends to be a much over-used term. It originally signified some monumental and revolutionary change in current thinking, but more recently it has come to mean a change in attitudes that people are all too eager to attribute to themselves. They want to be seen as the prime mover in some sort of quantum shift in current thought, simply because they had a bright idea themselves or because they used someone else's bright idea to provide a new angle from which to view something.

Table 4.1. Emerging packages for policymaking.

Type	Package	Cost	Reference
Cognitive science	*COGNITA.*	?	Epinasse, 1994
Expert system	*CESA*	?	Landsbergen, 1997
Expert system	?	?	Davidson, 1997
Expert system + Neural network	*NEULONET*	?	Quah *et al.*, 1996
Genetic algorithm	*GENIE*	?	Chambers and Taylor, 1996
Genetic algorithm	*What'sBest!*	?	http://www.palisade.com
Genetic algorithm	*Premium Solver!*	?	http://www.palisade.com
Genetic algorithm	*Evolver*	< $1000	http://www.palisade.com
Genetic algorithm + Neural network	*Braincel*	< $1000	http://www.palisade.com
Intelligent agent	*QuickKeys, Tempo II Plus*	< $1000	Miley, 1993

Worse, some people appear to become confused even as to what a paradigm is, and Rosenhead (1989*a*, p.2) shows signs of this when he broadly defines a paradigm as:

a set of implicit rules for identifying a valid scientific problem, and for recognizing what would constitute a solution to it.

That is, he sees paradigms in terms of problem solving. The irony of this is that, under certain paradigms, paradigms are not seen as problem solving.

Hence the word paradigm, at least initially, had a much deeper meaning than appears to be evident here (Stove, 1982). However for our purposes paradigm shifts, whether genuine or not, can still be useful. Hence sub-section 4.1.1 examines the 'soft systems methodology' paradigm, sub-section 4.1.2 deals with the boosterism approach to policymaking and sub-section 4.1.3 looks at the Cognitive Science paradigm.

4.1.1. Soft systems methodology

Much software described in this book shows evidence of having been affected by 'soft systems methodology'. The latter is an attempt to blunt the hard edges of traditional Operations Research when it is applied to human-oriented problems. This is because Operations Research is a form of applied engineering. It may be suitable for solving mechanistic, 'hard science' type, close-ended problems, but it tends to be abrasive and over simplistic when applied to the wicked, vicious and fuzzy problems.

Yet the birth of soft systems methodology was a difficult one, and Rosenhead (1989b) tells how it caused much dissension within the British Operations Research community during the 1970s. In the US it even prompted a rearguard action by some members of the 'Operations Research Society of America'. They called for the society to enforce profesionalization of the discipline and to punish members who did not practice traditional methods.

Eventually the debate split into three camps – the traditional Operations Researchers, the soft system methodologists, and the radicals. Rosenhead explains how the radicals saw Operations Research as a tool of the ruling classes, and so they called for a change in its clientele and an abandonment of its 'establishment' stance. They were particularly vehement in their criticism of the so-called 'rational comprehensive' approach to planning.

Regarding the latter, Rosenhead (1989a, p.3) claims that rational comprehensiveness moves through five stages. These are shown in the left hand column of table 4.2, and its right hand column shows how Rosenhead's conception of the rational comprehensive approach is not unlike the processes adopted by most of the software featured in this book, except that the latter adds an implementation or monitoring phase – 'anticipate'.

As we saw in Chapter 3, this last step involves anticipation that is additional to that performed during the 'choose' phase of the policymaking process. It involves anticipating what will happen now that we have chosen a policy. It therefore feeds back to the very start of the policymaking process – 'think', because as we have already mentioned, the policymaking process never ends. Indeed, many other perceptions of policymaking, even rational comprehensive perceptions, have recognized the existence of such a feedback loop.

Nevertheless, the radical Operations Researchers tended to criticize rational comprehensiveness on political grounds, saying it was the first step on the downhill slope towards totalitarianism and 'big brother' policymaking. This really tells us nothing helpful for improving the method itself, and the radicals thereafter continued to remain somewhat obsessed with political theory. Indeed, in terms of contributing to the practical advancement of policymaking techniques, many of them can be regarded as having descended into the unproductive depths of post-modernist and nihilistic relativism. Note however that they themselves would argue that what they do now is much more important, in a consciousness expanding sense, than Operations Research ever was.

Table 4.2. Rosenhead's view of the rational comprehensive approach compared to the approach taken by policymaking software.

The rational comprehensive approach (according to Rosenhead):	Policymaking software's approach:
1. Identify objectives, with weights. 2. Identify alternative courses of action.	1. Think
3. Predict consequences of actions in terms of objectives. 4. Evaluate the consequences on a common scale of value. 5. Select the alternative whose net benefit is highest.	2. Choose
	3. Anticipate

Now, the 'soft systems methodologists' had a more direct objection to rational comprehensiveness. They said it was infeasible. This is because there is a lack of data to support all of its five stages, and because there is a lack of theory about cause and effect within social systems. If social processes have never been adequately modelled, or even properly theorized, how can we plan for them? This is why Rosenhead developed his own, soft systems approach to policymaking, and he explained how it differs from traditional Operations Research.

In essence, Operations Research sees social problems as being tactical, whereas they are actually strategic. The difference between tactical and strategic, according to Rosenhead, is that the latter is plagued by uncertainty. This is not uncertainty that can be modelled using probability or expected utility calculations; it is the kind of uncertainty that people *feel*. Openshaw (1997*b*) would call such uncertainty 'fuzziness'.

One cause of such uncertainty is conflict, but the only Operations Research technique for analysing conflict seems to be Game Theory. We have already seen that this can sometimes be too esoteric for widespread adoption by practical policymakers. Alternatively, optimization might be of some assistance. But this assumes that there is only one, organization-wide objective function to be optimized. In human-oriented policymaking there are usually several.

Hence the soft systems theorists called for some sort of 'community' version of Operations Research to contrast to traditional Operations Research, which has remained stuck in its old institution-based rut. Its analyses are:

... used most often not for individuals but for organizations ... An organization is not an individual. It does not breathe, eat, or in any comparable sense have objectives. Decisions and actions emerge out of interactions between a variety of actors 'internal' to the organization. Each may, indeed will, have an individual perspective or world-view (Weitanschauung). (Rosenhead, 1989a, p. 9)

In other words, for as long as Operations Research sees problems as unified and company-based rather than collective, the traditional form of the discipline will remain inappropriate. Rosenhead argues, therefore, that the policymaker needs to make a number of decisions regarding what sort of style he or she adopts. More specifically, whereas the traditional Operations Researcher tends to adopt the style shown in the left-hand column of table 4.3, the soft systems methodologist should take the stance described in the right hand column. The powerful influence that such thinking has had on the software selected for this book should be plain for all to see.

So far so good for soft system methodology. It seems to have pulled the traditional form of Operations Research away from the 'thinking' end of the spectrum towards a people-reflecting, 'feeling' style. But it begins to get into trouble when its followers try to extend it in order to solve real-world problems (a little like Marxism).

Table 4.3. Traditional Operations Research compared to soft systems methodology.

Traditional Operations Research:	Soft systems methodology:
Single-objective optimization	Non-optimizing, multiple solution policymaking
Overwhelming data demands	Reduced data demands through the combining of hard, soft and socially judgemental data
Depoliticization of processes and assumptions about consensus	Simple and transparent observation in order to clarify the nature of conflicts
People treated as passive objects	People treated as active objects
Single-person planning within a hierarchical chain of command	Facilitation of bottom up planning by all participants
Attempts to abolish future uncertainty	Acceptance of uncertainty and an attempt to keep options open for later resolution

For example, Checkland (1989) strongly supports soft systems methodology by arguing that old-style Operations Research is basically 'means-ends' analysis in which the ends are always assumed to be known. But, says Checkland, what about the Anglo-French 'Concord' project to build the world's first supersonic passenger aeroplane? What was the end in view here – Providing employment for

British engineers? Collaborating with the French? Beating the Americans in at least one area of technology? Avoiding cancellation (as costs soared)? Or what? He therefore proposes to set up a loose, goal-seeking model in which various possible actions are assessed in view of the prevailing environment.

But this, at least in a policymaking sense, seems to be losing one's way. It is tantamount to setting up a simulation of the situation in order to understand it better, rather than deciding what should be done about it. It is simply modelling the situation and the possible ways in which it might change. This is science, not policymaking. The analytical tradition reasserts itself.

Similarly Rosenhead (1989c), in his attempts to operationalize soft systems methodology, appears to fall into the same trap. His 'robustness analysis' is supposedly tailored to better navigate the turbulent and uncertain waters of current policymaking. It is above all a flexible approach because there is a need in the current world to plan for multiple futures. Accordingly, he defines robustness as 'flexibility with an eye on the future' and he claims that concentration on policies that are robust enables certain intermediate actions to be performed. This is because robust policies are compatible with a greater range of possible future commitments.

But clearly, Rosenhead is over emphasizing just one of many possible policy-evaluation criteria. That is, evaluation solely in terms of robustness is unwise because it only covers a small part of the story. Rosenhead makes no mention of the *quality* of alternatives, and quality is measured by other criteria besides robustness.

To see this more clearly, consider Rosenhead's example. It concerns the situation where one needs to choose a restaurant for several friends to dine in. The traditional Operations Research approach would involve doing a survey of all restaurants, having the prospective guests rate each dish served at each restaurant, and then booking the highest-scoring restaurant. By contrast, robustness analysis would survey the prospective guests' likes and dislikes and then go to the restaurant that has a sufficiently wide-ranging menu to satisfy everyone.

Now, Rosenhead says the first approach could never be finished on time. Moreover, it would fail to handle the possibility that people's tastes might change between their filling in the questionnaire and going to the restaurant. That is, Operations Research's 'optimal' solution would probably be spurious. By contrast, robustness analysis is far less hungry of data, yet it works just as well.

Lesson 21: Eschew novelty

Fashionable changes in policymaking method, as peddled by writers using entertaining examples, are often not as good as they first seem. One needs to examine any new approach most carefully before deciding to forego an older, but verified approach.

There is usually no intrinsic value in novelty.

However, robustness analysis only looks better. It has simply redefined the problem to one of versatility (robustness) rather than of quality. And it is quality, a much more sophisticated concept, which was aimed for by Operations Research. That is, robustness analysis uses less complicated information because it reaches a less sophisticated solution – a solution that is robust rather than of high quality. Moreover, Rosenhead surely does not want us to take seriously his argument that people might change their long-held preferences. Even if they did, it would probably torpedo robustness analysis just as effectively as it would invalidate Operations Research, provided such changes were substantial.

Lesson 22: Be human

In many workplaces, strictly hierarchical and tyrannical procedures have been supplanted by workers' rights, equal opportunity, freedom of information and flatter line management structures. There is little doubt that the majority of people are happier under these new conditions than they were under the old.

However, there are still reactionary tendencies at work. For example, there has been a movement towards 'economic rationalism' during the 1990s, and the result is that much tyranny is now being justified on the grounds of greater efficiency, global marketing, increased competition and the need to keep pace with international competition. In short, it has led to domination of people's lives by socially unaware accountants.

Although it has brought some positive benefits, economic rationalism has also caused considerable damage to the social fabric of many organizations and communities – all in the name of the new world economic order. Such damage is bad news for sustainable and sensible policymaking. Indeed, the growing control of increasingly debt-ridden, poor nations by the world's increasingly rich nations has been described as 'modern slavery'.

Sensible policymaking therefore needs to be on the lookout for situations where a zeal to manipulate short term costs and profits does irreparable damage to real people. Policymaking practice needs to be human.

4.1.2. Boosterism

Taking the appeal of novel approaches one step further, some authors seem to think the best way to improve policymaking is to write 'pep talk' books. As mentioned in the Preface, these usually take the form of motivational texts that convince the reader they can do a world-beating job at policymaking both in daily life and at work. Such books seem to be everywhere that managers are likely to go, and they seem to have a particularly strong presence in airport bookshops! Their underlying message is often 'positive thinking conquers all'. Some are very seductive, and this is frequently achieved through a spectacular turn of phrase, plus an adoption of the latest jargon and name dropping.

Lesson 23: Flirt less with fashion

The level to which policymaking is fashion prone cannot be over emphasized. The sheer turnover of books on the subject is testimony to this. But what have the fashions of yesteryear achieved? Most of them have been forgotten.

Practitioners therefore need to dampen their natural tendency towards over enthusiasm for the latest approach. Most of the so-called new approaches are simply old approaches dressed up in new words.

Self delusion, to the point of always trying to be absolutely up to date, means that one is likely to spend too much time learning about 'new wave' techniques. Meanwhile, other people will get on with the more important task – policymaking. Resist being seduced by the fickleness of fashion.

An example is Wilson (1993) which is full of conceptual diagrams that, at least to this reader, appear to lack depth. Yet potential buyers are reassured that the book is part of the 'fast-track MBA series', it is 'published in association with AMED', the author works at the Henley Management College and he also runs courses for the American Management Association. Moreover, the cover is full of zip words and phrases like 'innovation', 'teamwork', 'effective techniques', 'up-to-the minute', 'accelerate your career', 'improve your skills' and 'develop your knowledge'. We are all guilty of too much hype at times, but this seems to be going over the top. There are a lot of valuable lessons to be learned from such books, but one needs to choose them carefully in order to separate out those offering more glitter than substance.

However, Cunningham (1994) has written a motivational book that does actually impart considerable useful advice. Other than the plausibility of their apparent logic, the book may not contain a lot of evidence to support the validity of its arguments, but it makes several potentially valuable observations none the less. Part of its charm is that it is crammed with interesting anecdotes, such as the one about good preparation being of utmost importance.

The story concerns three people who were offered the choice of opening one of two doors. Behind one door were vast amounts of gold, jewels and cash, and behind the other was a person-eating lion. The first subject refused to play the game and went home, thereby foregoing her chance of fabulous wealth. The second person had been to business school. He therefore conducted an exhaustive study of the situation using probability theory, utility analysis, simulation, forecasting and decision trees. He then opened one of the doors and was promptly eaten by a low-probability lion. The third person, and it is always the third person who wins in stories like this, took courses in lion taming.

Although Cunningam's book seems to be more about organizational development than about organizational policymaking, it gives some interesting pointers towards

Lesson 24: Look out for misconceived attitudes

Humans like to surround themselves with their own kind. It makes colleagues more predictable and facilitates a more harmonious working environment. But predictable personnel can stunt any organization's potential, as pointed out by Cunningham (1994).

For instance, some people become too theoretical – the world of theory has taught them to make generalizations in a classroom where they learn systems analysis, specialized subjects and specific skills. By contrast, others become 'too practical' – they learn 'on the job', from problems, people, patterns and processes.

The result is that on the one hand theoreticians have an 'S to P' problem where they know solutions and so go looking for people or problems to which to apply them. Worse, they might distort problems just to fit the solution. For example, a chemist looking at mental illness would probably prescribe a chemical solution rather than psychotherapy. This problem is currently being exacerbated by increased specialization of disciplines in the name of greater knowledge.

On the other hand, practical policymakers often have the reverse, 'P to S' problem, as epitomized by the hard-nosed manager who wants nothing to do with policies contributed by a bunch of academics. But they assume they have learned it all, from experience, which is to assume the future will be the same as the past, but Cunningham argues this is an erroneous assumption.

Indeed, modern society's young people have less reverence for aged people than did young people within traditional, agrarian societies. In the latter, things changed little, and so the older people were valued for their long and useful experience. In modern societies the young are growing up in conditions vastly different to those experienced by their elders, and so the latter's advice is less relevant.

However, such an argument could be the 'turbulence of modern societies' assumption surfacing yet again (see below). It is possibly erroneous. Be careful. Policymakers should never let misconceived attitudes blunt their performance.

improving the latter. For example, it preaches the virtues of life-long learning, by all members of any organization, to ensure that there is harmony, flexibility and growth within an institution. This allows it to progress and flower with the times, and such fluidity gives the organization 'eyes' and 'ears', because people from different age groups and cultures pay attention to different things:

Organizations lose a great deal by trying to be comfortably homogeneous (usually by hiring young, white, able-bodied, middle-class, heterosexual males for managerial positions). It makes superficial communication easier, but the reduction in the organization's learning capability through this strategy is enormous. (Cunningham, 1994, p. 55)

Such insights are typical of the boosterism genre of business policymaking textbooks. They may be over subjective, and they may be over hyped, but they are frequently grounded in considerable real-world experience and clever observation. In this sense, their justification is not light years away from the 'school of hard knocks' justification used by this book to defend its software-derived pronouncements.

4.1.3. Cognitive science packages

Another source of policymaking insight is Cognitive Science. But like the soft systems methodologists, some cognitive scientists are less keen on prescriptive policymaking than they are on descriptive policymaking (Winograd and Flores, 1986; Best, 1992). To them, understanding is everything. They prefer to examine policymaking not with the aim of formulating a prescription but with the aim of studying it as an activity.

But there is a 'cognitive' twist to such proposed activities. They actually see policymaking as an innate human skill that has somehow been corrupted by politics or whatever. Therefore, careful, 'cognitive' study of this activity is needed to unlock our awareness of the skills that we have lost. This is why Belton and Elder (1994) say a neglected part of decision support is the facilitation of users' learning about the problem. They therefore advocate visual interactive modelling as an effective way of perceiving and 'seeing through' complicated policymaking situations.

Visual interactive modelling involves the user constructing various sorts of pictures of the relevant data, on a computer screen, in the hope that some of these pictures will lead to new and fresh insights into the nature of the problem being faced. It allows transparency, understanding, insight into the 'sensitivities' of influent variables, clarification of one's subjective views and potential for changing the latter.

More exactly, Belton and Elder argue that a decision support system acts within three 'spaces', as shown in the left hand column of table 4.4. Note that again, this table has a right hand column to indicate that their ideas seem to conform with the

Table 4.4. Belton and Elder's decision support spaces compared to the approach taken by policymaking software.

Decision support's 'spaces':	Policymaking software's phases:
Decision space	1. Think
Solution space	2. Choose
Values space	3. Anticipate

policymaking process adopted by much policymaking software. Belton and Elder then outline the types of learning that the visual interactive modelling (VIM) approach should facilitate:

1. Discovery – understanding links between 'decision space' and 'solution space';
2. Explication – designing links between 'solution space' and 'values space';
3. Clarification – exploring and understanding these explication links;
4. Change – redrawing some explication links;
5. Creation – enlargement of 'decision space'.

So here we have some authors, who started out looking at the potential of visual interactive modelling for better policymaking, eventually recommending what we ourselves have been recommending in this book. Specifically, they advocate looking for more explication type links between 'decision space' and 'solution space', which is what much software does when it 'thinks'. Moreover, they advocate forging links between 'solution space' and 'values space', which is exactly what some software does when it predicts how different people, with their different values, will respond to different policy choices – 'anticipate'.

Lesson 25: Stay decisive

Although most policymaking practitioners start off their careers enthusiastically, many become bored with their mission. It is as if they have spent too many years making policy decisions that are never adopted because of human selfishness, perversity and jealousy, and so their crusading zeal eventually becomes blunted.

Such policymakers frequently drift into a more 'scientific' mode. They attempt to find the key to better policymaking. They study the processes and the actual policymakers themselves rather than persisting with trying to improve the process. Many adopt approaches like soft systems methodology and Cognitive Science, particularly if they switch to a university environment where such inquiry is encouraged.

But for those who remain back at the office, those who are still charged with the responsibility of making decisions, this drift towards description rather than prescription needs to be kept under control. If they, or their colleagues, begin to let science interrupt their policymaking too much, a loss of decisiveness inevitably follows.

This will not necessarily be a bad thing, providing one is aware that it is happening. Awareness enables one to counter the drift whenever urgent decisions are required. Retain your decisiveness.

Epinasse (1994) also presents a Cognitive Science-inspired view of policymaking. He too he sees it as an alternative to the rational comprehensive approach that has hitherto, according to him, dominated policymaking too much. He believes the Cognitive Science approach involves trying out lots of different forms of problem expression, and different ways of solving the problem, in an attempt to discover links between 'decision space' and 'solution space'. He then outlines how the cognitive approach to policymaking differs from the traditional, rational comprehensive approach – it is not explicit, voluntary or positive but 'largely unconscious'. It does not use 'progress' as its justification; it unifies situations by searching for 'coherence'.

The point to remember is that such searching for coherence probably corresponds to the way in which humans make sense of the world. That is, we all seek an equilibrium that assures integrity within our retained knowledge of our environment. This naturally leads to simplification in order to reduce complexity. But it is a form of simplification that is different to that attained by the 'rational' decision maker. Whereas the latter sees independent problems, the cognitive scientist sees a global explanation for them. Therefore, rather than make probability calculations, the cognitive scientist will resolve the problem using previously acquired beliefs, procedures and solutions. That is, in order to preserve perceptual coherence, certain processes of learning and reinforcement are required.

Lesson 26: Dream practically

The day might may come when software can, all by itself, 'learn' what the best policies are. This may sound like science fiction, but many of today's artefacts sounded like science fiction some years ago.

However, computers as we know them will never feel in the same way that a human feels, and so a computer will never learn in exactly the same way that a human learns. Hence the best that we can hope for is software that acts like an 'interesting' robot – a program that comes up with valid and perhaps unthought of policy suggestions, but whose recommendations we should never follow slavishly.

Only a human, at least in human-oriented policymaking, is able properly to evaluate software's suggestions – on the basis of their social intuition. Despite some software being made to be more 'feeling' in its style, by learning more and more about *how* humans actually decide things, such programs are unlikely ever to substitute for humans completely.

Therefore, although it is essential for policymaking's advancement that its practitioners keep dreaming up better and better artefacts and methods to help, this should always be done with the brakes on.

Epinasse then sketchily presents his prototype software, *COGNITA*. It seeks to act as a bridge between a symbolic module, in this case a cognitive map, and a connectionist module, in this case a neural network that tries to learn new things about the problem and its solutions. This is certainly a very worthy ambition, but the lack of detail proffered, about both the actual procedures used and the substantive results obtained, suggests that the software is, as yet, very preliminary. Perhaps the Cognitive Science formulation of how policymaking should proceed is not yet unambiguous enough to be operational.

Nevertheless, Cognitive Science's attempt to model the connections between problem perception and the discovery of a solution could be a pointer to the future of policymaking software. Indeed, many spin-off packages have resulted from this push towards operationalization of Cognitive Science, and it is to some that we now turn.

4.2. Innovative Software

Some packages are so clever that it is only a matter of time before they become more fully integrated into policymaking software. Accordingly, sub-section 4.2.1 looks at Artificial Intelligence-based packages, and sub-section 4.2.2 describes some Distributed Computing-based packages.

4.2.1. Artificial intelligence packages

It should always be remembered that policymaking is not the only complex discipline. Many fields are just as complicated, and so people in such areas have been studying ways to overcome complexity for a long time. One of these areas is Artificial Intelligence (Barr and Feigenbaum, 1981; Fetzer, 1990), the discipline that tries to get computer programs to perform human-like, intelligent things such as learning and planning. Some of its principles might therefore be useful in our quest for improved policymaking practice.

A once promising sub-area of Artificial Intelligence is 'text understanding' – getting computers to make sense of stories (Shank, 1984). It is in fact closer to policymaking than one might imagine, since the most favoured way of ensuring that a computer program 'understands' a story is to attribute some 'plan', or policy, to each of the story's characters. If the motives of the main characters cannot be inferred, then a story will simply not make sense. Hence this area of Artificial Intelligence research is knowledgeable about plans and policymaking. This is why there has been considerable overlap between research in text understanding and research in the field of robot planning – getting a robot to plan its actions (Sacerdoti, 1977).

There are also other parts of Artificial Intelligence that are potentially useful for policymaking, such as 'expert systems' (Landsbergen, 1997; Davidson, 1997). These have already been mentioned a few times above. They are basically collections of 'if-then' rules, as supplied by some acknowledged expert in a discipline, for giving advice as to what is applicable within different situations. The system begins by asking the user to describe his or her own particular situation, and it then responds with 'policy' advice derived from its store of if-then rules. Note that although they were very fashionable during the 1980s, expert systems have since fallen into relative disrepute in some quarters, and there are two main reasons for this.

The first is that experts frequently cannot tell an expert system builder the exact form of the if-then rules that they use while they are functioning as an expert. The expert system builder therefore finds it difficult to write into his or her system the rules used by the person whose expertise they are supposed to be replicating. Hence any system that does get built tends to be inaccurate. Such a difficulty is known as the 'knowledge bottleneck' – the problem of getting rules out of a human expert's head and into a computerized system.

The second problem is the inherent epistemological weakness of such a reductionist approach. Within the human-oriented domain, many enthusiasts quickly learned that distillation of human policymaking into a finite number of if-then rules is over idealistic and too simplistic. If human knowledge can be distilled into something so simple it does not say much for the subtlety and sophistication of such knowledge.

Nevertheless, some detailed research reported by Landsbergen *et al.* (1997) is still encouraging. It purports to show that users of expert systems, although they tend to have less confidence and commitment towards their own policymaking decisions, actually make better decisions. It is as if using an expert system alerts one to the extent of one's own lack of knowledge, but it also leads to higher quality performance. Perhaps this is one reason why expert systems have been widely used, along with people's desperation to use absolutely anything that could possibly help when problems are wicked, vicious and fuzzy.

However, most reported applications have been in 'simpler' problem areas. For example the US taxation office, the IRS (Internal Revenue Service), apparently uses an expert system to help answer taxation queries, and General Motors Holden has used an expert system to diagnose engine problems. Moreover, the Blue Cross medical benefits company used an expert system to evaluate plans and to expedite claims review, and the US Department of Defence has used one, called *CESA*, to assist in the sensible granting of research contracts.

Besides these, there are some more publicly accessible expert system packages. One is described by Davidson (1997) and it gives advice to financial traders. It claims to be able to get around the knowledge bottleneck by querying an expert using complex, interactive procedures so as to uncover their deeper thought processes. This works better than simply writing down if-then rules. But alas, no details are supplied of how this approach actually operates.

Another method that exists within Artificial Intelligence is 'simulated neural networks'. These are predictive mechanisms that absorb lots of information, thousands of times if necessary, about a set of inputs and their associated output(s). They then teach themselves, or 'learn' to replicate any relationship that might exist between patterns of inputs and their associated output. Hence they learn to predict what is likely to result from any pattern of inputs, even a previously unseen pattern. They learn in a relatively assumptions-free, information-soaked, evolutionary and 'soft' sort of way. They therefore constitute an attempt to make silicon-based computers 'feel' in the more organic manner of animals.

Such a style of learning has several advantages. One is its ability to still learn even when the 'training' data are inaccurate or incomplete, just like humans can. For instance, humans can learn to recognize hand-written symbols despite their shapes often being inaccurate or even partially missing, and it is similar with simulated neural networks. Thus the program used to recognize hand written postcodes, on letters to be sorted at the local post office, is usually a simulated neural network. Unlike more traditional statistical programs, such software is less likely to come to grief when it encounters inaccurate or partial information. Therefore, in a problem area like human-oriented policymaking, where data are often inaccurate and partial, simulated neural networks seem to have considerable predictive potential for use within the 'anticipate' phase of the process.

Lesson 27: Watch developments

In fields like Artificial Intelligence it often seems paramount to not 'give too much away'. Authors are keen to sing the praises of their new systems, but they are increasingly coy about providing exact details about how such systems work.

Such a situation was probably predictable, at least within the Western world. Growing privatization of government and higher education has stemmed from increased global competition for scarce development funds and it has led to an increasingly frequent demand for research to be self-financing. Under such conditions researchers will always be loathe to provide too much information that gives a competitive advantage to their rivals.

This is bad news for science. If people are too secretive about their methods, new knowledge is not disseminated quickly or effectively. Hence many policymaking innovations are now, presumably, being made within large and relatively wealthy management consultancies and passed on to their own clients rather than to the world in general.

Hence any individual policymaking establishment, if it wishes to keep up with world's best practice, has the choice of either using an expensive management consultant or trying to develop its own in-house expertise.

But the latter, whilst at first sight appearing 'unproductive' in cost accounting terms, could actually be cheaper in the long run. That is, employing a few young and bright policymakers might be less expensive than it has been in the past. This is because of competition for policymaking jobs, the relative cheapness of microcomputers and the huge growth of data available on the world wide web have, paradoxically, made it easier for small-scale efforts to achieve real success.

Hence a final statement on this issue would be premature. On the one hand policymaking methods have become more of a secret, but on the other hand the explosive growth of the Internet threatens to blow all this apart. It will be interesting to watch developments over the next decade. Keep your ear to the ground.

Quah *et al.* (1996) have actually tried to amalgamate simulated neural networks with an expert system in their *NEULONET* package. Once it has been trained it can answer questions by predicting a 'yes', 'no' or a 'don't know' output for any pattern of inputs. More specifically, the neural network program contains input nodes, into which various parameters of the policymaking situation are fed, along with their truth value – (1,0) means true, (0,1) means false and (0,0) means don't know. The network's links, from the two input nodes to the output node, have two weights on them, and the output node's net score is then calculated as the sum, over all inputs, of 'the first number times the first weight' minus 'the second number times the second weight'. This generates a value for the output node that is compared to the value that it should have been, as provided by the training data. Corrections that are proportional to the error in the output node are then made to all weights.

In this way, after many adjustments, the network trains itself to emulate the chained reasoning within an expert system. That is, it learns what trained weights ought to be put on the expert system's reasoning network. The point of bothering to do this is, presumably, to enable the expert system to work even when it receives incomplete or slightly unconventional input data.

It should be cautioned that neural networks have one major disadvantage – their 'black box' nature. That is, they may work in terms of predicting things, but we do not know *how* they work. Unlike traditional statistical models, a trained neural network is simply too complicated to be able to look at the weights on its components and so deduce which inputs had the most effect on the outputs and by how much. This is especially so when one remembers that whether or not any internal node within a neural network is activated during prediction depends on whether or not it has attained a certain threshold value. But the network is so hugely complicated it is difficult to keep track of which nodes are firing and which nodes are not. Hence the operational logic of the model remains a mystery.

This is a great drawback in policymaking because we usually want to be confident that we have a system that is 'reasonable'. By the latter we mean that its logic is plausible enough for the model to be likely to keep on predicting accurately in the future when it is confronted with novel input data. This is why Westland (1995) proposed an alternative to neural networks. It retains all of the features that attract users to neural networks yet it is much more 'transparent' – a Bayesian model. This mirrors the behaviour of neural networks but also enables one to use statistical performance measures that are useful for determining how prediction is actually being achieved.

Yet another potentially useful Artificial Intelligence technique is 'genetic algorithms'. These are a response to the inability of traditional optimization methods to find a globally optimal policy within ultra-complicated situations. The genetic algorithm may not be able to find a globally optimal solution either, but it can approach one as closely as desired by simply leaving the computer to search towards a better solution for a longer time.

More exactly, the genetic algorithm selectively 'breeds' whole generations of possible solutions. Each new generation of solutions has offspring that have inherited the features of its generation-leading parents and this makes it almost certain that the next generation will contain better solutions than did the previous generation. Hence the ultimate, globally optimal solution can be approached.

Such a potentially powerful approach underlies such programs as Chambers and Taylor's (1996) *GENIE* system that successfully found solutions to complex policymaking problems within the urban and transport planning fields. Moreover, Palisade Corporation (http://www.palisade.com) markets some genetic algorithm-based software that claims to be able to solve many problems that were previously unsolvable. These include *What's Best!*, which is software for linear and non-linear optimization and which is able to handle up to 32,000 variables along with 16,000 constraints, even though it is just a simple spreadsheet add in.

Another genetic algorithm-based package from Palisade is *Premium Solver!*, a program that fits into a spreadsheet seamlessly and handles up to 800 linear variables or up to 400 non-linear variables. But their best product is possibly the medium-priced *Evolver,* which claims to be able to find optimal solutions very quickly. The standard version can handle 80 variables, the professional version can handle 256 and the industrial version can handle an unlimited number of variables. Moreover, by using its 'evolver watcher' module, one is able to inspect charts that show the quality of each generation of solutions as they evolve.

So promising is this genetic algorithm-based search tool that its promoters even give an example of how it might be used, not for finding optimal solutions to specific problems, but for finding new 'theories' in a number of disciplines (http://www.palisade.com). Their example involves trying to find the best rule for stock trading which will maximize profits. If one has historical data about trading volumes, closing prices and changes in the price of related securities over the past few months, then one is able to ascertain the profitability that would have resulted from virtually any investment rule if it had been followed.

Such candidate rules constitute the search space. A plethora of rules can be searched, the better ones can be 'married' to other good ones, and so their 'child' rules will probably be better still. For example, one could always test, by computer of course, the profitability that would have resulted from a rule like:

If trading volume is up by at least 20% AND,
if the price of stock is up by at least 1% AND
if T-bill rates are up by at least 0.3%
THEN buy, OTHERWISE sell.

Moreover, other rules can be tested, for example 'If trading volume is up 15% . . .' and so on.

Such is the power of modern computers. Here we have a machine, a humble (but very powerful) computer actually generating alternative theories, testing their levels of predicability, and 'evolving' better and better ones. It is still too early to tell whether such procedures can actually lead to new and useful notions, but if they do, theory building will no longer be an exclusively human activity. What does this suggest about the future role of computers in the process of policymaking as we know it?

Openshaw (1997a) became so excited by all this that he wrote a fascinating book about it. His text is the first ever book about the application of Artificial Intelligence techniques to geography, and his approach is so radical that it has made him unpopular with certain theorists within that discipline.

Specifically, he points out that we are presently awash with huge amounts of geographical data coming from remote sensing systems. These data have overwhelmed the spatial sciences. They have not even been able to develop theories about where to begin looking for patterns within such data – pattern recognition being the initial, first step within any science. Therefore, just as the investment analyst of the previous paragraphs used a powerful computer to look for theories and patterns, why should we not get computers to tell us where to start looking for patterns, and scientifically testable theories, amongst overwhelming masses of spatial data?

Openshaw (1997b) has actually had some preliminary success finding new theories for prediction of road traffic. This is no mean feat, since human transport policymakers have, for decades, been developing their own traffic-prediction theories to a high level of sophistication (Hayes and Fotheringham, 1984). Yet by using computer search of alternative traffic-prediction formulae, Openshaw found new equations which he claims perform better than the traditional ones do.

Note that Openshaw enlisted the aid of 'fuzzy logic' (Zadeh, 1986). The latter assigns entities to several categories at once, but to different extents. Hence ambiguous situations where in some ways an entity can be assigned to one category, but in other ways it should be assigned to a different category, are tracked. All such ambiguity can then be resolved at the end when final membership strengths for the different categories are totalled.

For those who either do not believe this, or who think that computers can never perform theorizing, Coffee (1994) describes some more concrete, but equally spectacular achievements of software based on Artificial Intelligence methods. His first example is the Mellon Bank of Chicago's 1993 adoption of a neural network system to predict disturbances in patterns of credit card usage. The neural network reduced the amount of credit card 'warnings' by 90% over earlier, less intelligent methods. It was able to spot, for the very first time, the habit of credit card thieves to use stolen cards for making small purchases of fuel at service stations in order to test the cards.

Moreover, at about the same time a genetic algorithm was used to find the optimal course for a spacecraft on a long distance mission. The problem was to use course-correcting thrusters in such a way that, given the gravity of nearby planets, the craft would arrive in a minimal amount of time and use as small an amount of fuel as possible. This was a huge optimization task involving 10180 possible solutions! Yet a small genetic algorithm package was able to converge on a 'nearly optimal solution' after examining only 500 of the possible combinations.

Lesson 28: Fuzzy policymaking

Fuzzy logic has considerable potential in policymaking practice. This is because it is sometimes sensible to place alternative policies into more than one category. The 'fuzzy' (multiple) way of categorizing policies' performance might be a more accurate representation of reality, and this could ultimately lead to better decisions.

Be warned, however, that this could get out of hand. The soft, fuzzy model could eventually show everything and nothing – it might become so loose and undefined that it is unable to make definite recommendations about how to proceed. Use fuzzy logic cautiously.

Note that some packages actually combine a simulated neural network with a genetic algorithm. This is because simulated neural networks do not work very well until the researcher has experimented with several network configurations in terms of how many layers and how many nodes per layer they have. Correctly configuring a neural network is still more of an art than a science. Hence the genetic algorithm is used to evolve a close to optimal configuration for the neural network. It 'breeds' generations of network structures, and each generation suggests better networks than the previous one.

An example of a neural network plus genetic algorithm package is the medium-priced *Braincel* (http://www.palisade.com). This attaches to an *Excel* spreadsheet and outputs its predictions in the form of charts. Also, *Braincel for Excel* does much the same thing but does not have a genetic algorithm to help choose the best network structure. Instead, it has a routine called *Best Net* that simply tests a number of standard neural network structures to see which one 'learns' the most effectively.

Such software is, of course, extremely easy to use because the whole predictive process is so automatic. One simply designates the input cells and the output cells; the neural network trains itself on this information and so, for any new set of inputs, the predicted output(s) simply appear on the spreadsheet. We will surely hear much more about these Artificial Intelligence-based packages in the future.

4.2.2. Distributed computing packages

An approach with many similar characteristics to the neural network and genetic algorithm is the long-standing, but increasingly fashionable method known as 'distributed intelligence' or 'distributed computing'. It involves trying to understand information, and policies, through the use of a large number of simple mechanisms that are individually dumb but collectively very powerful (Bond and Gasser, 1988). Ekenberg *et al.* (1997) call such elements 'intelligent agents'. The agents combine their judgements about what policy seems best, in a fuzzy-scoring sort of way. Moreover, the latter adjusts the final decision according to the assumed validity of each agent's input.

Lesson 29: Use technology astutely

Human-oriented policymaking is so incredibly difficult to perform well that it is always tempting for practitioners to adopt the latest technology and so become intoxicated by the hype that surrounds it.

For instance, during the 1980s many people really believed that expert systems would be able to solve policymaking problems within any field. It was only the cold hard light of dawning hindsight that revealed expert systems were useful for just a few, limited problem domains. Therefore, although they proved to be a blessing in some circumstances, for many people expert systems meant a large amount of wasted time that could have otherwise been spent more productively.

It is likely to be similar with currently novel technologies such as simulated neural networks and genetic algorithms. Right now they are experiencing the initial flush of enthusiasm and it seems that they can, in theory, be applied to almost any problem that involves prediction and optimization respectively. But we will probably find that they are useful for solving only certain types of policymaking problems and not others.

Yet this is no reason to hold back from such techniques while everyone else takes them up. Indeed, the more people who are testing new technologies, the sooner we will all learn about suitable and unsuitable areas of application.

Whether or not to take the gamble of setting aside time and money to test some techniques that are currently peripheral to mainstream policymaking practice is a decision that only individual policymakers can make. Use technology astutely.

Also, Ekenberg *et al.* make the point that calculating maximum utility, as traditional Operations Research does, is not always the best route to the best policy. Maximum utility is artificially holistic and so tries to search across all of the unimaginably complex, 'infinite' possibilities. Yet this differs from what happens in the real world. Some policies will never even be considered because they are just too risky – they violate security constraints. Therefore, why waste time considering them? Accordingly, distributed computing adopts a 'soft' approach to computing in which the analysis 'feels its way' towards a solution, in the soft systems methodology manner, rather than being brutally and artificially optimal.

In passing it should be noted that Eckenberg *et al.* quote Simon's contention that rational decision making is really a series of steps. This is shown in the left hand column of table 4.5 along with policymaking software's approach shown, again, in the right hand column. Such steps appear to be similar to the approach taken to policymaking in this book. Note however that steps 2 and 3 on the left, taken together, are equivalent to step 2 on the right, that is, Simon's steps 2 and 3 are equivalent to our step 2. Also, we actually take the process a step further by looking at the consequences of our choice (step 3). The latter will, of course, ultimately feed back and so change our choice of policy (step 2). That is, we have reiterated the importance of feedback in policymaking, just as we did when discussing table 4.2 above.

Table 4.5. Simon's view of rational decision making compared to the approach adopted by policymaking software.

Rational decision making (according to Simon):	Policymaking software's approach:
1. List the acts	1. Think
2. Determine all their consequences	1. Think
3. Make a comparative evaluation	2. Choose
	3. Anticipate

But returning to distributed computing, Doran (1992) has argued that the relationship between distributed intelligence and social science is the same as the relationship between Artificial Intelligence and Psychology. In other words, distributed computing has the potential to automate some of social science. It could serve as a computer-based simulation of society.

More exactly, each intelligent agent could have declarative knowledge to simulate a person's beliefs and procedural knowledge to simulate a person's abilities; it could collect information about its environment, and it could then decide what actions to perform on the basis of its individual goals. In other words, all agents could act concurrently to form a 'social' environment. The latter is called a MAS (Multiple Agent System). It needs to be equipped with complex communication rules, and it relies on agents having some knowledge both of one another and the total agent community (Sycara *et al.*, 1996). Such an approach has obvious potential for making better policy in fields such as cooperating expert systems, air traffic control, concurrent as distinct from traditional, sequential engineering and team-based design. Note however that the latter would require the inclusion of specialist knowledge about conflict resolution.

Kitano (1996) claims that such systems could reduce the workload and enhance the quality of policymaking by eliminating human error. This seems to be an extravagant claim, but he does point out that such systems can behave more reasonably within a wider range of situations than can conventional software.

In fact, some forerunners to these systems have in fact already been built. For example, *QuickKeys* and *Tempo II Plus* (Miley, 1993) are programs that observe users' keyboard habits and then make tentative suggestions for improvement. We are therefore moving closer to the time when we will have systems that can gradually learn what sort of data a user prefers and then find them for him or her. That is, we are approaching the science fiction ideal of, say, an intelligent television set that learns the tastes and preferences of its user and then combs the world's cable networks until it locates suitable programs to keep its user happy.

There are obvious problems foreseeable with such technology, such as controlling how intrusive we want these 'helping hand' programs to be. Other problems are discussed by Miley, such as the problem of inappropriate learning by the software in situations where the user changes his or her requirements and preferences due to radically altered circumstances.

However, there are theoretical ways around many such problems. For example, one could connect distributed systems to a data warehouse that contains case histories of the successes and failures of other systems. Then, one could search this warehouse with a genetic algorithm to 'evolve' an optimal multi-agent system (!). Again, we have probably not heard the last of distributed computing and related packages.

4.3. Summary

This chapter took an excursion back into the theory of policymaking software. It briefly examined soft systems methodology, along with other efforts to make traditional Operations Research more 'feeling' and less 'thinking' in its style. It demonstrated how Operations Research partially overlaps with both the boosterism and the Cognitive Science styles of improving policymaking. Such approaches provide many insights for possible improvements to practice, but they can sometimes degenerate into featureless description rather than inspired prescription.

Some Artificial Intelligence and Distributed Computing packages were then introduced. These are based on methods like expert systems, simulated neural networks, genetic algorithms and intelligent agents. All of them have huge potential to perform activities that have hitherto been performed by humans exclusively, such as theory development and cooperative planning. Indeed, some of this software's early results have been extremely promising. But it is important not to get swept away in an uncritical, first burst of enthusiasm for such packages.

Chapter 5

Frontier Software Case I: *CyberQuest*

We now come to the first of our four 'research frontier' packages – *CyberQuest*. This system is useful during the 'think' phase of the policymaking process because it is electronic brainstorming software. Yet it is an advance on other brainstorming packages because of its thoroughness, its ease of use and, most of all, because of its 'multi media' attributes. That is, because the whole idea of brainstorming is to stimulate users' creativity using whatever means possible (Van Grundy, 1985), *CyberQuest* enlists the support of many stimuli, including videos, music, sound, pictures, paintings, proverbs, thesauri and even (descriptions of) smells. This is over and above the usual matching of key words with databases, as performed by *IdeaFisher* and other more standard packages introduced in Chapter 2.

More specifically, *CyberQuest* comes with two associated programs, *Cristal* and *Quantitative CyberQuest*. These allow the user to flip in and out of spreadsheets, painting and drawing software, the Internet and other aids to analysis. However, our main thrust here is to describe the core of *CyberQuest* – the mechanisms by which it prompts users to come up with possibly good ideas.

CyberQuest was originally nourished during the 1970s by the development of *TIM – The Ideas Machine* (Dickey, 1995). The latter was actually one of the first multi-media packages to be used in human-oriented policymaking. It consisted of not only computer software but also of video and music CD's, electronic and paper encyclopaedias, picture books, thesauri and aromic disks that actually emanated odours.

The aim was to trigger in the user's mind a plethora of potential policy suggestions. Moreover, the approach was always predicated on an assumption – the more 'bright ideas' we can stimulate a human to come up with, the more likely it is that good policy will follow. Such an assumption has been echoed by several writers within the field of creative brainstorming, for example Rawlinson (1994), yet this notion – 'more *quantity* leads to greater *quality*', has probably never been tested rigorously. Nevertheless, many writers, as well as the author of *CyberQuest*, would probably defend such an assumption on the grounds of its logical plausibility and statistical probability.

However, the early versions of *CyberQuest* had a much more pressing problem – the multimedia equipment for playing videos, music and aromas was expensive, both for people to buy, and for John Dickey to take on the road to his clients. Eventually such a problem prompted development of the 'PC version', which we discuss here. In it, the stimulation potential of movies, music and smells may have been sacrificed in favour of reliance upon disk-based storage of key words, concepts and proverbs.

However, two comments are in order. Firstly, at least the new system is portable. Secondly, the use of videos and music on computers is becoming increasingly common, and so the latest versions of *CyberQuest* come with many sounds, images and videos, courtesy of the accompanying *Cristal* software, and they are all neatly held on the computer's hard disk. This has made *CyberQuest* a very useful and comprehensive tool for assisting human brainstormers.

Table 5.1. Some problems that have been addressed by *CyberQuest*.

Anticipating a transportation system's economic impacts	Improving performance in manufactured food processing	Finding markets for capital investment
Learning mathematics through real-life examples	Facilitating computer-assisted language instruction	Increasing the appeal of teaching handicapped children
Increasing funding for urban transportation	Importing and exporting to Eastern Europe	Reducing overcrowding in prisons
Revitalizing a depressed rural area	Manufacturing bridge decking that is durable	Fostering leadership in global society
Appointing a director of a hospice	Facilitating community-based child care	Facilitating wider usage of information
Improving students' problem solving skills	Improving people's access to CD-ROM databases	Reducing uncertainty of auto parts supply
Boosting the image of commuting	Improving health care and insurance for employees	Providing shelter for the homeless
Applying household insecticides	Marketing Soviet films	Motivating corporate recycling
Motif design	Reducing court delays	Working with at-risk students
Rearranging some of Bach's music	Planning a 21st century school	Improving student performance
Designing a sports complex	Encouraging innovation in the workplace	Evaluating a company's alternative energy supplies

The result of this is that a large number of companies and organizations have used *CyberQuest* to address an extremely wide variety of problems. This is why the 'Recent Cases', which come supplied with the software, list a large number of ideas generated when addressing a vast range of problem domains, as shown in table 5.1.

5.1. Analysing the Situation

Whenever users start *CyberQuest* and indicate that they wish to create a new 'case' they are presented with the screen shown in figure 5.1. One can see that a user has typed in a brief description of a policymaking problem – '(how to) reduce the incidence of war'.

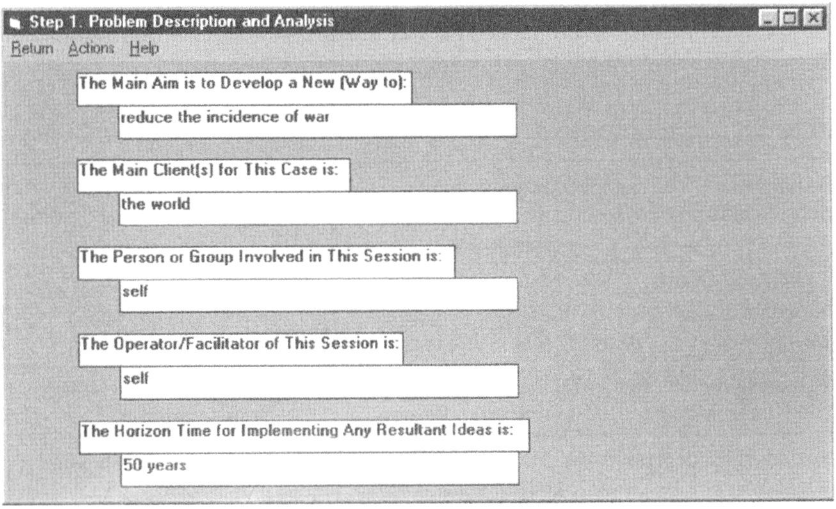

Figure 5.1. *CyberQuest* beginning a new case.

After the user clicks 'Return', *CyberQuest* begins by tolerating considerable informal discussion of the problem and of the issues surrounding it, so that users do not jump to premature conclusions about their situation. More exactly, it asks users to take part in 'situation structuring' as a preparation for nominating key words that sum up the nature of the problem.

After that however, *CyberQuest* opts for a prescribed and clear brainstorming procedure. If it simply facilitated informal discussion between its users, by having them type in random thoughts about their policymaking situation and possible ideas for addressing them, the whole exercise would become unwieldy. Then, the package would find itself being heavily maligned for indecisiveness and lack of direction. *CyberQuest* therefore directs users what to do quite closely.

For instance, figure 5.1 shows that *CyberQuest* asks the user to state clearly why he or she is undertaking policymaking, and the user is able to answer only by cryptically nominating the overall goal, the client and the policymaking horizon. This might seem surprising given that the various subtleties and nuances of the policymaking situation might be better captured when users are allowed to type in long descriptions, thereby boosting the chances of more incisive policymaking. But *CyberQuest* needs a short headline to describe the overall goal for no other reason than it fits onto the computer screen. But as with most policymaking software, *CyberQuest* users are allowed to type in longer answers so that subsequently they can access the longer descriptions in order to refresh their memory.

Lesson 30: Proceed with clarity

CyberQuest gives us many pointers to exemplary policymaking practice. Firstly, short summary phrases to describe alternative policies are mandatory. They are easier to handle and move between. However, longer and richer descriptions of alternative policies must also remain instantly accessible, just in case participants forget their exact nature and subtle characteristics.

Secondly, recording who exactly the client is seems to be a good idea. If the client is not known, sensible policymaking is unlikely to occur, because the client usually influences the available possibilities. For example, if the client is the 'local school', policies for achieving peace at school will be very different from those for achieving peace in the world at large. In turn, policies will be different again if the client is the 'household' or the 'factory'.

Indeed, lack of clarity about who the client is has often been disastrous. It frequently transpires that there are multiple clients, and so one set of policymakers emphasizes one client's needs while another emphasizes another and their different needs. There then follows an argument over policy between the two sets of policymakers that could have been so easily defused by simply establishing who the most important client is or, at least, which client should be concentrated on for the present.

Thirdly, nominating the policymaking horizon is also a neat clarification tool. The time horizon gives an indication of how strategic one's policymaking should be. This is important because sub-goals in strategic exercises are likely to be different from those in less strategic exercises - even when the overall goal remains the same. For example, the sub-goals for achieving strategic, long-term financial profit are likely to be different to sub-goals for achieving tactical, short-term financial profit.

In short, exemplary policymaking involves short statements along with identification of the aim, the client and the time horizon. Such tactics bring clarity to one's tasks.

Now, its main menu continually shows *CyberQuest* wanting to take users through the following sequence of steps:

1. Problem (description)
2. Key words (nomination)
3. Idea generation
4. Idea screening
5. Idea packaging
6. Reporting

Moreover, the user is able, at any stage, to generate a help message that outlines what to do if one is confused. In other words, *CyberQuest* gives participants a 'map' of the steps they are expected to go through.

Hence our initial impression is that *CyberQuest* is a 'thinking' sort of package that forces users to conform to a strict procedural model. However, as we shall see later, the package actually has an overwhelmingly 'feeling' style because of the way it interacts with its users. Nevertheless, *CyberQuest* does present clear and unambiguous menus because of its underlying belief that policymaking should work to a definite agenda.

Lesson 31: Manage people carefully

There is no one clear answer to the question of whether policymakers should arrange unstructured or structured meetings. We have seen that Mintzberg (1994) is a strong advocate of less formal meetings. He believes that meetings which conform like clock work to cryptic agendas are often mere rubber stamping exercises set up to enforce decisions that have already been made, secretly and behind closed doors, by the power brokers within an organization's kitchen cabinet.

Also, controlled and contrived meetings often bristle with suppressed value differences, where paranoia torpedoes any chance of workable compromises being hammered out; where entrenched, unenlightened positions are adopted by each side.

Yet policymakers' choice on this issue will obviously depend on the stage that their policymaking has reached. In the beginning, when participants have only just met, it is probably a good idea to have one or more informal meetings to enable people to get to know each other and their respective value systems. But later on in the process, after people's value differences have become known, any policymaking manager who continues to just have 'getting to know you' meetings will do so at his or her peril. Such sessions will generate so much continuing debate, as well as re-affirmation of value differences, that clear policymaking will become unlikely.

Properly managing participants, and caring for their prickly egos so as to get the best possible contribution from them, can be one of the policymaker's most difficult tasks. Perform it carefully.

In practice, many readers will have endured the alternative - no agenda. Whenever a policymaking meeting's chair suggests that an informal meeting style is about to be adopted in which participants will be setting their own agenda, it is, more often than not, a signal that a 'talkfest' is about to begin. One can almost guarantee, therefore, that issues will be discussed in no particular order of priority, and tangible outcomes in the form of clear, succinct and committed decisions are extremely unlikely.

5.1.1. Exploring concepts

After nominating their problem, *CyberQuest*'s users' first task is, as we have already seen, 'situation structuring'. This involves the user identifying elements (issues) that seem to surround the problem, nominating 'dimensions' on which such elements should be 'scored', and then using such scores to have *CyberQuest* cluster the situation's elements into 'themes'.

One of these processes is shown in figure 5.2 where *CyberQuest* is prompting a user to list the issues, or the 'situation elements' that characterize the problem. The user types elements into the space near the top left, and he or she might be helped by the standard suggestions on the top right. Moreover, the bottom left window shows the problem elements that they have already chosen so far. Hence in our example, where the problem is how to reduce 'war', figure 5.2 shows some possible situation elements – 'military group', 'political group', 'natural environment' and so on.

The user is also asked to nominate dimensions along which these elements might be measured. The program then helps the user to do this. It nominates, at random, trios of situation elements and asks why two of these elements are similar, but different to the third one in some respect. For example, in the 'world peace' problem, there could be other situation elements like 'children', 'overcrowding' and 'profit' because they each have some role to play when it comes to the causes and outcomes of war. If so, 'children' and 'overcrowding' might be nominated as similar because they are both associated with economic underdevelopment, whereas 'profit'

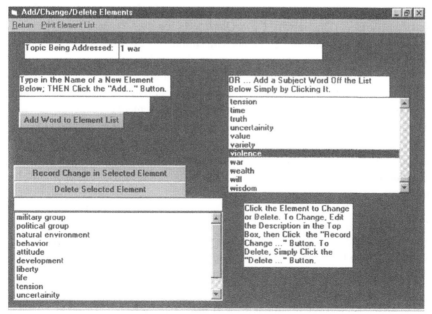

Figure 5.2. *CyberQuest* entering situation elements.

is different to both of them because it tends to be associated with developed nations.

This means that *CyberQuest* has now elicited a 'problem dimension' from the user. In other words, a thread within the (war and peace) problem's situation elements has been uncovered which is related to different nations' different stages of development. Thus a possible key word for the problem being addressed might be 'development' and this, in theory, has a chance of leading to a location in *CyberQuest*'s databases where ideas are stored that might be useful for addressing the problem.

Such a detailed process demonstrates *CyberQuest*'s determination to 'get inside the head' of its users. It delves into what they really see as the problem and its associated, problematic elements. This method, whereby policymakers nominate contrasts between trios of problem elements, is sometimes referred to as the 'repertory grid' procedure (Shaw, 1980). Users can persist with this for as long as they think they need to. The eventual result will be an exhaustion of the *CyberQuest*'s ability to make the user think of new dimensions. That is, *CyberQuest* simply keeps presenting random trios of situation elements, to prompt the user eventually to generate another new dimension, for as long as the user thinks fit.

5.1.2. Clustering concepts

However, cluster analysis will ultimately be necessary. This is because there will usually be too many situation elements for policymakers to handle sensibly, and one way out of such information overload is to organize the situation elements into a smaller number of relatively similar clusters. Clusters of situation elements, rather than the situation elements themselves, can then be compared with clarity and confidence. This is why *CyberQuest* asks the user to score each situation element on each dimension – elements with similar scores on the same dimensions are probably so similar that they ought to be clustered together.

For our current example, the optimal number of clusters seems to be three or four, and they might be termed something like 'bullying', 'vulnerability' and 'competition'. The point to note is that such a three-element typology of the 'war and peace' problem is certainly a more succinct description than that provided by the original situation elements. Based on these clusters of situation elements, users can now click 'Key Words' with greater confidence that they have carefully thought about their problem. Hence their nomination of key words should be more apt.

5.1.3. Nominating key words

Having deduced what the problem is, *CyberQuest*'s next step is to ask the user to volunteer some key words in order to encapsulate the problem in a succinct way. This is shown in figure 5.3. *CyberQuest* needs to do this if it is to have any chance of suggesting good ideas for the current user's problem. No software can have a list of all possible problems that it is likely to encounter, let alone a list of suitable, bright ideas to match. But it can have a list of probable key words, as shown.

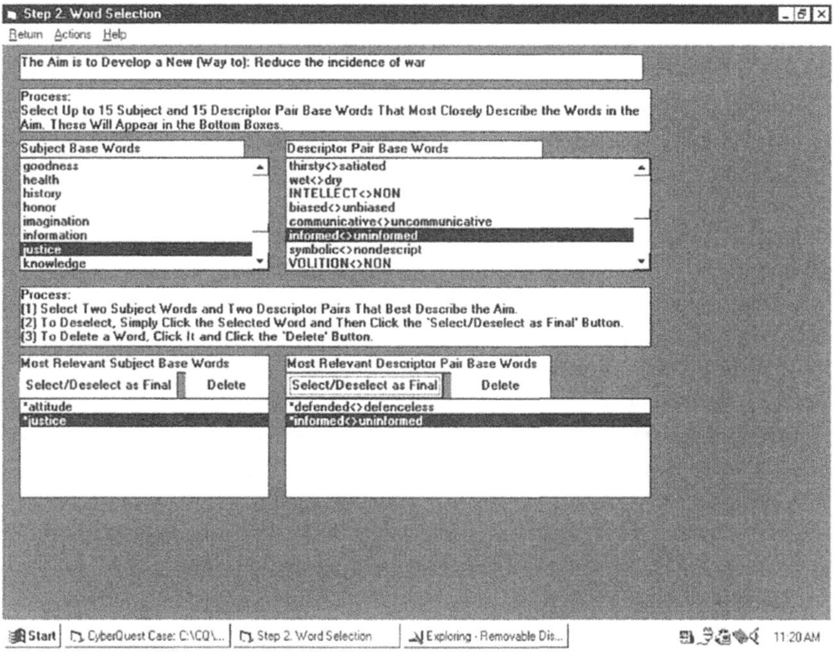

Figure 5.3. *CyberQuest* choosing key words.

Lesson 32: Analyse thoughtfully

Good policymaking practice will always use as much information as it can find and then clarify it. The *CyberQuest* package illustrates this when it uses cluster analysis to try to zero in on a situation's essence.

However, cluster analysis is arbitrary in the sense that it does not incorporate a hard and fast rule for determining what the optimal number of clusters is. It depends on the structure of the data set.

Hence simply throwing cluster analysis at policymaking is simply not good enough. One needs to think very carefully about its results. One can then settle on that number of clusters which succinctly sums up the situation but which does not lose too much information doing so.

Specifically, note that in the top half of the screen *CyberQuest* is suggesting many key words and many 'descriptor pairs' which the user could find helpful for summing up the 'war and peace' problem. Eventually four terms were chosen with the key words being:

'justice'
'attitude'

and the descriptor pairs being:

'defended <> defenceless'
'informed <>uninformed'.

Lesson 33: Activate your intuition

Without a focus on key words, it is difficult for policymakers to access their experience of similar problems that they have previously encountered, along with the various solutions that they tried, and the eventual wisdom of trying them. Such memories, or data banks of concepts, are what enable policymakers to make suggestions in new circumstances.

Yet it is no good having such suggestions inside one's head if one does not have a viable method for accessing them. Always use computer assistance to fully activate your intuition.

This finally brings some sort of succinctness to the process. Until now, *CyberQuest*'s style of smothering the user in lots of situation elements, dimensions, scores and clusters, in an attempt to get them to describe their problem in detail, was probably quite confusing to the user. But eventually, the package has managed to encapsulate the essentials of the problem into two key words and two descriptor pairs.

Again, remember the package's ever present, underlying assumption – greater quantity of thoughts eventually leads to greater quality of ideas. Such a philosophy means that it encourages a richly detailed policymaking process. One might quibble about the assumption, but few would dispute its plausibility. Again, the alternative is probably worse – a small quantity of thoughts along with a possibly forlorn hope of generating high-quality ideas.

5.2. Generating Ideas

The user can now progress to the crux of *CyberQuest* – matching key words with terms describing concepts within its databases. If matches can be found, then *CyberQuest* will suggest that the user should think more about these concepts, and such a process can sometimes cause the user to come up with a policy suggestion never previously thought of.

5.2.1. Matching key words with words in databases

The process is begun by clicking on 'Generation/Idea Generation/Internal' in the main menu. The term 'Internal' contrasts to an alternative item called 'Own Experience', and it leads users to *CyberQuest*'s internally stored lists of:

general concepts
definitional concepts
relational concepts
proverbs, and
aromas.

Users search through such databases using their key words (remember that in our example they are 'justice', 'attitude', 'defended<>defenceless' and 'informed<>uninformed').

Hence when the 'relational concepts' database was searched using our key words, *CyberQuest* found one match – 'Run a contest'. Such a match was derived from the 'informed<>uninformed' descriptor pair. That is, it was generated because *CyberQuest* had, stored within its 'relational concepts', the notion that one way to separate 'informed' people from 'uninformed' people is to run a contest. On the face of it, running a contest hardly seems sufficient to solve the vexing problem of 'world peace', and so it might seem wise to reject this idea.

Yet on the other hand it may not be so irrelevant after all. Remember that some historians have argued war itself is a contest – a necessary contest for the continued evolution of human kind. This is because the intense effort to win wars leads to all manner of technological and organizational breakthroughs. Indeed, we have already noted that computer software itself was first written during World War 2. It follows that if some way could be devised to ensure that competition takes place between nations, without leading to the horrors of war but which constitutes genuine competition none the less, such competition might take us a long way towards the attainment of world peace. The contest would, to some extent, be a substitute for war. Hence we have been prompted to come up with the idea of staging say, a 'technology Olympics'.

5.2.2. Thinking laterally

Such an idea is certainly a lateral one and it is possibly useful and worthwhile. After all, previous ideas that have been suggested by international strategists have not had much impact on the world peace problem. That is, international policymaking is in dire need of laterally thinking and innovative ideas. The thought-association methods employed by *CyberQuest* are an effective way of generating such ideas.

Note that for some years brainstorming facilitators have realized that thought-association can trigger originality, provided of course that the facilitator does not let thought-association mechanisms become so eccentric that they lose touch with the original problem. But the personal computer version of *CyberQuest* does not come with an accompanying, human facilitator. There is, therefore, no compulsion for *CyberQuest* users to check themselves in order to examine whether their thought processes are becoming too 'wild' and 'off the wall'.

Yet in practice it is reasonable to assume that people themselves are their own best managers. This is because it is difficult to imagine users persisting to the point of wasting too much time when the ideas-generation process stops bearing fruit in the form of potentially useful, policymaking ideas. Such inappropriate persistence would only occur if users became addicted to the ideas-generation mechanisms within policymaking. No case of this amongst practitioners, to the author's knowledge, has ever been reported.

Some people might point out that many academics are habitual idea generators – thinkers rather than doers as described in figure 1.1 above, but it was probably not the *CyberQuest* package which caused such a situation! In the hands of practical policymakers, *CyberQuest* is more likely to do good than harm, and even for the said academics, the package just might improve the quality of the ideas they are so fond of generating.

Now, getting back to our example problem, in terms of the 'technology Olympics' idea, some might argue that the free market already constitutes such a contest. But real-world collusion, shady practice and politics invariably corrupts market mechanisms. By contrast, the ancient Greek Olympic games were conceived of as being above politics (and wars and commerce), and so the idea of a 'pure', non-commercial and non-political, technological Olympics might be well worth pursuing. The point to remember is that people who were working without *CyberQuest* would probably not have generated such an idea – it took *CyberQuest*'s idea-generation procedures to stimulate the idea within an ordinary human's mind.

A key word search was also run on *CyberQuest*'s other databases listed above. Some interesting ideas were so generated. For example, figure 5.4 shows that a match was found, both with 'attitude' and 'informed<>uninformed', for the 'Transducer' concept. *CyberQuest* is telling the user that this concept means 'representation of a quantity by another quantity'. Such an explanation then triggered the idea of having simulated warfare. That is, real war could be represented by simulated war, fought either in virtual reality or by robots. Computerized war games could be a harmless surrogate for the real thing.

Such an idea was then added to other, fairly conventional ideas for reducing warfare, like a United Nations peace-keeping force, a corps of volunteers to spread the message of pacifism throughout the war-torn areas of the globe, disarmament policies and a world court of justice. But all these latter ideas have been tried with only limited success, so the need for some new, fresh and innovative suggestions remains.

It is therefore pleasing to note that *CyberQuest* found a match between the 'defended<>defenceless' descriptor pair and the concept of 'immunity'. This concept of immunity is used all the time within democracies – the majority rules but minority safeguards are always incorporated whenever it is likely that the wishes of the majority will cause minorities to suffer. Minorities are made immune from persecution. Why not do this among nations?

That is, it might be a good idea to have some sort of military version of the world heritage list. The weak and vulnerable parts of the world could be listed, so long as their uniqueness is agreed to by the wider community of nations, as especially worth preserving. They would be then granted immunity and protection from war. Morally, the UN should, right now, be granting such protection to all people in all places, but it has sometimes proved inadequate to the task. A cultural world heritage listing might therefore grant at least some layer of protection to some countries that are currently getting none.

For example, such a mechanism might have at least preserved Dubrovnik during the war in Bosnia throughout the early 1990s, and it may have protected many other 'priceless' places and cultures as well. Protection of cultural and religious treasures already happens to some extent in wartime through a mechanism whereby combatants aim only at military targets rather than at civilian or cultural targets. They presumably do this partly because of their fear of incurring the wrath of world opinion. Formalization and international acceptance of a cultural world heritage list might reinforce this.

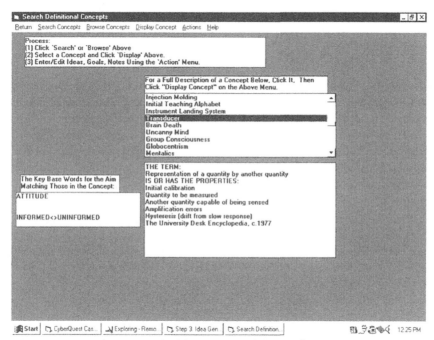

Figure 5.4. *CyberQuest* in idea generating mode.

5.2.3. A richness of ideas

Before proceeding with our review of *CyberQuest*, it is worth reviewing the other ideas thrown up by this particular session with the software. Some are shown in figure 5.5 below. They include satellite surveillance information being made freely available to anyone. This would ensure that aggressive build ups of troops and weapons are no longer secret but simply there for all to see. This would surely reduce world tension through the resulting, political lobbying aimed at dampening the threat of actual warfare.

Also, the idea of requiring people to participate in international volunteer services to fight against desertification by planting trees, or to fight against poverty and injustice through local community service is worth considering, as is the idea of 'nation adopting'. The latter would involve each strong nation being required to take a vulnerable nation 'under its wing' by having free movement, trade and development cooperation between them. The stronger nation would act just like a parent protecting and nurturing its child against a hostile outside world. Hence in theory, there would be less international bullying. For example, the US could adopt and protect Mexico, Australia could adopt and protect Papua New Guinea and Canada might adopt and protect Greenland. Naturally, controls would be necessary to prevent such mentoring from degenerating into colonization of the old and discredited sort, but nation adopting/mentoring might still be useful.

Moreover, it might be sensible to work on some of the underlying causes of war, such as borders. If there were no international borders, and people were allowed to move freely around the globe, there would presumably be no wars. It would probably mean that the more desirable parts of the world would become very crowded. But it might be possible to make such crowding work to the advantage of all parties living within the locality. That is, if strong local controls and proper management of squatter settlements was achieved, immigrants would be close to where they want to be and the local economy would prosper.

In a way, such a strategy would be substituting international war for local 'wars' in the sense that this option would require a strong local police force and land use controls. Moreover, juxtaposing the very rich with the very poor in one place, as happens to some extent already in cities like Los Angeles and Caracas, might increase rather than decrease the chances of (class-based) warfare. Nevertheless, the idea of a borderless world might be worth considering and, in any event, such a situation is already evolving to some extent.

Another cause of war is cultural and religious differences. Hence it may be desirable if a world monoculture could somehow be superimposed over the top of the various separate cultures, maybe using resources such as the Internet and the 'universal' education that such a facility can increasingly deliver. Monoculturalism could preach tolerance for all people and customs so long as everyone adheres to certain rules, and so a major source of world conflict would be removed.

Finally, another idea might be to repair the damage which war-like actions have already caused and will continue to cause. For instance, if the Internet could be used to publicize war crimes, thereby short circuiting the repression that results from non-free presses within the nations of the perpetrators, then the outrage produced, even amongst people within the aggressor nations, would surely have a huge dampening effect on further damage.

In the same vein, an international war insurance fund might be an idea worth investigating. That is, lots of suffering could be removed if all the countries of the world agreed to pay premiums in order to insure themselves against the ravages of war. Countries that were invaded could then claim compensation from the world war insurance fund; aggressor countries would be deemed liable for the damage and so lose their 'no claim' bonus and incur a much heftier premium the next year, and so the incidence of war might decrease. Having a common world currency could perhaps raise the necessary capital for such a venture. It would siphon off those huge amounts of money which, every day, go into the hands of international speculators. It would presumably be put to a better use – world peace.

But alas, readers hardly need to be reminded that many of these ideas are hopelessly idealistic. Indeed, it is unrealistic to expect any software to make progress of any kind against such a daunting problem – a problem that has remained unsolved, by the best of human minds, since the beginning of time. Yet our purpose here has been to demonstrate the fertility of suggestions which *CyberQuest* can come up with, some of which may have potential for at least making some inroads into the problem.

5.3. Packaging Ideas

Perceptive readers will have noticed the irony that drips from the previous section. Here we had an example problem, war, which is the ultimate example of a vicious problem. Yet we have been suggesting single, insight suggestions to help solve the problem, despite having advised against doing this in Chapter 1 above. But singular ideas can act as seeds for more comprehensive, multi-faceted ideas which, fortunately, *CyberQuest* can help us develop.

That is, although *CyberQuest*'s great strength is its innovative way of generating new and fresh ideas, it is also very proficient at assembling such ideas into more 'marketable' packages of ideas, or policies. This packaging process is twofold. Each idea is first 'screened' in order to evaluate its intrinsic merit, and then it is actually 'packaged' with other ideas into some maximally palatable policy.

5.3.1. Rating ideas

Whenever 'Idea Screening' is clicked, a screen like that shown in figure 5.5 appears. Here *CyberQuest* is asking the user to assign a 'predominant status' to each idea. This is an important part of idea screening; it is useful to know whether each idea has been tried, whether it has been successful or unsuccessful, whether it is actually a goal, whether it is an ill-defined 'muse' and so on. Also required from the user are ratings, for both the idea's 'importance' and 'effort that will be required for its implementation'.

Clearly, the author of *CyberQuest* regards such considerations, 'importance' and 'effort', as the most crucial things that a policymaker needs to know about each policy. This now suggests that *CyberQuest* is veering towards the 'thinking' end of the 'thinking versus feeling' dimension – it is telling users what evaluation criteria to use rather than asking them to nominate their own.

In any event, once the user has input his or her ratings, between zero and ten, for importance and required effort, *CyberQuest* calculates an overall assessment of that idea using the following formula:

Overall Rating = 5 * (Importance Score - Effort Needed + 10)   (5.1)

Hence the 'universally available satellite imagery' idea shown in figure 5.5, whose score for importance is 6 and whose score for effort needed is 3, comes out as scoring 65 overall, as shown on the bottom right.

Lesson 34: Cultivate originality

Haefele (1962, p. 166) once listed many of the questions that older, more conservative policymakers ask whenever they hear their less experienced and more enthusiastic colleagues put forward new ideas. Their questions are usually designed to stifle such upstart enthusiasm.

That is, conservative guardians of the comfortable *status quo* are fond of asking young Turks questions like 'How much will it cost?', and 'Is it practical?'. Moreover, not only does Haefele list the comment 'We tried that, unsuccessfully, some time back' as typical, but he also states that it is the response which discourages people twice as much as do all of the other comments combined.

Consequently, it may be wise to desist, on the grounds of blunting the potentially brilliant contributions from young idealists, from asking whether or not a suggested idea has been tried before. It can cause conservatism and a failure to exploit important opportunities.

Such a sentiment is at the back of Arthur C. Clarke's 'first law' (quoted in Hampden-Turner, 1970). This states that when an elderly and distinguished scientist claims that something is impossible, the chances are that he or she is almost certainly wrong. The reason is that 'experts' are always skilled at seeing why something cannot be done; they are less skilled at seeing how things can be done, and so the brilliant breakthrough perceptions of how to see around problems are often made by 'ignorant amateurs'.

Therefore, policymaking ought to tread carefully whenever it evaluates bright people's new ideas. Originality ought to be cultivated by policymakers, not suppressed.

But why only 65? Why not more? Or less? That is, readers hardly need to be told how arbitrary this is. If one really wants an accurate indication of an idea's overall worth, why not score it as the score for 'importance' minus half the score for 'required effort'? Or perhaps the formula could be 'importance' minus ten times 'required effort'; or the square root of 'importance' minus the cube root of 'required effort' or whatever.

An ideal formula has long been the Holy Grail of evaluation researchers (Wyatt, 1989, chapter 6) but it remains undiscovered. Hence it has to be said that *CyberQuest*'s attempt to calculate numerical scores smacks of spurious accuracy. Why then, have the package's many users tolerated it?

The answer surely has something to do with policymakers' desire for numbers – any numbers. Numbers have a remarkable ability for seeming to clarify over-complicated, policymaking situations that humans find difficult to handle intuitively.

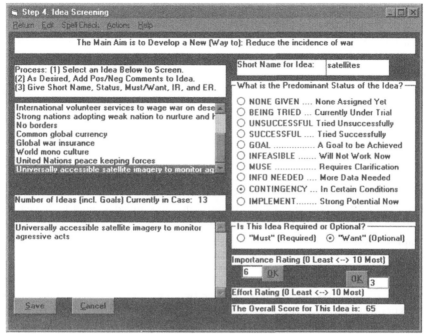

Figure 5.5. *CyberQuest* in idea screening mode.

Indeed, over 40 years ago Miller (1956) argued that assessing more than seven alternatives in one's head simultaneously is impossible for most people. The only way out therefore, if there are eight or more alternatives, is numbers.

If numerical scores can be assigned to each alternative, their relative desirability levels instantly become obvious. It is this prospect of bringing order out of chaos that has caused policymakers to be less critical than they should be about methods that involve numbers. Hence programs like *CyberQuest* continue to get away with arbitrarily assigning numerical scores to ideas.

Lesson 35: Be wary of software

We may have implied above that policymaking software, since it has been fired in the crucible of hyper-critical evaluation by its users, will perform satisfactorily at all times. If so, this was obviously an overstatement.

Users might well hone the software that they criticize to a high level of excellence according to them, but if they themselves have weaknesses, the software that reflects their demands will be similarly flawed. An instance of such a flaw is people's desire for numbers no matter what.

Therefore, policymakers should be ever mindful that software's recommendations can sometimes fall seriously short of validity. Policymakers should treat packages, which are only human artefacts after all, with due disrespect.

Note however that when it comes to scoring suggestions numerically, some software does better than *CyberQuest*. It forces users to make several, mutually consistent, paired comparisons of the alternatives, and it then calculates valid numerical scores from the totality of such comparisons. This method will be described in subsequent packages, but in the meantime simply note that packages like *CyberQuest* frequently get away with over-hasty numeration.

The *CyberQuest* package therefore seems to have slipped up in both ways. On the one hand it can be accused of being too 'feeling', in the sense that it likes to interact with users by smothering them with concepts and encourage detailed explorations of their thoughts. This has the danger that users can become drowned in so many concepts to the point where they become indecisive. Yet when *CyberQuest* gets to the ideas-scoring phase it seems to be too 'thinking'. It is extremely willing to use numbers arbitrarily in a misguided attempt to decrease the users' discomfort that always accompanies their responsibility of making complex evaluations.

Lesson 36: Be disciplined

In much policymaking software, flipping between pedantry and simplicity occurs frequently. It is also endemic throughout policymaking practice. That is, in their zeal to achieve the best possible policymaking, practitioners tend to vacillate between over-complicating things and over-simplification.

Policymakers therefore need to be acutely aware of when detailed analysis is required and when glib summarisation is called for. This requires disciplined recording of what stage one's policymaking exercise is currently at.

5.3.2. Reviewing ideas

Note that a *CyberQuest* user can also click on 'Make Report/Ideas Screening' to generate, either on the computer screen or in hard copy, information like that shown in figure 5.6. The primary purpose of such output is to give some sort of feel for what might be the more productive ideas to pursue, the arbitrariness of the numerical scores notwithstanding. Also, it is possible to print out a report showing each idea along with the concept that triggered it. As such, *CyberQuest* preserves a partial record of the user's thought processes. Therefore, on inspecting such a report at a later date, the user can speculate down other idea-exploration paths that he or she' lacked the time to go down on the first occasion.

In fact, this is standard practice in non-computerized, brainstorming workshops. At the latter, every suggestion is written onto a paper flip chart, and at the end of the session the problem's 'owner' is able to roll up the flip chart and take its ideas away for further exploration at his or her leisure. This is particularly useful for revisiting those ideas that seemed promising but were not explored fully by the brainstorming group when it went down some other path of idea development instead.

Now, in figure 5.6 it is suggested that for the world peace problem some of the higher scoring ideas are the cultural world heritage list, universally available satellite images, a peace corps and the United Nations. Note that 'United Nations' is hardly an innovative idea and so it was not discussed above. However, it was added to our list, along with some other traditional ones, for completeness. Hence of the four ideas, only this last one has actually been tried; the other three are, of course, plagued with implementation difficulties related to world politics and world trade. Therefore, although it would probably do no harm to try to make some progress towards the first three ideas, perhaps the world peace problem will remain unsolvable until politics and trade have become non issues at the global scale. We will, of course, have to wait a long time for this.

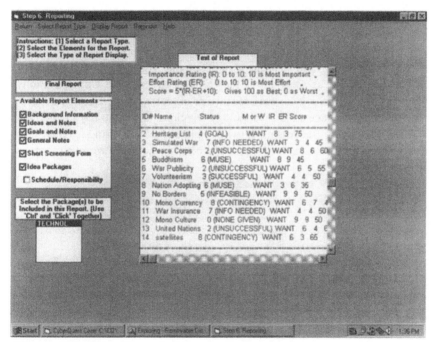

Figure 5.6. *CyberQuest* in idea reporting mode.

But before we give up in despair, *CyberQuest* has one more lesson for us. It goes to considerable pains to ensure that its top-scoring ideas are not simply wasted. It tries to prevent users simply rushing off to management with 'half baked', impractical versions of them. Instead, the user is encouraged to think very carefully about how such ideas might be 'sold'. This is *CyberQuest*'s final stage, it is called 'Idea Packaging' (figure 5.7), and it encourages the user to amalgamate some or all of their ideas into various 'packages' of related ideas. Such amalgamations can then, perhaps, be sold by taking advantage of the fact that a suite of interconnected ideas can be more persuasive than single ideas presented individually.

Lesson 37: Selling policy

Obviously, if the 'marketability' of innovative ideas is boosted, policymaking practice will improve. Alternatively, if one cannot convince the power brokers of the wisdom of one's recommendations, even though the policymaking is of high quality, then the policy is of little use.

Therefore, it is well worth noting the methods that *CyberQuest* uses to 'package' its best thoughts into saleable amalgamations of related ideas.

Four amalgamations for addressing the world peace problem have been assembled – 'Non-government Organizations (NGOs)', 'Technology', 'Actions' and 'Radical Ideas', and figure 5.7 is addressing the second of these. That is, the package is asking for an assignment of some of the ideas to the Technology package. Now, since both universally distributed satellite imagery and simulated warfare using computers or robots are contingent upon a certain amount of technological progress being made, both ideas are assigned to the 'Technology' package.

Likewise, the ideas assigned to the 'NGOs' package are United Nations, volunteers to wage ecological warfare and a peace corps. Also, the ideas assigned to the 'Actions' package are the technology Olympics, the cultural world heritage list, nation adoption, Bhuddism, and wide publicity of war crimes. Finally, the ideas assigned to the 'Radical' package are no borders, monoculture, mono currency and war insurance.

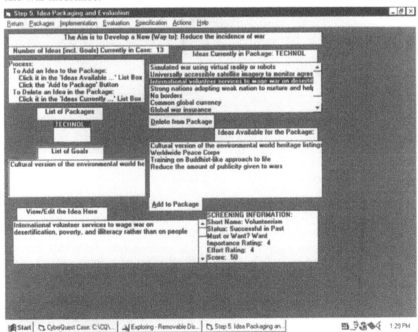

Figure 5.7. *CyberQuest* in idea packaging mode.

Once these packages have been identified, users' thoughts will then turn to their advantages, disadvantages and ways of convincing others that they are worthwhile. Such speculations may then trigger yet more ideas about what to do, which is why *CyberQuest*'s 'idea packaging' routines encourage users to make such speculations for as long as they can keep thinking of new ideas.

More specifically, users' imaginations are stimulated by all the different sorts of ways that idea packages can be assessed. These include:

➤ *Design* (e.g. usefulness, trade off with alternatives and degree of improvement over current packages)
➤ *Organizational Environment* (e.g. who will evaluate it?, who will support it?)
➤ *Alternatives*
➤ *Goals and Constraints*
➤ *Fit to On-going Activities*
➤ *Timing, and*
➤ *Uncertainty*.

The important thing to remember is that as a by-product of such evaluations *CyberQuest* keeps users actively thinking about possible new ideas. Indeed, the software generates a virtual plethora of criteria that might usefully be taken into account during policymaking. There are so many criteria that they have to be stored under headings:

➤ *Technical* (e.g. complimentary technologies, availability of trained people)
➤ *Economic* (e.g. general market conditions, financing arrangements)
➤ *Managerial*
➤ *Political*
➤ *Social*
➤ *Cultural*
➤ *Intellectual*
➤ *Religious/Ethical*
➤ *Ecological*
➤ *Health*
➤ *Sensual*, and
➤ *Legal*.

Perhaps the criteria are too comprehensive. Dealing with so many is likely to divert the user from constantly thinking about how the idea under consideration affects the overall goal. What does it really matter if the current idea has bad 'health' or 'sensual' connotations – to choose two at random? What really matters is how useful the idea is, in terms of helping one to attain the overall goal – world peace. If it has associated difficulties, then these can be addressed at another policymaking session.

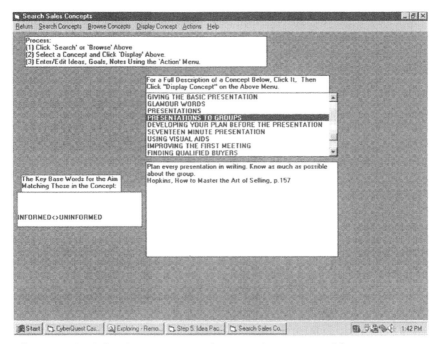

Figure 5.8. *CyberQuest* attempting to trigger more ideas

In short, *CyberQuest* seems to have strayed away from being a policymaking package to one which wants to solve all the world's problems at once. This is impossible. But in its attempt to examine the saleability of each worthwhile idea, *CyberQuest* has been led down a quixotic path. There is, of course, great value in going to so much trouble to make sure good ideas can be successfully sold, but such gymnastics are of less relevance to the subject of this book – policymaking.

On a more positive note, remember that *CyberQuest* will (again) search its databases for matches between concepts therein and the original key words, along with the various amalgamations of ideas that have subsequently been developed. An example of how this might stimulate the user to come up with still more, useful ideas is shown in figure 5.8. In this, any number of possible databases could have been selected:

➤ *Program Linkages*

➤ *General Law*

➤ *Banking and Finance*

➤ *Organization*

➤ *Personnel and Labour Relations*

➤ *Contracting*

➤ *Cost Reduction*

➤ *Sales Concepts*

➤ *Marketing,* and

➤ *Training*

and the one chosen was 'Sales Concepts'. Moreover, a match has been found between our original 'informed<>uninformed' descriptor pair and 'presentations to groups'. Such a concept is basically about being more convincing if one knows, intimately, the characteristics of the group that one wishes to engage with.

Such a concept could generate yet another idea in the user's mind. For instance, in our example problem we need to sell the 'Actions' package of ideas. It contains new suggestions that, for proper adoption, would require people partially to change their current ways of thinking. Moreover, we need to sell such a package to the world's different countries and cultural groups. It would therefore be in our interest to know as much as we can about the world's different cultures. Hence it seems like a good idea to set up say, a 'Peace Studies Institute' in order to learn as much as we can about different cultures, and their attitudes to war, and how the latter's incidence might, accordingly, be reduced.

Such is the tenacity of *CyberQuest* in its mission to stimulate new and innovative ideas. It appears to leave no stone unturned in its search for idea stimuli and continues this right up until the very end of its processes. Such a quest for novel suggestions is extremely important in policymaking practice

5.4 Summary

It is difficult to imagine policymaking software that is more exploratory. As such, *CyberQuest* is extremely general and applicable to the full gamut of policymaking problems. But such generic versatility comes at a price. *CyberQuest* is only able to achieve its broad applicability by addressing just the broad, initial, idea-generation phase of the policymaking process. Although it utilizes a very rich set of considerations in the later stages when it is ruminating on the consequences, strengths and weaknesses of ideas generated earlier, such considerations serve mainly as discussion points rather than as elements to be evaluated rigorously. Indeed, right until the very end, emphasis is on the generation of still more ideas, and this is surely *CyberQuest*'s trademark. In short, the package opts for a comprehensive approach, but it only concentrates on the generation of ideas.

However, it succeeds in its mission, and so it enjoys considerable status as an inspirational system that is versatile enough to be able to straddle a plethora of application fields. But if it moved on to the 'choose' stage of policymaking by insisting on rigorous, computer-based analysis of all the ideas that it prompts human users to think of, it would become enormously unwieldy. *CyberQuest*, therefore, stops short of over-ambition and so it avoids the common trap, succumbed to by many software packages, of trying too hard to replicate the reality of the full policymaking process.

Chapter 6

Frontier Software Case II: *STRAD*

A package that pushes closer to the 'choose' part of the policymaking process, is *STRAD*. Its special status in the world of policymaking stems directly from its being based, over 30 years ago, on long-term observation of a major, real-world, policymaking exercise. Specifically, in the 1960s John Friend and William Jessop closely observed and monitored the various committees at Coventry City Council, UK, and they eventually wrote up their findings in their ground-breaking book of 1969, *Local Government and Strategic Choice*. In it they floated the so called 'Strategic Choice' approach which inspires today's *STRAD* package (Friend, 1989, 1992).

This approach involves assembling a group of people for workshop-based discussions about the policymaking problem. The group is led by a facilitator and it uses many felt pens, overhead slides, flip charts and cups of coffee. In 1987 a manual for running such workshops was produced, in book form, by Friend and Hickling – *Planning under Pressure*. This book has since gone to a second edition (1997), and it has been translated into several languages.

STRAD actually stands for 'strategic adviser'. Its emphasis is on the alerting of users to the probable consequences of implementing various policies or 'schemes' and examination of the nature, extent and possible counters to the various kinds of uncertainty that surround the problem. In other words, *STRAD* records how important and how urgent each policymaking issue is and then evaluates large numbers of possible, sequential chains of actions. It investigates the detailed aspects of how various policies, for addressing different problem 'issues', will impact on other policies. Therefore, as well as generating a recommended policy, a valuable part of *STRAD*'s output is the increased state of awareness that it generates amongst the people using it. Its attention to detail is quite remarkable.

This is why it too has been applied to many problems, a selection of which is supplied along with the software, as listed in table 6.1. Note that *STRAD* is probably one of the most 'feeling' of all the packages described in this book. It is entirely dependent upon reflecting all of the problem details and implications of possible actions, as provided by its users. It reorganizes such input in a neat way, but its main contribution is to record as much data as possible and search, most exhaustively, through all the various combinations of possible actions.

Table 6.1. Some problems that have been addressed by *STRAD*.

Protecting an urban environment: a depressed, urban district houses about 10,000 people who are heavily dependent on the local steel mill which will probably close soon. It is proposed to resume houses for a new industrial highway to be built through the area, as well as a new, more concentrated shopping centre. Residents want the local council to defend their neighbourhood.	**Closing a district mental hospital**: there is a need to investigate the best ways to look after discharged patients and their carers within the community after closure. The closure is in fact very problematic and influenced by the capacities of local groups, general practitioners and alternative institutions.
Managing a consulting contract: a contract has been won to analyse a public authority which is two hours drive away from the consultant's office. A delay in awarding the contract has resulted in many of the staff of 12 becoming committed to other jobs in the meantime. Decisions are therefore required about whether to set up some kind of project team, its leadership, a project office and ways of providing administrative support. All of these decisions might affect the long term policies and success chances of the total firm.	**Managing a printing business:** because of slow turnarounds some directors want to scale down or even eliminate this part of the company. Other directors favour investment in new colour printers and a larger advertising budget.
Managing a marine technology firm: two factories are presently operated, one making marine instruments and the other making polystyrene packaging, and local environmental regulations, along with traffic congestion, are forcing decisions on whether to relocate one or both factories. Such decisions are complicated by more immediate concerns about whether or not to invest in some new polystyrene packaging machinery this year and whether or not to seize an opportunity to purchase a bankrupt transport company at a bargain price.	**Managing an internal consultancy**: a special projects group, which used to act as a problem-solving consultancy for other sections of this privatized, public corporation, could be incorporated into a large information services department. Alternatively, the group, along with its in-house, policymaking software, could be commercialized as a separate company, perhaps with a joint partner, even though some people feel this would leak valuable company expertise to rival firms.
Policymaking a holiday: decisions need to be made about destination, timing, mode of travel, accommodation, duration and the sort of companion to take along.	

6.1. Recording the Issues

STRAD begins by having the user(s) record a description of their situation. To illustrate, a demonstration problem that comes with *STRAD*, but which we have not shown in table 6.1, concerns a village within a developing country. This village's population has recently been enlarged by an influx of refugees, and in order to boost the village economy, a cooperative of farmers and villagers has been formed to produce white lime fertilizer. Policies therefore need to be made about the fuel that the limestone kiln should use, about arrangements for transporting the product, about management of the business and about marketing.

STRAD therefore begins by asking the user to nominate 'issues' and to say which issues are 'Decision Areas'. The latter are designated thereafter on the computer screen with a shorthand label and a question mark. In this example the full set of Decision Areas, along with each one's 'options', or alternative goals, is:

> ➤ TRANSPORT? – hire a truck OR buy a truck?
> ➤ PRODPROCES? – improve the existing kiln OR buy a new mill?
> ➤ FUELSOURCE? – get fuel from reservation OR get fuel from farms OR use an alternative type of fuel?
> ➤ MKTEXPND? – keep selling fertilizer only to citrus growers OR sell to banana farmers as well?
> ➤ COORDINATN? – have a management committee OR have a manager OR have a rotating manager OR have an independent cooperative OR have a cooperative of members OR should it not?
> ➤ AGRIC COOP? – should the cooperative's farm be cleared as a fuel source for the mill?
> ➤ TRAINING? – have a training scheme OR do not have a training scheme?

Note that users enter such Decision Areas by activating an 'Issues' window. The latter allows one to type in any new issue one can think of, and it is stored even if the user is not yet sure whether it is a Decision Area.

When any issue is so stored, a retrievable window appears. One can then click on this window at any subsequent time to check all the information that is connected with this issue. Such connected information includes its 'importance', its 'urgency' and which organizational unit has the most responsibility for it. Also stored is its headlined caption, its more detailed description, and the different alternative options along with their descriptions and their associated notes. Moreover, if *STRAD* has already been worked through sufficiently, one is able to store proposed 'actions' that are related to this issue. The latter consist of recommendations about what option(s) should be implemented, by whom, when, and using what resources or authority. The package certainly tries hard to get a comprehensive 'feel' for the problem situation.

6.1.1. Neutralizing conflict

Moreover, *STRAD* is particularly keen to record Decision Areas in which there are likely to be different views about which option to take – conflict. If such areas of possible differences are recorded early, users can begin thinking about them early and, consequently, not be taken aback when someone else mentions, and argues strongly in favour of some option later on. That is, the chances of surprise will have been minimized.

Lesson 38: Heed hidden agendas

'Open' policymaking is often implemented to stop participants harbouring 'hidden agendas'. These are secret desires, and they have often proved to be a deadening hand. They cause participants to refrain from telling others what their real motives are. Consequently, it is difficult for the group to understand why such people are arguing certain points in a certain way.

Thus there is little chance of the group being able to come up with policy that allays everybody's hidden concerns. Hence all good policymaking must strive to incorporate some effective mechanism for revealing all participants' hidden agendas.

Also, *STRAD*'s approach is eminently suitable for revealing hidden values. This is because in a typical *STRAD*-based session the facilitator would get users to nominate Decision Areas, plus each Decision Area's alternative goals, in a strictly neutral manner. In other words, recording would precede in a non-threatening, non-judgemental way that is predicated on the facilitator's stated need to document *everything*, simply for 'completeness'. Indeed participants, once reassured that they are in no way being judged in terms of what they contribute, could become quite enthusiastic contributors and really get carried along by the group energy of the workshop. Yet the process of recording all details about the various possible goals, like their importance, urgency and resources to be used, actually reveals to the facilitator considerable information about what participants really favour.

Note that all issues are recorded, for later retrieval by the software. Such retrieval, after participants may have forgotten details about what had previously been agreed to as a way of describing some part of the policymaking situation, is essential in all good policymaking. But *STRAD* goes even further. Sometimes the issue being discussed might not actually be a Decision Area but a 'Comparison Area'. This is a little like a criterion for assessing the desirability levels of policies, and it can reveal much about participants' hidden agendas. Accordingly, all such Comparison Areas are stored, along with their associated information.

Alternatively, an issue might actually be an 'Uncertainty Area', which is a set of related considerations that throw doubt on the wisdom or otherwise of pursuing the various goals. Again, these reveal much about people's hopes and fears, and they are stored by the software along with their characteristics.

The latter include Uncertainty Areas' levels of 'prominence', levels of 'tractability' and appropriate organizational units ('sectors') of responsibility for reducing the uncertainty. Also noted are the actions that could be taken to reduce

the uncertainty (if known), general notes and what type of uncertainty it is anyway
– environmental (UE), values-based (UV) or uncertainty about related actions (UR).
The actions to be taken are called 'exploratory options'. They are listed in headlined
as well as in a more fully descriptive form; and so are estimates of their 'cost',
severity of consequences if pursuing such an action is delayed (= 'delay'), and
'gain' that will result if such an uncertainty-reducing action is implemented.

6.1.2. Grouping decision areas

It is therefore obvious that the approach of *STRAD* to policymaking is very much
one of 'lay it all out on the table'. By the time all of the Decision Areas, Comparison
Areas and Uncertainty Areas have been detailed and recorded, all participants should
have a very good grasp of the problem and its issues. Hence by immediately
recording, most comprehensively, all details in a neutral manner, *STRAD* avoids the
artificiality and over-simplification that characterizes much policymaking practice.

The latter, naturally, tends to make people less warm towards the policymaking
problem. They are therefore less likely to solve the problem and so, eventually
they will become more suspicious of the policymaking process in general. By
contrast, *STRAD* panders to the natural tendency of humans to want to discuss
straight away all the details and intricacies of the policymaking problem. This is the
interesting, 'juicy' part of policymaking with which people like to become involved.

To see this, note that the result of a user nominating all of a problem's issues
can be seen by activating *STRAD*'s 'Windows/Overview' menu item. For instance,
in the village example a screen will appear like that shown in figure 6.1. Decision
Areas are on the top left, Comparison Areas are along the bottom and Uncertainty
Areas are on the top right.

It should be remembered that any typical session with *STRAD* is actually awash
with a very large number of goals. This is because goals can actually exist not
only within the Decision Areas but also within Comparison Areas and Uncertainty
Areas as well. In other words, some Comparison Areas, despite constituting, in a
sense, a criterion on which to judge goals, are really implicit goals themselves.
For example, the so-called Comparison Areas 'sustainability' and 'employment',
shown in figure 6.1, can also be looked upon as goals to be pursued.

One might counter that we are being less than rigorous in our terminology and
that there are actually fewer goals because what we are referring to as goals are
really 'actions'. Hence the real difference between Decision Areas' options and
Comparison Areas is that the first are actions and the second is a criterion for
evaluating such actions. But this would be simply playing with words. Presumably,
if one re-phrases the word 'sustainability' to 'achieving sustainability', it has then
become an action – which we, of course, call a goal. Moreover, the same argument
can be used to suggest that possible actions for reducing the level of uncertainty
within Uncertainty Areas can also be thought of as goals.

Hence there really have been lots of goals identified in our example, and so a
problem is that such a plethora of goals can become unwieldy. Moreover, because

they have been fed into the software using free-ranging discussion that is designed to instil confidence and energy amongst participants, *STRAD* will always tend to be working with goals at different levels of abstraction – it will not organize goals hierarchically. Such is the price of having software that is 'feeling' in its style.

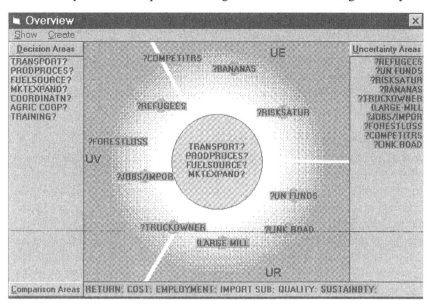

Figure 6.1. *STRAD*'s overview window.

But fear not. *STRAD* actually has a mechanism for unravelling its self-inflicted chaos. It becomes more 'focused' by actually having users activate a 'focus' window. This window encourages people to concentrate on just a few inter-related goals at a time. That is, the user is asked to indicate which Decision Areas are closely interconnected to which other Decision Areas. One decides this by asking whether considering them together is likely to lead to a different decision from considering them separately. If so, they must be interconnected

Users can specify such inter-connected (sets of) goals using a chart type mechanism that is reminiscent of the cognitive maps that were discussed above in Chapter 2. They specify whether or not a connection between two Decision Areas is 'strong', 'weak' or 'non-existent'. Moreover, those Decision Areas whose 'importance' has been designated as being above a 'critical level' are printed in red, and all Decision Areas whose 'urgency' has been designated as being above a critical level are framed within an ellipse. Such punctuation is presumably used to prompt the user to notice, and to think more about possible interconnections between goals that are important and urgent.

Eventually, *STRAD* records all links between all interconnected Decision Areas within a series of charts that show strong interconnections using strong blue lines and weak interconnections using weaker, red lines. The idea is that the user can now address different groups of strongly-related Decision Areas, in turn, as the temporary focus of the moment. Users can therefore derive policy for such areas, move on to the next focus, and proceed until the complete set of Decision Areas has been worked through.

Note that by clicking 'Focus/Selection Aid' it is possible to get assistance from the software to determine what the successive focus areas should be. A points-scoring mechanism appears for alternative singles, pairs or triads of Decision Areas that are shown in successive charts. This grouping of Decision Areas into singles, pairs or trios is based on the number of links they have between them, whether such links are via strong or via uncertain interconnections, and whether importance levels and urgency levels of the Decision Areas concerned are high.

6.1.3. Decomposing the problem

Hence *STRAD* records people's intricate concerns in a thorough and detailed manner so that the policymaking process is as wide-ranging as possible. However, it then tries to simplify things because the focus windows act, in some ways, like a goals hierarchy. To see this remember that whenever some Decision Areas are at a similar level of abstraction, that is, at the same hierarchical level, they will tend to have more interconnections between them. Hence these Decision Areas and their goals will probably be designated as part of the same focus area. Moreover, if Decision Areas are at the same abstraction level they are also likely to have similar urgency levels, making it even more probable that they will be part of the same focus. In other words, the sequential, focusing procedure of *STRAD* is likely, at least partly, to replicate the more conventional movement of one's focus down through a goals hierarchy.

An example might help. When policymaking in a large city one might decide that 'better public transport' is a worthwhile overall aim, and that to achieve such an aim one needs to achieve say, 'more buses', 'extra trains', and 'integrated timetabling'. Moreover, to attain say, 'integrated timetabling', one needs to achieve 'optimization models', 'more educated staff' and so forth. A typical goal hierarchy-based approach would therefore approach this problem piece by piece. It would first consider the problem of whether or not 'better public transport' is a good idea, then, if 'better public transport' is a good idea, the problem of whether to aim at 'more buses' or 'more trains' or 'integrated timetabling' would be addressed. Then, if 'integrated timetabling' was favoured, whether to opt for 'optimization models' or for 'educated staff' would be considered, and so on.

STRAD does not work like this; it simply feeds all options into its analysis regardless. But it later 'sorts out' the ensuing confusion by adopting various problem foci in turn. For example, 'better public transport' and its competing, city-level goals are likely to be designated as one focus because of the obvious interconnections between them and their similar levels of urgency. For similar reasons (the choice between) 'more buses', 'more trains' and 'integrated timetabling' are also likely to be designated as another focus. Likewise, 'optimization models' versus 'educated staff' will probably be another focus. Hence, although *STRAD* might look like it eschews the goals hierarchy concept, its problem-focusing mechanism appears to serve a similar purpose. The difference between *STRAD* and our other software packages is only that its simplification mechanism is implicit rather than explicit.

6.2. Comparing Goals

STRAD has other simplification mechanisms as well – it needs to because it is so incredibly 'complex' in other ways. For example, it incorporates 'option bars'. That is, for any set of Decision Areas which are currently the focus, whenever the user clicks on the 'Windows/Compatibility' menu item *STRAD* asks them which of the associated options are incompatible. Incompatible options should then be 'barred' from occurring together within the same scheme.

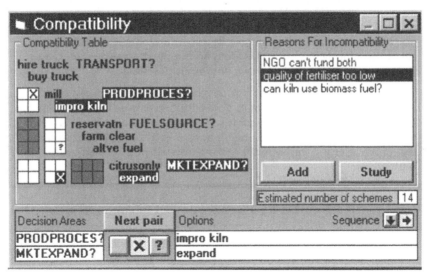

Figure 6.2. *STRAD* using option bars.

This is illustrated in figure 6.2, which shows the use of option bars when addressing the village problem. The 'X' near the top left is an option bar because one option, 'buy a truck', rules out the other goal of 'purchase a new mill' and vice versa. Buying a truck and purchasing a new, modern mill are incompatible because the UN will not fund both of these. Accordingly, the user inserts a cross in the grid cell at the intersection of the 'buy truck' row and the 'new mill' column.

Note that the villagers should also insert a cross at the intersection of the 'improve (existing) kiln' column and the 'expand markets' row. This is because using the existing kiln, no matter how much it is upgraded, means that marketable, higher-quality fertilizer will always be impossible to produce and sell. Moreover, users should probably insert a question mark, as distinct from a cross, to signify that the 'improve kiln' goal is possibly incompatible with the 'alternative fuel' goal, since it is unknown whether or not the existing mill could ever use bio-waste as a fuel.

Obviously, *STRAD* is here reducing the effects of the 'combinatorial explosion' that bedevils any package which, like *STRAD*, is complicated because it tries to examine all possible combinations of all possible goals. In large problems there are simply too many combinations to consider within a reasonable time, so *STRAD* reduces their number by ruling out all schemes that contain incompatible actions. In other words, option bars are an attempted simplifying mechanism for (partially) steering *STRAD* towards a shorter search for policies.

Lesson 39: Of babies and bath water

In practice, policies are frequently ruled out of consideration in a careless or even emotive way. This is because participants sometimes baulk at the hard work they will need to undertake in order to find out whether certain policies should, or should not be removed from consideration. So to make their lives easier, they simply rule out unfashionable ones on a whim. All of the slightly less attractive ideas are simply dismissed en bloc, even though some might, in fact, have enormous potential.

Therefore, in the interests of not passing up some great policymaking opportunity, practitioners would do well to never ever remove a policy from consideration until after some sort of option bar argument has been mounted against it. Never be over-eager to jettison an idea that could still prove useful. This would be like throwing out the baby with the bath water.

Note that it is conceivable the villagers could think of ways to get a truck AND a new mill. Indeed, simply by pointing out the incompatibility between these two goals *STRAD* might prompt lateral thinking amongst its users so that they find a way around the problem. If it does, such suggestions could be added to the list of options. But generating still more goals cannot go on forever without the risk of hopelessly complicating the exercise. The idea of option bar analysis is to reduce the number of (combined) goals rather than increase them. Hence the attempt by *STRAD* to reduce the complexity of its approach could actually be counter productive.

However, when all the incompatible combinations have been weeded out, after going through all the different problem foci, *STRAD* is in a position to see how many combinations of goals, or policies, or 'schemes' are still available. Accordingly, users can always see what schemes are still feasible by clicking 'Window/Schemes', and in the village example the screen so generated is shown in figure 6.3.

6.2.1. Assessing actions

STRAD will eventually get users to choose between these remaining schemes. It can be seen that in our example there are twelve possible schemes and two uncertain schemes. These latter two are uncertain because of the possible incompatibility between 'improve kiln' and 'using bio-waste/alternative fuel' for its power source. More specifically, when figure 6.3 was generated there were four decision areas within the current focus:

TRANSPORT?
PRODPROCES?
FUELSOURCE? and
MKTEXPAND?

and in the TRANSPORT? Decision Area there were two options:

'buy a truck' and
'hire a truck'.

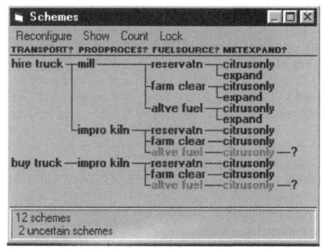

Figure 6.3. *STRAD* generating available schemes.

But, as we have seen, if a truck is bought a new mill cannot be. Hence if a truck is hired rather than purchased, there remains a choice between the existing mill and improving the kiln, but if a truck is bought there is no choice other than persisting with the existing mill. Moreover, if the kiln is persisted with, then market expansion is impossible, which leaves only one option - persist with the citrus-growing market exclusively. By contrast, if a new mill, and not a truck, is purchased, market expansion becomes a possibility. Finally, all three fuel sources – fuel collected from the forest reservation, fuel collected from farm clearing and fuel from the alternative source of bio-waste products, are possible no matter what type of mill is used, although there is some doubt about using the 'alternative' fuel in the existing kiln.

Hence twelve schemes are possible, two of which are uncertain. *STRAD*'s approach is to then evaluate all of such possible schemes. One might begin by changing the order of the Decision Areas as we move from left to right in figure 6.3. For example, if Decision Areas were arranged in order of importance, the FUELSOURCE?

decision area would actually be the most leftward one. But the number of schemes would always be the same no matter what the order. There would always be ten valid schemes and two uncertain ones.

In practice, this kind of exhaustive search approach to policymaking can be just that – exhausting. Keeping track of all possibilities is in fact impossible within large practical projects unless one uses a computer running software such as *STRAD*. Whether or not subsequent search of the totality of all possibilities is in fact then the best way to proceed we will defer judgement upon until later in this chapter. For now we will simply note *STRAD*'s comprehensiveness and the fact that it is here that it most clearly displays its origins in the field of Operations Research. Classical optimization methods used in Operations Research always incorporated 'smart' search of the 'domain of feasible solutions' until the best possible solution was found. In many ways, *STRAD* makes a valiant effort to persist with such a tradition within people-oriented policymaking, but it is probably impossible to sustain.

6.2.2. The perils of popularity

Note that *STRAD* counts how many of the possible schemes a particular goal figures in, and this could fool some people into believing that these counts are actually relevant in goal evaluation. For example, figure 6.3 shows that the 'buy a truck' goal is part of only three schemes, whereas the 'hire a truck' goal is part of nine schemes. Therefore, users could conclude that buying a truck is a far less robust goal. That is, because it is less popular it must combine less well with other goals and so it must not be as desirable – it must have 'implementation difficulties'. But such a conclusion would be false.

Lesson 40: Forewarned is forearmed

The ultra thorough information that current policymaking software provides can lead to false conclusions. For example, users often believe that since a particular policy features frequently in the list of possibilities, it must be a more popular or desirable one. Simply noting its frequency of occurrence, in an unthinking way, encourages them to believe this.

In other words, there are dangers whenever certain artefacts, like comprehensive policymaking packages, are put into the hands of people who are fallible humans. Therefore, everyone needs to be alerted to the dangers of complicated software.

Some might even reject policymaking software outright, but this would be misguided. As we saw above, such an attitude would have resulted in humankind still living in caves because people would be too afraid to make bows and arrows – just in case the technology fell into the wrong hands and was misused.

For the moment, concerned awareness of policymaking software's dangers should suffice. Forewarned is forearmed.

To see this, note that in figure 6.3 the only reason that 'buy a truck' occurs within fewer schemes is because spending available funds on a truck precludes purchasing a new mill along with the six schemes that emanate from this. But if the latter six schemes were all deficient in some way, buying a truck might still be the best thing to do. The fact that it leads to less possibilities does not necessarily mean that it is an inferior goal.

6.2.3. Rating goals

In order to rate goals the first thing a *STRAD* user must do is nominate which Comparison Areas he or she wants to use in order to evaluate the goals. Note that Comparison Areas are designated by the users. *STRAD* does not come with pre-set, or 'universal' evaluation criteria because, like most policymaking software, it works on the assumption that selection of suitable evaluation criteria will depend on the problem being addressed. Hence the user nominates such criteria.

For example, in the village example there were six Comparison Areas nominated by participants:

return
cost
employment
import substitution
quality (of fertilizer produced), and
sustainability.

'Import substitution' actually refers to a goal of the central government to reduce the drain on currency reserves which comes from importing fertilizer. Moreover, with regard to sustainability, case notes stored by *STRAD* record that a larger amount of debate took place within the community about whether or not environmental sustainability should be considered separately from social sustainability. It was eventually decided to consider them together. It is also recorded that the UN looks very favourably upon the pursuit of goals that score highly on the sustainability criterion.

STRAD's rating mechanism is thus a three-stage process. The first stage is, of course, selection of those Comparison Areas that are relevant to the current problem, and the second stage involves recording the 'impact' of each Decision Area on each Comparison Area. This is achieved by clicking 'Windows/Assess' and then altering the width of rectangles, using the computer's mouse, to represent different levels of impact, as shown in figure 6.4A. The user also designates the correct units of measurement for measuring the impact on each Comparison Area.

After the impact assessments for each Decision Area on each Comparison Area have been recorded, *STRAD* 'averages' such impacts for each Comparison Area across all Decision Areas. Such averaging is achieved by adding the squares of all the separate Decision Area-specific impacts and taking the square root of the resulting sum. This gives an estimate of the total 'influence', or the 'importance weight' within the current problem focus, of each Comparison Area.

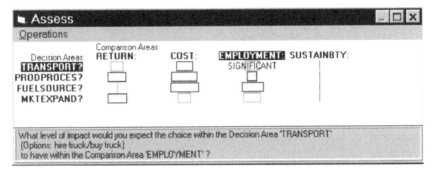

A

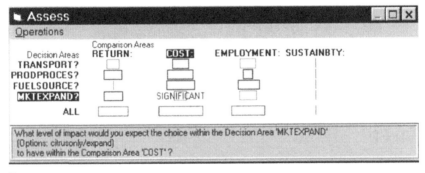

B

Figure 6.4. *STRAD* manipulating Decision Areas' options' impacts on Comparison Areas to derive the latter's importance levels.

The user can see these levels of importance at any time by clicking 'Windows/ Assess/Operations/Weights' which makes a set of rectangles appear along the bottom of figure 6.4.A. Their widths correspond to the overall 'weight' of each Comparison Area, at least in terms of the current problem being focused upon. This is shown in Figure 6.4B. Users can then manipulate any of these lower rectangles if they want to change the relative 'weight' of any Comparison Area. It is done by stretching the width of the appropriate rectangle, using the right button of the computer's mouse, and the program will proportionately scale the separate impact levels, of each Decision Area, on that Comparison Area.

At first sight this procedure of deducing criteria weights, by aggregating the 'impacts' of all the goals upon them, seems like the reverse of the process performed by most other policymaking software. The latter usually assigns importance levels to the criteria and then uses such assigned values to evaluate goals. But in another sense, *STRAD*'s procedure is quite logical. As we have pointed out, the criteria, or

Comparison Areas, can actually be thought of as goals - goals at a higher level of abstraction than the Decision Areas' options. If so, the impacts of the options on their parent goals will of course measure such parent goals', or criteria's 'importance levels'. A parent goal that is impacted on by a lot of goals will be more important in the total scheme of things.

Now, the third and final step of comparing goals is to rate each Decision Area's goals on each Comparison Area. This is performed by double clicking on 'Decision Area/Comparison Area' for the pair concerned. Such an action generates an 'Option Assessment' window, as illustrated in figure 6.5. A bar chart can be seen showing the ratings for the two 'Market Expansion' options – 'citrus only' and 'expand market', in terms of the Comparison Area being considered – 'cost'.

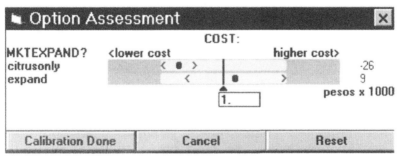

Figure 6.5. *STRAD* calibrating a score for each option.

The user is able to 'mouse drag' the dot within each option's bar in order to show the relative desirability levels for the two options, along with confidence margins around such ratings. Then, by mouse dragging the small black triangle, followed by clicking the 'Calibration Done' button, the user is able to set an actual numerical score, if known, for one of the dots or for anywhere else along one of the bars. This causes the program to re-calculate the actual numerical ratings, for all the other goals, according to where their own respective blue dots have been placed along the bar of possible scores.

It is worth reflecting on figure 6.5. It gives a further hint of *STRAD*'s origins within the Operations Research discipline. Most policymaking practice is concerned only with noting goals' scores on criteria, like 'cost'. But *STRAD* wants more than this. It also wants to know the significance of such scores, as shown by figure 6.5's error margins. This is similar to the traditional statistician's approach to say, regression analysis. He or she wants to know not only the strength of a relationship between two variables, as given by the 'R' statistic, but also the latter's significance.

Now, put brutally simply, 'significance' really means extent to which the measurement should be taken notice of. It is of no use recording a low or a high score if the significance of such a score is low. Hence not only the score, but also its significance are what must be known. Such an insistence on knowing the significance of scores seems to be yet another ploy to narrow discussion of options down to the more significant, or important ones. It joins the mechanism noted above – that of putting ellipses and different colours around those goals which rate highly for 'importance' and 'urgency', as another way of leading user's thoughts and efforts to the options that matter. It is part of *STRAD*'s attempt to make its rather informal approach more formal.

6.3. Crafting Good Schemes

STRAD now knows the score for each goal within each Decision Area in terms of each Comparison Area, and the latter's importance weights are also known. Hence desirability scores for each bundle of goals, or desirability scores for each 'scheme', can be calculated directly. Users can view the results of such calculations in two ways. The first involves clicking 'Windows/Assess/Operations/Select all/ Assessment', and the result of doing so, for the village example, is shown in figure 6.6.

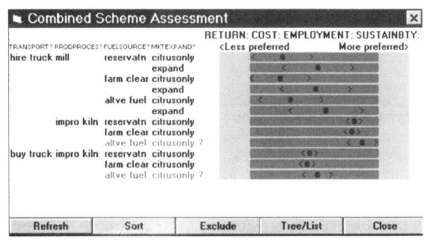

Figure 6.6. *STRAD* assessing available schemes.

Here we can see straight away that the most preferred schemes (policies) are the three shown near the middle. They all involve hiring a truck, improving the existing kiln and selling fertilizer exclusively to the citrus industry. However, the next highest-scoring policy, shown sixth from the top, involves all of these things except that it includes market expansion rather than selling exclusively to the citrus industry. Note that this is a much more radical and brave policy, as shown by the width of the uncertainty interval that surrounds its rating.

STRAD calculates such uncertainty margins by taking the square root of the sum of the squares of the uncertainty margins around each option that is part of the scheme. But such a 'grand averaging' procedure is based on an implicit assumption that the different types of uncertainty do not affect one another, which is surely false in some circumstances.

For example, consider the impact, on the 'Cost' criterion, of using bio-waste. This is quite uncertain because using bio-waste involves striking out into unknown technology. It is therefore difficult to imagine such uncertainty not being affected by the uncertainty of the impact, on cost, of purchasing a new mill, because purchasing a new mill also involves exploring new territory. That is, if the uncertainty surrounding a new mill was reduced, so too would be the uncertainty surrounding the costs of using bio-waste. Alternatively, if the uncertainty surrounding the mill was increased, so too would be the uncertainty surrounding bio-waste's impact on total costs.

Nevertheless, it is still important at least to take note of the 'averaged' uncertainty margins around each scheme's desirability scores - even though such averaging might be slightly inaccurate. When we do, it rapidly becomes evident that favouring the fourth best scheme in figure 6.6 would need to be done with extreme caution.

6.3.1. Eliminating schemes

One might therefore be tempted to eliminate from consideration the bottom three schemes in figure 6.6 on the grounds that, although fairly accurately scored, they are considerably lower scoring than the middle three. One might also eliminate the six schemes at the top of figure 6.6 on the grounds that they are probably slightly lower scoring than the middle four and they are, possibly, very inaccurately scored anyway.

Two comments apply to this. Firstly, *STRAD*'s approach is certainly an advance on 'satisficing' which, the literature tells us involves policymakers simply opting for *any* strategy which is a slight improvement over the current situation. By contrast, *STRAD* really gets to grips with searching out all of the possibilities within the solution space. It sorts them, and it forces detailed comparisons to be made between many more of them than it would be possible to compare using less rigorous methods of policy search. *STRAD* has no peer as a searcher of possible solutions.

Secondly, even when a policymaker has such a powerful searching and comparing mechanism, he or she might still be reluctant to remove, from all subsequent consideration, several of the possible schemes simply because of figure 6.6. For instance, one might still have nagging doubts about prematurely dismissing the sixth scheme from the top of figure 6.6. There is a chance, albeit a slight chance, that this scheme might be the second highest scoring scheme of all, given the upper limit of the uncertainty margin that surrounds its rating. In other words, serious policymakers will be reluctant to 'let go' any potentially useful scheme too early.

Accordingly, *STRAD* takes a much more conservative and measured approach when it comes to eliminating schemes. More specifically, users can click the 'Windows/Balance' menu item to compare each scheme with every other scheme – pair by pair. If it then transpires that two schemes making up some particular pair are very similar in terms of their chosen options but widely different in terms of their overall desirability rating, then there is little sense in continuing to consider the lowest scoring, but hardly unique one. Accordingly, few users would have any qualms about eliminating it from consideration. That is, eliminating similar, but much lower-scoring schemes means that most options are still being retained for further consideration, yet there are now less schemes to worry about.

Such an approach constitutes elimination of policy possibilities by attrition. This is probably better than a sweeping elimination of whole blocks of policies because doing this would run the risk of eliminating some particular policy that further analysis reveals as having enormous potential. *STRAD* accommodates planners' natural caution, which is based on a desire to leave no stone unturned in the search for the best policy. All good policymakers fear 'throwing out the baby with the bath water' when they dismiss possible policies too willingly and too early.

An example is shown in figure 6.7. This compares the two schemes that are at the top of figure 6.6. They are similar in all respects except that the first involves selling fertilizer only to citrus growers whereas the second involves expanding the fertilizer market. Both involve hiring a truck, using the existing mill and exploiting the existing reservation as a fuel source. Consequently, they score about the same for all the Comparison Areas except that the second scheme probably has a significantly higher financial return, albeit with a large margin of doubt around this. *STRAD* is therefore asking the user whether or not they wish to eliminate the first scheme, because the second is very similar yet has a higher combined score, as shown on the bottom line.

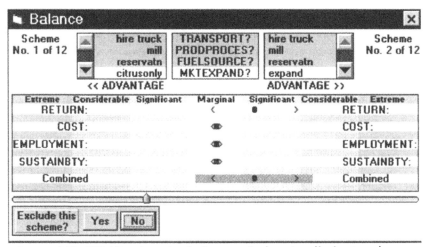

Figure 6.7. *STRAD* using the balance window to eliminate schemes.

Note however that the pointed brackets on either side of the middle three Comparison Areas' dots show that uncertainty margins have not yet been activated for 'Cost', 'Employment' and 'Sustainability'. Goals have not yet been scored on the latter, and so the equality of scores shown in figure 6.7 is simply a default, as are the uncertainty margins around such (non) scores.

Hence respective schemes' combined scores and their estimated margins of error, as shown in the bottom line, are actually unknown and based only on the scores for the schemes' respective goals on the 'Return' Comparison Area. In other words, the extent or otherwise of scheme 2's superiority over scheme 1 will remain unknown until actual scores for all of both schemes' goals, on all of the Comparison Areas, are known. Thus figure 6.7 may or may not provide sufficient grounds for eliminating scheme 1, it depends on whether the user wants to take a small risk by eliminating it now, based only on information about Return.

Yet users could never complain that *STRAD* does not 'lay everything out on the table'. It certainly is much safer and more open than many packages where wholesale elimination of whole rafts of policies, on flimsy grounds, is common. *STRAD* does not eliminate any scheme unless the user, who is always supplied with full information on what he or she knows and does not know about every scheme, says so.

Moreover, *STRAD* allows users to drag the positions of the dots in figure 6.7 and watch the effect this has on the comparative advantage for one of the schemes in terms of combined rating. Such a facility is very useful for analysing the sensitivity, or consequences, of small alterations in previous judgements about the score by a Decision Area goal on some Comparison Area.

6.3.2. Managing uncertainty

After the user has compared all possible pairs of alternative schemes, eliminated many of them from consideration and so settled on just a few for possible implementation, *STRAD*'s final step is to look at sources of uncertainty. Note that *STRAD*'s instructions manual emphasizes, when it is explaining figure 6.7 above, that once users become serious about considering just a few schemes they should focus on the margins of error by asking themselves 'surprise limit questions' – how much it is conceivable that a surprising result could occur. This is, of course, asking about levels of uncertainty.

But the explicit tactic used by *STRAD* for analysing sources of uncertainty is the identification of Uncertainty Areas at the very start. For instance, in the village example the nominated Uncertainty Areas were things like the future size of banana exports, continuity of UN funds, future extent of illegal fuel gathering in the forest reserve and several others shown in figure 6.8 below. Again, these Uncertainty Areas can always be explored by clicking 'Windows/Overview' to produce an overview screen like that shown in figure 6.1 above.

Notice in figure 6.1 how each Uncertainty Area is headlined using a word preceded by a question mark. Moreover, if their 'prominence' is high, such words are placed closer to the problem focus, and if their prominence is lower they are located further away from the problem focus. They are also placed in a 'clock position' according to whether they represent uncertainty about the environment (UE), uncertainty about related decisions (UR) or uncertainty about the values of other players (UV).

Moreover, the user can alter Uncertainty Areas' names, descriptions, prominence levels, positions and so forth by clicking 'Windows/Uncertainty'. The result of doing this in the village example is shown in figure 6.8. This provides a more detailed description of each Uncertainty Area as well as adjustable bars whose widths represent each one's 'prominence', along with an arrow showing its 'tractability'.

Note that if the widths of the bars are altered, the Uncertainty Areas can then be sorted in order of prominence by clicking on the sort button. Users can also click the bottom right button to indicate that they wish to add a new Uncertainty Area. This will generate a window that has boxes for a headlined name, a more detailed description and notes, along with adjustable bars to represent prominence and tractability. Moreover, the window for existing Uncertainty Areas can at any time be generated by double clicking any Uncertainty Area's short label.

Given that few other policymaking packages deal with uncertainty at all, and given that much policymaking practice only discusses uncertainties in a fairly vague and poorly-documented way, it is no wonder that *STRAD* has earned a reputation for being the package that is most suitable for 'management of uncertainty'. Its industrious detailing of all the aspects of uncertainty that surround a problem, along with what might be done about them, is unprecedented.

An example of such detailing is shown in figure 6.9. Note how the user can, by clicking on windows, easily alter headline descriptions, detailed descriptions, sector (of responsibility) and notes. 'Prominence' can also be altered by changing the

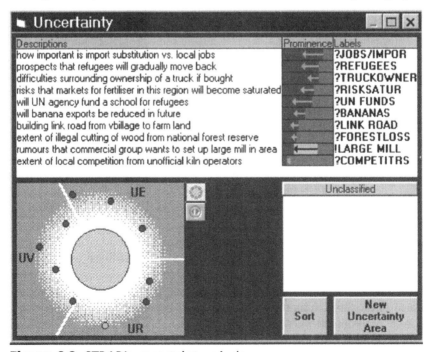

Figure 6.8. *STRAD's* uncertainty window.

width of the prominence bar, and 'tractability' can be adjusted by altering the width of the left-pointing arrow. Also and most importantly, there is space provided for the user to type in suggested actions for reducing the Uncertainty Area's prominence.

For instance, in the village example there have been two suggested actions for reducing the uncertainty surrounding rumours about a large, commercial group wanting to set up a fertilizer mill in a neighbouring village. One possible action would be to inquire about such proposals at the regional development agency. Another would be to lobby the government to not permit such a mill. Both actions have been assigned similar cost estimates, but the second action is shown as having more serious consequences in terms of delaying decisions if it is not carried out. Moreover, the width of the gain arrow is longer for the 'press government not to permit' action. Also, it has been estimated (by some user) that such an action will reduce the 'prominence' of this Uncertainty Area to the width of the band on the left of the gain arrow.

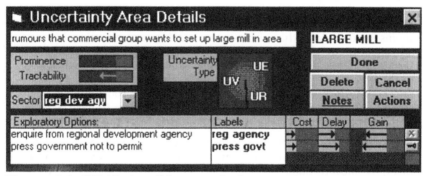

Figure 6.9. *STRAD* describing a typical Uncertainty Area.

Accordingly, such an action has been 'locked', as indicated by the key sign, as something that ought to be pursued forthwith. This is why, in figure 6.8 above, the prominence band of the '?LARGE MILL' Uncertainty Area was reduced, as shown by the left-pointing arrow, and its headline title was changed to '!LARGE MILL'. The action has been locked into policy and so this Uncertainty Area's prominence has been reduced. Note finally that by clicking on the 'Actions' button in figure 6.9, a space appears where users can type whether, and which action has been chosen, who will undertake it, when, using what authority and what resources.

6.3.3. Policymaking amid turbulence

It is worth considering that *STRAD*'s preoccupation with uncertainties and threats could actually cause a policymaking exercise to become bogged down in trivia. If one becomes obsessed about immediate threats to the *status quo* one can lose sight of the overall policies that are possible. In other words, the removal of all sources of uncertainty could become an obsession. Indeed, we noted above how this fixation on the 'limitation of surprises' has been highlighted in the literature as a major fault of practice (Mintzberg, 1994) – it can lead to conservatism and a lack of inspirational policymaking. Hence *STRAD* could be accused of encouraging a

Lesson 41: Current turbulence?

Short-term policymaking practice is often justified on the grounds that the world has become a much more turbulent and uncertain place. Under such conditions, long-term, 'light on the hill' policymaking is becoming less and less appropriate. Indeed, in many of today's 'down-sized' and 'out-sourcing' institutions the definition of policymaking seems to have changed from 'moulding the future' to 'preparing for the future'.

Some packages seem to be well placed to take on this new role by facilitating adaptive, contingency type policymaking. They focus on uncertainty, and ways of reducing it, in order to gain us just a little breathing space. But two comments are in order.

Firstly, most policymaking software can always be used flexibly. It can be used for schemes analysis whenever long-term policymaking seems appropriate, and for managing uncertainty whenever the environment seems so turbulent that short-term, contingency planning is more advisable. Better still, software might be used with an experienced human facilitator to lead users towards schemes analysis whenever participants become too obsessed with uncertainty management, and towards uncertainty management whenever they become too obsessed with schemes analysis. As such, packages like *STRAD* appear to have covered both ends of the policymaking spectrum – long term and short term.

Secondly, there is actually a huge debate about turbulence. Mintzberg (1994) makes a powerful case that all eras regard their own period as being the most turbulent yet, and so the current era is probably no more uncertain than any other has been. It therefore follows that packages with detailed mechanisms for management of uncertainty, although they fuel a fashion for the short-term thinking of the 1990s, might actually be misconceived. Policymaking practice that places too little emphasis on the longer term will ultimately prove disastrous for the preservation of the social fabric and the natural environment.

Policymaking is an activity that demands considerable contemplation. As Solzhenitsyn (1971) reminded us, it is difficult to achieve this when looking at the turbulence of a babbling brook. But if one slows down the water by diverting it into a tranquil pond, then deep reflection becomes possible.

Hence for maximum performance, policymakers need to desist from making quick decisions that are justified by the supposed turbulence of current times. They should pause to reflect on present day conditions by taking into account as many arguments as possible, including those that they had insufficient time to explore during the babbling, policymaking process itself. Most of the policymaking software considered in this book acknowledges such a need.

negative aspect of much current practice – over emphasis of immediate threats and an unwarranted concern for the short term.

However, at any stage users can get *STRAD* to print out a 'progress report'. They can then take such a report away for quiet reflection somewhere else at some other time – reflective analysis after the heat of the moment has passed. More specifically, users generate a report by clicking 'Window/Progress', and for the village example such a report would look like that shown in figure 6.10. We can see the actions that need to be carried out now, as well as those needing decision in the longer term. So far, there has been a decision to implement one action immediately – press the government not to permit the large mill in a neighbouring village. Such an action can, of course, be supplemented later by different Decision Area goals taken from the highest-scoring schemes, along with actions that should reduce uncertainty within various other Uncertainty Areas.

| | NOW | | FUTURE | |
Sector	DECISIONS	UNCERTAINTIES: Explorations	Decisions	Uncertainties
General				
coop			TRANSPORT? PRODPROCES? FUELSOURCE? MKTEXPAND? COORDINATN? AGRIC COOP?	?RISKSATUR ?TRUCKOWNER ?JOBS/IMPOR ?COMPETITRS
ngo			TRAINING?	?UN FUNDS
reg dev agy		[LARGE MILL press govt]		?REFUGEES ?BANANAS ?FORESTLOSS ?LINK ROAD

Figure 6.10. *STRAD* generating a progress report.

Note that if users click the 'Adopt' menu in the top left hand corner they will be asked whether or not they want to adopt such a set of actions as a 'Commitment', as a 'Recommendation' or as a 'Strategic Option'. If one adopts a set of actions as a strategic option, they can be saved as a separate file, along with other strategic options that can subsequently be developed and separately saved as alternatives. That is, one might use *STRAD* to generate feasible and desirable policy options and, if one has reservations about *STRAD*'s ability to test properly their desirability levels, take such policies to other software.

After all, we have emphasized how *STRAD* is extraordinarily thorough in its recording of details, but we have had less to say about the quality of its policy evaluations. There is little doubt that the package is excellent for searching through all possible policies and for gaining a thorough understanding of the nature of relevant uncertainties. But such qualities do not necessarily equate with a top-of-the-range ability to evaluate alternative policies.

6.4. Summary

STRAD's tactic is to detail immediately all the intricacies of the situation. We have noted how this contrasts to many policymaking packages which take a more hierarchical approach. They begin by first evaluating overall, conceptual policies and, once some have been chosen, performing more focused analyses of the details. *STRAD* eschews this. It favours a 'boots and all' approach to get users deeply involved in the problem's intricacies from the very start. This almost certainly makes participants 'feel good', but in terms of coming up with the best policies, it may or may not be the best way to proceed.

Perhaps *STRAD* goes too far towards trying to replicate reality. Even for the relatively simple village example outlined above, its analyses are enormously complex, and users have considerable opportunity to change parameter scores and uncertainty margins at will. Hence the recommendations emanating from any *STRAD*-based analysis can really be whatever one wants, depending on the extent one is willing to alter the various scores. It is therefore easy to imagine users becoming confused, or worse, fooled by unscrupulous and dominant workshop participants who hide behind the smokescreen of complicatedness to 'pull the wool over the eyes' of other participants in order to get their own favoured policies recommended.

The alternative argument is that *STRAD* has actually been set up to clear much of this smokescreen, *STRAD* can cut through it so that everyone can appreciate the nature of the situation as it truly is. Yet ironically, by doing this so industriously, *STRAD* may sometimes overkill its clarification procedures to the point where they begin to make things less clear again. Again, one might counter that if reality is so complex, then we must replicate it regardless. But policymakers are only human, and so sometimes a more considered, hierarchical approach to interpreting reality might be more easy for them to understand.

Yet there is little doubt that *STRAD* makes a valiant attempt to sort out the desirability levels of all possible policies. Indeed, it has no peer as a searcher of solution space. But we are left with the feeling that it may give too much attention to extraneous detail. At a time when users' efforts could be better spent examining only the important choices, they are led towards trying to compare all possible choices. It is perhaps not focused enough and is too 'feel good' in its approach. Yet *STRAD* baulks at too much focus because of its justifiable fear of over simplicity. It seeks to avoid premature decision making about what actually is important. However it may sometimes go too far in this direction, and so err on the side of over elaboration. Hence we remain in search of a package that can clarify the essential choices and then directly help us make such choices.

Chapter 7

Frontier Software Case III: *Expert Choice*

We have seen that *CyberQuest* focuses users' hearts and minds on the generation of ideas, and *STRAD* forces users to assess possibilities and to deal with uncertainties. *Expert Choice* has a different emphasis – alternatives evaluation. It helps policymakers choose, by converting their comparative ratings for alternative policies into ratio scale scores. That is, *Expert Choice* focuses users' hearts and minds on rating policies.

But what sets this package apart from other policymaking software is its ability to monitor inconsistency within its users' ratings. It will then warn them if their inconsistency level is high. *Expert Choice* is also able to incorporate, into a goals hierarchy, the impacts on policy choice of different scenarios and their likelihoods. It can also incorporate the impacts and likelihoods of different 'players' and their different attitudes. Moreover, *Expert Choice* has extensive sensitivity testing capabilities in which users can see clearly how small changes in their ratings of policies, on criteria, will change the ultimate conclusion about which policy is best.

Table 7.1. Categories of problems that have been addressed by *Expert Choice*.

Corporate executive decision making	(e.g. strategies, mergers, marketing, investment)
Corporate managerial decision making	(e.g. advertising, public relations, hiring)
Small business	(e.g. bids, new products, time allocations)
National policy	(e.g. legislation, budget allocation, military planning)
Public administration at the federal, state and local levels	(e.g. resource allocation, tactical planning, legal decisions)
Personal decision making	(e.g. career planning, geographical location, voting)

Expert Choice was originally developed by Thomas Saaty, a mathematician who worked in the Wharton Business School at the University of Pennsylvania and later at the University of Pittsburgh. He has written many books about his

Analytic Hierarchy Process (AHP) approach, which utilizes complex analysis of users' preference matrices (Saaty, 1994; 1996; Saaty and Vargas, 1994) and underpins the *Expert Choice* package. Such an approach draws upon the paired comparisons method of rating policies, as mentioned above, and which Saaty himself pioneered as a way of dovetailing qualitative judgements with quantitative ones.

Saaty consults widely, and so the *Expert Choice* software has been applied throughout North America, China, Japan, Africa, the Middle East and, indeed, most other parts of the world, particularly within the business policymaking sector. In fact, so many are listed in the instructions manual that they have to be amalgamated into categories, as shown in table 7.1. *Expert Choice* has even been applied to various peace initiatives and hostage crises around the world, and such applications are frequently described in the *Expert Choice* Newsletter (http://www.expertchoice.com).

7.1 Identifying Alternatives

In its earlier versions, *Expert Choice* used to be much more 'thinking' in its approach. It straight jacketed any problem into a traditional hierarchy of goals. This was·in contrast to both *CyberQuest*, which undertook situation structuring, and *Strad*, which asked users to suggest 'issues' – *Expert Choice* simply asked users to input 'alternatives' directly. The latter were then placed along the lowest level of the goals hierarchy, the overall goal was placed at the very top, and up to five intervening layers of 'other considerations' could be inserted in between. The main thrust of *Expert Choice*'s approach was to then score the bottom-line alternatives according to how much they affected the intervening considerations and how 'important' the latter were.

However, *Expert Choice* now includes a 'structuring module' which is similar, in many ways, to *CyberQuest*'s 'situation structuring' routines. That is, the package now has a more relaxed and 'feeling' approach than it had hitherto. It still builds a goals hierarchy for the user, but the user is now more stimulated to think, very carefully, about the policymaking problem before doing so.

7.1.1. Structuring the problem

Figure 7.1 shows *Expert Choice* in problem setup mode. Figure 7.1A indicates how users can enter their problem either by following the lead of some other problem, or by 'structuring', or by simply inputting their hierarchy directly. When users click on 'structuring', they have a choice of building their hierarchy from the top goal downwards (figure 7.1B) or from the bottom line alternatives upwards (figure 7.1C).

Expert Choice then presents the user with a few aids to thinking about the problem being faced, such as a facility for entering the pros and cons of each alternative. But such aids are nowhere near as extensive and as sophisticated as the mechanisms used in *CyberQuest*'s situation structuring routines. Therefore, we will not discuss the *Expert Choice*'s situation structuring procedures any more – we will move on to explain its unique features.

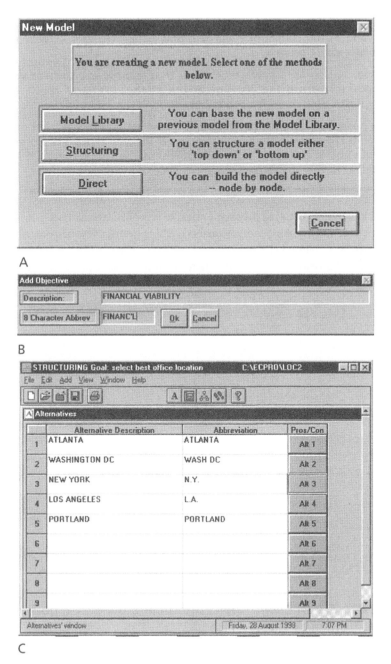

A

B

C

Figure 7.1. *Expert Choice* describing the problem.

Lesson 42: Have patience

Policymaking is actually a very sophisticated activity. Hence although many readers have access to books like this one, it does not follow that everyone in the community will feel that policymaking is actually an understandable process.

Indeed, it is simply naive to assume that people everywhere will immediately grasp the concept of the goals hierarchy. Hence all enthusiastic policymakers need to have copious reserves of patience.

Thus policymaking practice needs to proceed with a slowness that may be painful for some professionals to endure. The alternative is to proceed faster. But in this lurks a danger of losing the commitment of lay participants, thereby torpedoing any chance of useable outcomes.

After situation structuring the user is asked to type their overall goal in less than 65 characters. Such a number of characters could be restrictive when describing a very complex problem, but the user is always able to add 'notes' to elaborate on any input, as shown in figure 7.2. From here on, the process of problem description – entering the other nodes into layers of the hierarchy, is easily completed.

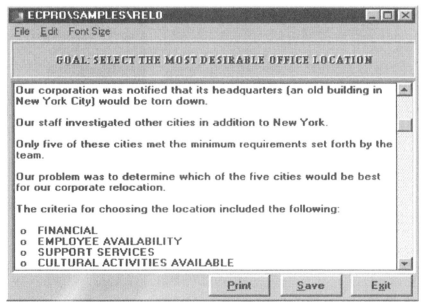

Figure 7.2. *Expert Choice*'s notes attached to the overall goal in the office relocation example.

However, it is still difficult to imagine novice users, who have a completely fresh problem, which they do not wish to structure in the same form as some other problem, being able to build a goals hierarchy without prior knowledge of the concept. Readers of this book certainly have some understanding of the concept, but not everybody does. Even for readers it is still probably a good idea at this point to reiterate the key feature of goal hierarchies – any goal's sub-goals must be at roughly the same level of abstraction before they can be validly compared.

Lesson 43: Sort out the goals

Huge amounts of time are wasted by participants arguing about the relative merits of what are, supposedly, comparable sub-goals which are not comparable at all. Such goals are often at different scales, and so they are fundamentally different in terms of what they are aiming towards. Yet a simple arrangement of the policy problem into a goals hierarchy would have immediately revealed this.

Hence shared knowledge amongst the participants of what the goals hierarchy is, and consequent agreement as to which policies can actually be compared to one another, is strongly recommended. The hierarchy is a most effective instrument for clearing the hopeless confusion with which policymaking projects are frequently afflicted.

To see this, look at a properly conceived goals hierarchy in figure 7.3. Note in passing that *Expert Choice* is able to draw goal hierarchies in several different ways and figure 7.3 shows just two of them. Anyway, figure 7.3 presents the hierarchy for the 'Relocation' problem, which is one of the many 'past cases' supplied with *Expert Choice*. Its overall goal is to 'select the most desirable office location', and the selected location needs to be financially profitable, close to available employees, accessible to support services, near to cultural facilities close to leisure opportunities and in a geographical region that has an acceptable climate.

Note however that achieving these sub-goals might not necessarily involve actual relocation of the existing office. For example, it might be possible to achieve financial profitability by using mail order distribution of products, and so it might not matter where the actual office is. Hence the existing office could presumably be kept. Similarly, access to employees may be achievable by a means other than physically shifting the office close to some labour pool. For example, it might be possible to arrange a company bus to travel from areas of high labour availability, or to import 'guest workers' on the European model.

Yet it seems to have been assumed, at least in this example, that we need a new office location. We will therefore assume that there is something about this problem situation which says a move is absolutely necessary and that the existing office is completely unsatisfactory for some reason. This is an especially plausible assumption given that, as we have pointed out, the latest version of *Expert Choice* includes a situation structuring module for canvassing an extremely wide range of alternative policies before actually entering them into a goals hierarchy model of the problem's essence. That is, other policies, besides those that finally ended up

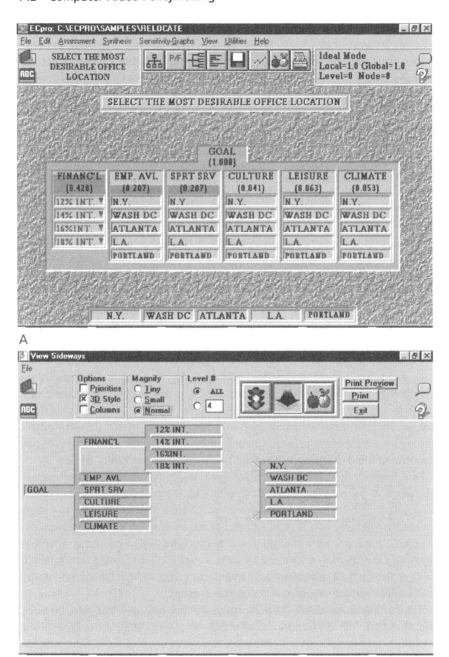

A

B

Figure 7.3. *Expert Choice* using a goals hierarchy.

in the given goals hierarchy, were probably generated but then rejected because
they were inappropriate.

Therefore, since this example seems to be addressing an office relocation problem, the policymaker needs to identify regions that are attractive financially, which have access to a large labour pool, and so forth.   However, there could still be a possibility of 'breaking the mould' – some room for innovative, and perhaps more attractive solutions than simple relocation.   For example, one could rent some cheap premises in a geographic region where rents are low precisely because it has very few leisure facilities. Thus the financial profitability criterion would be instantly satisfied, but the leisure facilities goal would not be. Yet if one used the financial savings to build company-operated leisure facilities the latter criterion would be met also. Such a crafted policy might be better than an office relocation. That is, it might be useful to build one's own solution to the office location problem, *CyberQuest* style, rather than simply choose between packaged relocations.

Lesson 44: Amplify your creativity

It is fallacious to assume that structuring a policymaking problem into a goals hierarchy will stifle users' lateral thinking ability. Indeed, the reverse is possibly the case. That is, it is perhaps a perverse aspect of human nature that whenever our hearts and minds are focused using a simplification instrument such as a goals hierarchy, we usually have a desire to break out of the mould to think about other possibilities as well.

Some people may not feel this need, but here we speak of those who are very keen to find the best possible solution for their policymaking problem. Often, if we did not set out the problem in a hierarchical way, many of the more innovative possibilities may never have suggested themselves.

Hence those who opt for 'feeling' rather than 'thinking' software, on the grounds that this puts greater emphasis on the contribution by the human user and so makes creativity more evident, could be wrong. Computers can sometimes amplify one's originality.

But choosing between packaged alternatives is what *Expert Choice* does well. Its name is no accident; its main emphasis is the making of *choices* rather than formulating new ones. Hence the task in our example is to choose between the packaged alternatives of – New York, Washington DC, Atlanta, Los Angeles and Portland. These can be thought of as policies, and the second-level goals, such as 'profitability' and 'access to a labour pool' can be thought of, if it is helpful, as evaluation criteria. In other words, each location, or policy, can be evaluated in terms of how well it scores on the various criteria. Obviously, the scores obtained by policies on the evaluation criteria will be multiplied by the relevant evaluation criterion's importance level. The numbers in figure 7.3A show the latter. Such products will then be summed in order to find which policy has the highest overall priority.

7.1.2. Accommodating possible scenarios

As foreshadowed above, layers of other things that need to be taken into account can also be inserted into the *Expert Choice* hierarchy. A partial example is evident in figure 7.4 which shows that under different interest rates (12%, 14%, 16% and 18%), the alternative locations are likely to have different scores for financial profitability. Thus in figure 7.4A it can be seen that if interest rates are 12% the most attractive location is Los Angeles. By contrast, if interest rates are 18% the best location is New York, as shown in figure 7.4B.

Hence the estimated probabilities, for the different interest rate levels, are multiplied by the relevant scores for each policy. The resulting products are then summed, for each policy, in order to calculate which one has the maximum 'financial utility'. That is, the best office location is the one whose amalgamated 'score times probability' product is highest.

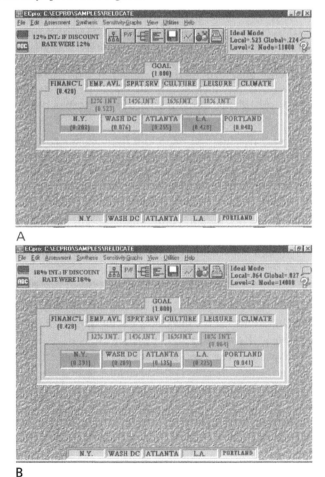

A

B

Figure 7.4. *Expert Choice* scoring alternatives under different scenarios.

7.1.3. Accommodating possible actors

Other considerations besides evaluation criteria and scenarios can also be inserted into *Expert Choice* hierarchies. For example, key persons or organizations are often included. This ensures that policies are scored according to how desirable they are likely to be from the point of view of different individuals or different organizations. Also, the latter's importance levels, or their levels of power, play the same role as probabilities do when scenarios are inserted into the hierarchy. That is, rather than evaluate each alternative goal in terms of 'expected utility' (score times scenario's probability), alternatives are compared in terms of 'acceptability' (score times actor's importance).

As a perhaps clearer example, another problem that comes with the *Expert Choice* package has an overall goal of easing traffic congestion within the Washington DC area, and the bottom level, alternative policies are:

➤ build a proposed outer belt way
➤ improve and expand rapid transit
➤ limit the extent of outwards urban development, and
➤ introduce flexible working hours.

Yet rather than the next layer upwards from the bottom being one of evaluation criteria, as is the usual case, this example introduces a layer of 'actors', or (possibly overlapping) groups of people in the Washington DC area who are likely to be affected, by each of the policies, in different ways:

➤ users
➤ land and home owners
➤ interest groups, and
➤ voters.

Numbers are then assigned to the latter in terms of their power or 'political clout'. When the alternatives are scored for desirability, they are scored from the point of view of each of the groups – each group of stake holders will have a different view as to the relative desirability levels of the alternative policies. Hence the evaluation of policies, at least in this part of the hierarchy, will involve looking for the one which has the best score in terms of 'community acceptability' (the sum of all the 'score times power' products).

In summary, *Expert Choice* is able to evaluate policies in several ways. Firstly, it is able to evaluate them using evaluation criteria, which users compare for 'preference', and so they are measured in terms of 'preferability'. Secondly, it is able to evaluate policies using scenarios, which users compare for 'likelihood', and so policies are assigned a score for 'expected utility'. Thirdly, it is able to evaluate policies using actors, who users compare for 'importance', and so policies are scored for 'acceptability'.

7.2. Rating Alternatives

This is perhaps why *Expert Choice* is, possibly, the most widely used policymaking package. It seems to be able to handle any sort of problem. Yet problems surface if the policymaking situation involves combinations of the three types of consideration – intrinsic preference, probability and political power. The *Expert Choice* approach is simply to mix all these considerations into the goals hierarchy regardless. That is, one simply constructs a layer, or layers for scenarios, other layers for actors and others for preference levels, and simply multiplies the scores for any bottom level alternative up its relevant branch of the tree. Hence each alternative policy comes out with a unitary score, and presumably the one with the highest score is the best.

Lesson 45: Beware of numbers

In policymaking, numbers appear to make life easier. Hence whenever there is a hard decision to be made, many people will simply accept numbers uncritically.

But this is dangerous. All numbers need careful interpretation – what logical meaning do they have? If they do not appear to have any validity, it is not acceptable simply to adopt the highest-scoring option as the best policy. Its high score might be a mathematical accident.

One needs to 'see through' an evaluation exercise to the point of being convinced that something valid about the different policies has been measured. Alternatively, if one is unsure about what has actually been measured, one should be extremely careful. Never adopt some policy simply because it scores more highly and so 'seems' to be better.

7.2.1. Scoring

But how to interpret such unitary scores is a deep source of worry to many people. An overall score might simply be an accident that has no valid meaning. Therefore, *Expert Choice* might do more harm than good by appearing to legitimize some policy as the best even though its high score might be a numerical fluke.

This is not to suggest that all numbers are useless. Some are very useful. For instance, if we multiply preferability (utility) by probability we calculate 'expected utility'. This has always been used in standard, 'decision tree' software as described in Chapter 2. Expected utility has always had plausibility as a measure of any policy's desirability because it is convenient to use in gambling type situations. One multiplies the size of the possible prize by the known probability of that prize in order to calculate whether or not a gamble is worthwhile. If the reward is high, but such a reward's probability is extremely low, it is probably not worth taking the gamble. Nor is it worth taking the gamble if a reward's probability is high but the actual reward is very low. Better gambles are those whose rewards, times their probabilities, are relatively high.

Lesson 46: Expected utility

People do not actually make choices in the way that the theory of 'expected utility' would predict. If they did, nobody would ever buy lottery tickets, which offer very high rewards but abysmal odds of ever being able to claim them. Nor would anybody ever take part in high-risk recreations, where catastrophically low, negative results have a reasonably high probability of occurring.

Yet lotteries and thrill sports are extremely popular. Clearly, reasoning that says 'expected benefit is equal to utility times probability' is only plausible in terms of its own internal logic. Its actual correspondence with the realities of people's behaviour seems to be mostly a mirage. Hence if policymaking practice adopts the expected utility approach for rating policy alternatives, it will run the risk of suggesting policies that people do not agree with.

To explain this, some researchers suggest that we all have a tendency to misjudge very high and very low probabilities. We overestimate low probabilities of success, which partly explains why we buy lottery tickets, and we underestimate high probabilities of failure, which partly explains why we participate in thrill sports – an optimistic streak. But we also have a conservative, pessimistic streak whereby we overestimate low probabilities of disaster, which partly explains the insurance industry.

Perhaps such a 'perverse' way of making choices is necessary in a depressing world where one needs to be optimistic if one is to remain active, yet conservative if one wants to stay safe. Or perhaps such 'irrational' behaviour is an evolutionary characteristic that ensures people will continue to evolve experimentally as well as consolidate what they have already achieved.

Yet the fact remains that any policymaking exercise, if it is predicated on the assumption that the best policy is the one with the highest expected utility, is unlikely to conform to the wishes of the people it is supposed to be serving. Expected utility should, therefore, be looked at only in the spirit of stimulating our thinking. Think carefully about expected utility.

But this only covers expected utility. Some of the other combinations generated by *Expert Choice*'s willingness to multiply things together, regardless, are far more worrying. For example, what does 'preferability times acceptability' mean? In some situations we might want to separate policies according to their preferability because acceptance is less important – it is something that we might need to be aware of only when it comes to implementing the policy. In other situations, acceptability might be very important, and theoretical preferability might not be so much of an issue. Hence always multiplying the two together might seem sophisticated, because it is taking advantage of all the data at one's disposal, but if some of those data are irrelevant, such 'automatic' multiplication is unwise.

Lesson 47: Carbon-based versus silicon-based judgement

Consider the problem in which alternative policies for dealing with a city's homeless may score differently according to the likely financial rates of interest pertaining at the time. These interest levels, along with their respective probabilities, simply have to be factored into the policymaking process. Moreover, various people from different organizations might have different views as to the desirability levels of the various policies depending on what interest rate regime is operative at the time. Therefore, overall community 'acceptability' becomes a necessary prerequisite for getting any policy implemented, and so this needs to be measured also.

The result will be an evaluation of policies based on interest rate scenarios, actors' importance levels, actors' scores for policies' desirability levels and scenarios' probabilities. Hence for each policy we would multiply its desirability level by each scenario's probability level by each actor's acceptability level and sum. That is, we will be calculating each policy's 'expected utility times acceptability' score.

Even though it is difficult to interpret logically, or defend the validity of the resulting, unitary score, some policymakers do not mind. They insist that all information must be used. They worry that leaving out either the interest rate scenario probabilities, or the acceptability levels of the different actors, means that our policymaking exercise is running on partial information.

Yet perhaps it would be better to score policies at least three times, say, once for average desirability, once for expected utility (average desirability times average probability) and once for acceptability (expected utility times actors' acceptability levels). The final, synthesizing decision can then be made by a human, who will be able to estimate the relative worth of each of the three specialized scores – something which a mechanical computer is less competent at doing.

Worldly judgement about the intrinsic worth of different ways of evaluating things cannot presently be replicated in computers. Simply having computers multiply the different scores together, as if such scores all had equal validity, is no substitute for human judgement. Thus some software's apparent synthesizing power is largely a mirage.

Indeed, multiplying scores for 'preferability' and for 'acceptance' can pollute both pieces of information and so obfuscate what was previously a clear policy choice situation. That is, it is not difficult to imagine policymakers working away at rating alternatives on the basis of say, preferability, when a well meaning team member suddenly points out that there are various, differently thinking stake holders who need to be included within the policymaking equation for 'completeness'. But including such stakeholders at this time, along with their importance levels, might thereafter damage, and possibly completely overturn an entirely satisfactory choice procedure. Sometimes it might be more important to find the most preferable, rather than the most acceptable policy.

A counter argument could be mounted that the policy which has the largest 'preferability times acceptability' product is the one most likely to be suitable for forging some kind of community consensus. But even this is by no means certain. How often does it happen that the seemingly best compromise fails to carry the day – it is shunted aside by a policy that has a pure and specialist appeal that captures all participants' imagination?

In short, an uncritical consideration of 'everything that one can think of' is not necessarily a good idea. It will often be better to run two separate analyses, to find, say, the most 'preferable' policy on the one hand and, say, the most 'acceptable' policy on the other. If these turn out to be different policies, the human brain is a far better instrument than a computer program for resolving which one we should go ahead with.

Likewise, one can think of situations in which it would be better to know the policy with the highest preferability, and the one with the highest expected utility, and the one with the highest acceptability, rather than the one whose score for 'expected utility times acceptance' is highest. The latter seems such an artificial construct that it is difficult to understand what it might be measuring. Nevertheless, this is what many exercises using *Expert Choice* measure.

7.2.2. Making paired comparisons

To enable any user to assign ratings to policies' preferability levels, to criteria's importance levels, to scenarios' probabilities or to actors' influence levels, *Expert Choice* uses the famous 'paired comparisons' method. That is, it does NOT let users assign scores directly to each one; it requires instead that they compare each alternative with every other one in turn. People often find it difficult, or even impossible, to assign scores to a set of things and if they are forced to do so they will probably do it inaccurately. By contrast, if they are asked whether one element is higher or lower-scoring than another, they can usually answer the question accurately and consistently. Hence by taking each pair in turn, asking which is higher scoring, and then asking whether it scores moderately, strongly, very strongly or extremely more or (less), *Expert Choice* is eventually able to calculate each element's overall rating.

Yet a closer inspection of Saaty's books (Saaty, 1994, 1996; Saaty and Vargas, 1994) suggests that the reason for insisting on paired comparisons is far more subtle. Basically, Saaty believes that people's feelings about alternatives, criterion weights, likelihoods and actor's levels of influence cannot be accurately portrayed by simply assigning a number to them in the way that most policymaking software does. Where is the starting point of such numbers? There isn't one. Therefore, how can we expect to be able to add and multiply the numbers in order to produce meaningful results? It is impossible, according to Saaty and, on the face of it, it seems that he is correct.

In other words, Saaty is adamant that we need genuine 'ratio scale' numbers if we are going to be able to add and to multiply scores. The arbitrary 'interval scale' numbers used by most policymaking software simply will not suffice, and indeed, if we do try to add and multiply these numbers we will get nonsensical ratings and misconceived policy recommendations. And the only way to get such genuine ratio scale numbers is to implement the paired comparisons method followed by matrix algebra techniques that are beyond the scope of this book.

An example of paired comparisons being implemented is shown in figure 7.5A where the user is being asked, in connection with the office relocation problem,

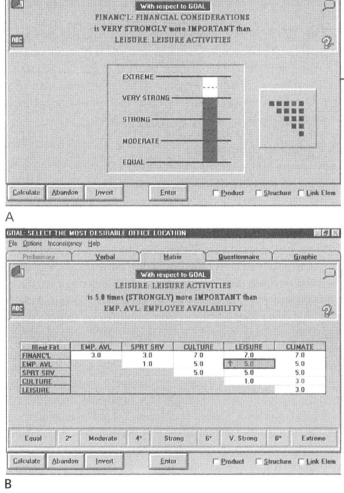

A

B

Figure 7.5. *Expert Choice* making a paired comparison.

whether 'financial considerations' are moderately, strongly, very strongly or extremely more important than 'leisure activities'. Note that *Expert Choice* gives the user a choice of several ways of making paired comparisons, and figure 7.5 shows just two of them.

The user is, therefore, able to click the mouse to mark the place that answers the question in figure 7.5A (or type a number in the relevant cell in figure 7.5B). *Expert Choice* will then ask about the desirability of 'financial viability', compared to 'support services', compared to 'cultural opportunities' and so on until all possible pairs of evaluation criteria have been so covered. The user's answers are converted to a numerical score between zero and nine and they are then aggregated across all pairs to attain an overall score for each evaluation element. Overall scores, for this example, are shown in figure 7.6. Financial viability has come out on top, followed by availability of support services and leisure opportunities.

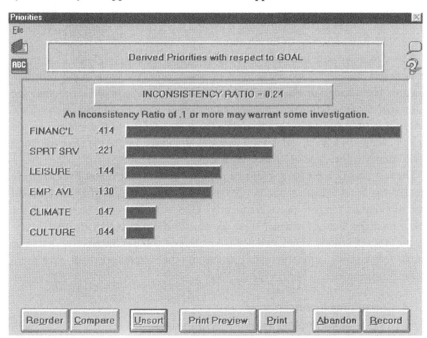

Figure 7.6. *Expert Choice* assessing importance levels of evaluation criteria.

Note that to calculate these overall scores the data had to be standardized, and *Expert Choice* users have a choice of two standardization methods – the 'distributive' and the 'ideal' modes. The 'distributive' mode standardizes according to each element's share of the sum of scores earned by all of its sibling nodes – each element's score is proportional to its share of the total. By contrast, the 'ideal' mode rates each element according to its fraction of the score attained by the best, 'ideal' element.

Although the *Expert Choice* manual points out that 90% of the time the two modes will generate much the same result, it gives some useful advice about the circumstances in which each should be used. Basically, it recommends using the 'distributive' method whenever one is doing general policymaking, and it recommends using the 'ideal' method whenever there are a number of policies that are very similar in terms of one, or a few of the evaluation criteria.

To explain this the manual presents an example where comparisons are being made between five diamonds using evaluation criteria like 'rarity', 'colour', 'hardness' and 'shape'. One of the diamonds is clear, but the other four are blue in colour and so they are very rare. Now, if the distributive, 'fraction of total scores' method is used, each of the blue diamonds would get a score for rarity of something less than 0.25. Therefore, if scores for the other evaluation criteria are fairly standard, the scores of all diamonds would be around 0.25 for all the other characteristics as well. Thus the clear diamond would have a good chance as coming out as the best alternative, even though it is extremely common compared to the blue diamonds, one of which should win.

Hence to make sure that each blue diamond is given the credit that its extreme rarity deserves, one should use the ideal, 'percent of the best score' standardization method. Here each blue diamond would be given a high score for rarity; the blue diamonds' scores would come out about the same but all would be well above the rarity score of the clear diamond. Hence the scores for the blue diamonds would all be elevated to a level which they warrant, and the score for the clear diamond would plummet because of its lack of rarity.

The fact that *Expert Choice* retains an option for its users to choose between the 'distributive' and 'ideal' methods of standardization suggests that the diamond type of situation tends to occur frequently. Hence users need to be watchful for policymaking situations in which there are several alternatives that are very similar on one or more criteria. They will need to be scored not in a 'distributive' but in an 'ideal' way in order to distinguish them from other alternatives that have more eccentric attributes.

7.2.3. Correcting inconsistency

Expert Choice goes to great lengths to ensure that such scoring is done with accuracy. It calculates and shows the user his or her 'overall inconsistency index'. The latter is obtained by analysing a matrix that shows, for each element, its score for superiority, or inferiority, compared to each other element. Such calculations take place deep within the *Expert Choice* software and they are not transparent to users. Basically, they involve identifying the 'eigenvectors' of the matrix of comparison scores, and the result can be interpreted as a measure of the extent to which some paired comparisons, as made by the user, are not reconcilable with other paired comparisons that he or she has previously made.

As an example, note that the inconsistency ratio shown in figure 7.6 is higher than recommended. This is because there are inconsistent scores in figure 7.5B.

To see this look at figure 7.5B and observe financial viability's score against two other criteria – employee availability and leisure opportunities. Financial viability has been scored as moderately more important than the first and strongly more important than the second. Yet the first, employee availability, has been scored as quite strongly LESS important than the second – leisure opportunities. This is inconsistent, and one feature for which *Expert Choice* is well known is its tenacity for reminding users whenever they are being inconsistent. Usually, users will alter their scores to make them more consistent.

Yet it is important to reiterate that the *Expert Choice* instruction manual advises users that whenever the package keeps telling them their judgements are inconsistent they should stand by their judgements if they still seem valid. It rightly points out some problems can be legitimately inconsistent, to the point where the inconsistency generates slightly intransitive rankings, as illustrated in figure 7.5B above. Such inconsistency must be retained if *Expert Choice* is to reflect the problem in a way that is sufficiently accurate to lead to possibly new and original insights.

There is something strange about this exhortation. If users leave their scores displaying unadulterated inconsistency, the 'rational' scoring mechanisms of *Expert Choice* will be violated, and so the final, unitary scores for the policies that it generates will be inaccurate. On the other hand, if users clear up their inconsistency, the manual is arguing that their ability to think laterally might be impaired. *Expert Choice* seems to have a split personality. It is primarily a generator of accurate scores for alternative policies, yet its manual says it is willing to sacrifice accuracy in order that it functions as an ideas stimulator.

Lesson 48: Persist

Whenever a problem is so mysteriously complicated that inconsistency is rife, policymaking's recommendations will probably be inaccurate.

One should therefore try to re-formulate the goal hierarchy in the hope that greater clarity is achieved. Alternatively, one could cut one's losses and go to a package like *CyberQuest* in search of new and different creative ideas. Later, after such ideas have been crystallized and clarified sufficiently into integrated policy alternatives, one might re-use evaluation software to choose between them.

Indeed, the best policymaking practice probably involves flipping from brainstorming to evaluation according to the stage in the policymaking process that has been reached. But in order to tame some of the more vicious problems, this may have to occur several times. Persist with the flexible approach.

In other words, *Expert Choice* appears to want it both ways. On the one hand its careful use of the paired comparisons method ensures that users score alternative policies as accurately as possible - its inconsistency coefficient even alerts users to when they may have lost concentration and so made some inaccurate judgements.

On the other hand it does not insist that users change their apparently inconsistent judgements. It holds off from doing this just in case inconsistency really does reflect a reality that is more complex than the reality that can be conveyed by 'consistent' software.

7.3. Reviewing the Ratings

Once the user of *Expert Choice* has made all the necessary paired comparisons, a bar chart of the policies' scores, like that shown in figure 7.7 can be obtained. It is important to understand what it is showing. The bars represent, for each policy, how much they scored in terms of contributing to their parent nodes, what the latter scored in terms of contributing to their own parent nodes, and so on. Remember that when there are many layers, that is, great grandparents and great great grandparents, scoring is continued all the way up to the goal at the top of the tree. And since all ratings on each layer have been standardized to a number less than one, the different ratings for each policy up the different branches of the tree can simply be multiplied together in order to calculate their total score.

Note that *Expert Choice* has several menu items that allow the user to study exactly why the scores for the alternative policies have come out the way that they have. For example, figure 7.8A shows why Los Angeles scored 14% better than New York – it defeats it on all criteria except the availability of business support services. Moreover, figure 7.8B shows why Los Angeles scored more than the Atlanta alternative by an even greater margin – it has been scored higher on every criterion, albeit only marginally for culture, leisure opportunities and climate.

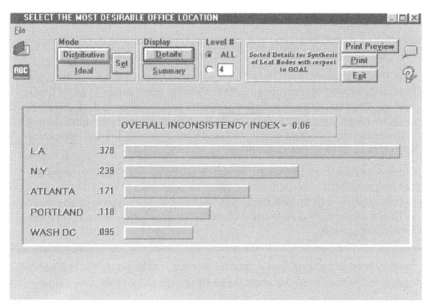

Figure 7.7. *Expert Choice's* showing alternatives' aggregated scores.

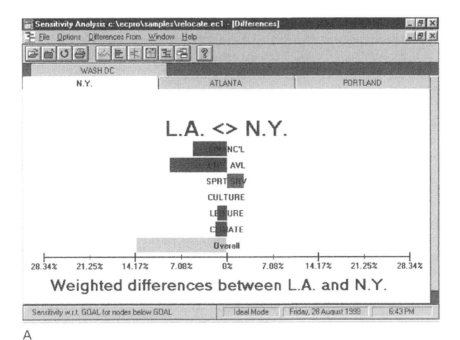

A

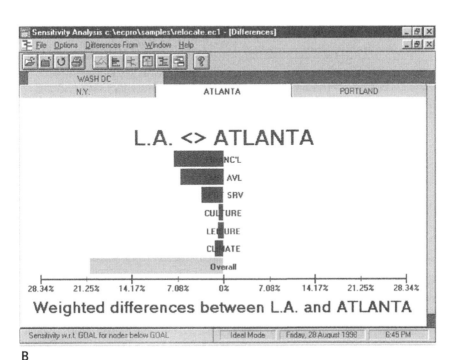

B

Figure 7.8. *Expert Choice* explaining the final result.

7.3.1. Re-scoring

It should be remembered that making the paired comparisons can be very tedious. This is because *Expert Choice* permits up to seven elements on any level of the hierarchy, which means it might take $6 + 5 + 4 + 3 + 2 = 20$ comparisons to score all of the elements in just one part of the goals hierarchy. This is quite demanding of any user's concentration, and if there are several levels in the hierarchy, the amount of comparing that needs to be done before one can get a rating for each bottom-line policy is prodigious. This is why the software allows users, if they are re-considering their ratings, to make comparisons in a quicker way.

A screen for verbally adjusting ratings is given in figure 7.9A, and an example of a screen used for adjusting ratings graphically is shown in figure 7.9B. In figure 7.9A the user is able to simply click on more accurate ratings, and this will change the words on the top of the screen. That is, the user sees the linguistic consequences of changes to scores. Alternatively, in figure 7.9B the user clicks on the dots on the bottom right in order to see the length of the horizontal bars, and the relative proportions of the circle, change in response. In this way, users can see the graphical consequence of changes to scores. In either case, whenever a bar or a segment is altered, the other one changes automatically to retain the totality of these two elements' original proportions. Screens such as those in figure 7.9 are made available mainly to save time. But also, some users feel more comfortable rating things graphically, whereas others prefer to do it numerically.

Lesson 49: Vary your methods

One needs to employ a variety of methods to extract from participants their views on alternative policies. This is because different people respond differently to different methods of software presentation - verbal, numerical, graphical and whatever, as school teachers have known for years.

Hence any one group of people, unless they have been psychologically tested and found to be very similar in terms of their preferences, should be offered a variety of policy-scoring methods.

If participants are given a choice, the chances of their being committed, interested and accurate greatly increase. Varied methods keep the participants interested.

7.3.2. Sensitivity analysis

As well as its ability to keep a close check on the consistency of its users' judgements, the other hallmark of *Expert Choice* is its ability to analyse the consequences of such judgements. This is achieved by 'sensitivity analysis', which the user can access by clicking on the 'Sensitivity-Graphs' menu item. As an example, figure 7.10 shows the 'dynamic' form of sensitivity analysis. Relative scores for the alternative office locations are shown by the figures and bars in the

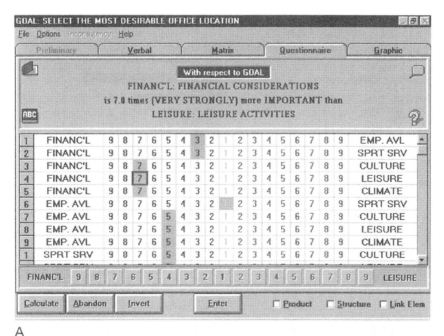

A

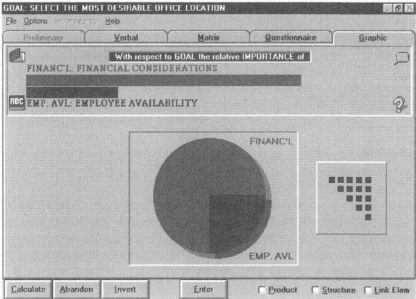

B

Figure 7.9. *Expert Choice* re-scoring.

right hand column, and the importance levels of the evaluation criteria, which were used to reach such conclusions, are shown in the left hand column.

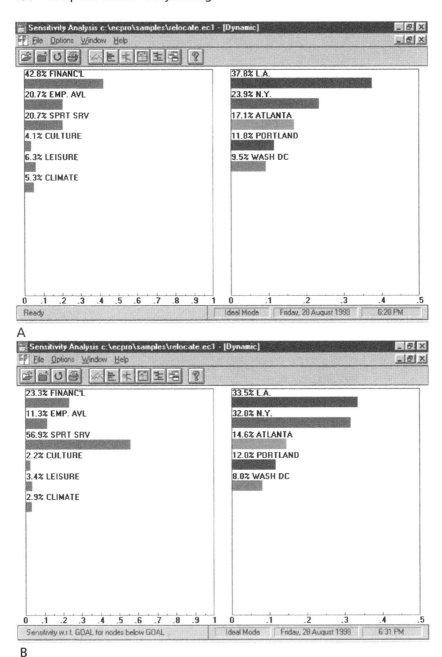

Figure 7.10. *Expert Choice* conducting dynamic sensitivity analysis.

Figure 7.10 is referred to as 'dynamic' because it is possible for the user to 'mouse drag' any bar on the left to increase, or decrease the importance of some criterion – the other bars will automatically adjust their lengths. Moreover, whenever this is done, the bars in the right hand column will also adjust their lengths. Hence the ratings of the alternative policies that result from changes in the criteria's importance levels are automatically shown – a clear picture is given of how sensitive any ranking is to changes in criterion priorities.

An example is shown in figure 7.10B where a user has mouse dragged the importance of the 'support services' criterion to a value of 56.9% and so the importance levels of the other criteria have correspondingly shrunk. Such a change boosts the desirability of New York to a level that approaches Los Angeles' rating, because New York is strong on 'support services'. Note that the importance of this criterion, because it has been boosted, now contributes more to each city's final score, although those places with less impressive scores for 'support services' are affected the least.

Another type of sensitivity graph which users can ask *Expert Choice* to generate is shown in figure 7.11. Here the slopes of the lines indicate how much the policies' overall desirability scores will alter if one changes the importance of the 'financial viability' criterion. Note that New York and Atlanta obviously have the largest scores for financial viability because their slopes are the greatest, closely followed by Los Angeles. Moreover, Washington DC performs in only an average way when it comes to this criterion because its slope is flat, and Portland performs poorly for financial profitability, as shown by its negative slope.

Hence the more importance that is assigned to financial viability, the more poorly Portland will score overall compared to the other policies. In fact, the user is able to move the position of the vertical line in figure 7.11 either to raise or lower the

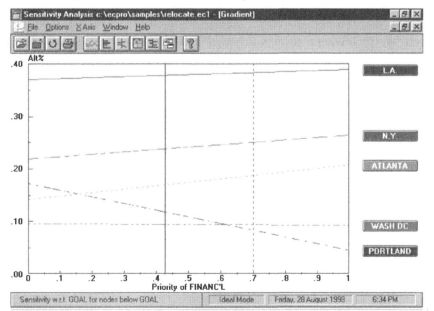

Figure 7.11. *Expert Choice* conducting gradient sensitivity analysis.

importance of financial viability from its current level of just over 0.4. If so, one can see that as soon as the importance of financial viability becomes greater than 0.65, Washington DC actually becomes a more desirable location than Portland.

This is further illustrated by the screen shown in figure 7.12A, which is generated by clicking on 'Sensitivity-Graphs/Performance'. Again, it shows that Portland has the lowest financial viability and this, along with its scores on the other criteria, means that it ranks second last overall. However, it can also be seen that Portland scores second highest on 'employee availability' and has the highest score of all for 'leisure facilities'. Therefore, if the user alters the importance levels of the 'employee availability' and 'leisure facilities' criteria, by mouse dragging their vertical bars in figure 7.12B to new heights (the heights of the other bars will adjust automatically), then Portland becomes second only to Los Angeles in overall desirability. Such a situation has plausibility because it may be related to the growth of 'high tech' industries in Oregon. The north-west of the United States contains many young, educated workers, and such workers place considerable importance on the environmental quality of the place where they are to live and recreate – 'leisure facilities'.

It should now be fairly clear that *Expert Choice* is very strong on detailed sensitivity analysis. Its instructions manual consequently recommends that users apply as much sensitivity testing as they can in order to see why the alternative policies' scores do not sometimes reflect anticipated levels of desirability. If so, users might wish to re-consider some of the ratings that they have assigned to criterion importance levels, to probabilities and so on. Alternatively, they might change their 'gut feeling' about the relative desirability levels of the alternative policies, because using *Expert Choice* has actually alerted them to various subtleties about the problem situation which they hitherto did not recognize. Such consciousness expansion is, after all, the aim of all software described in this book.

Lesson 50: Expand your consciousness

Policymaking is mostly about consciousness expansion. Thus when dealing with very wicked problems it can be misleading simply to assign scores to alternative policies. Such scores could be spuriously accurate and hence misleading.

It is better to try to increase participants' knowledge about the range of feasible options. Participants will then be well placed to exercise their powers of synthesis, based on worldly experience. Hold off from assigning scores until you are sure you have explored the full gamut of possibilities.

7.3.3. Extending the software

One should never underestimate *Expert Choice*'s versatility, or its rich potential for consciousness expansion. Indeed, this and all the other chapters have only

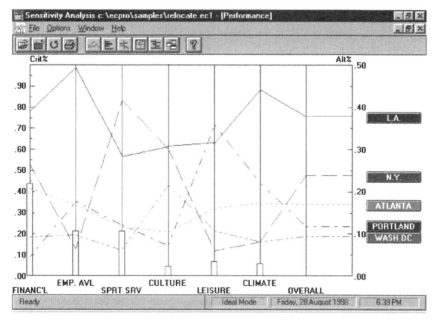

A

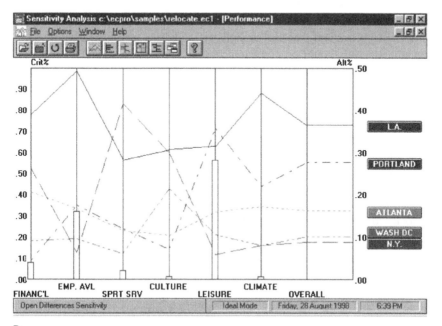

B

Figure 7.12. *Expert Choice* showing the performance of each alternative on each criterion.

conveyed the essentials of the packages described, and so they have not described many other menu items and their associated functions.

For example, *Expert Choice* can actually handle problems where there are perhaps hundreds of alternatives, even though there is normally a limit of seven alternatives in the standard application of the package. The instructions manual explains that this function would be useful, for example, when one is using *Expert Choice* to rate hundreds of job applicants in terms of their ability to perform.

One would proceed by setting up a hierarchy in the usual way, with nodes on the second level covering all the criteria that one might use to evaluate applicants' job suitability, such as 'dependability', 'education' and 'experience'. Moreover, one would compare such evaluation criteria for importance in the usual, paired comparisons way. Then, beneath such nodes one would insert *ratings*, as distinct from alternative policies.

For instance, ratings for the 'dependability' criterion might be 'outstanding', 'very good', 'good', 'below average' and 'unsatisfactory'. These would be assessed in the usual, paired comparisons way, to show their impacts on job performance. For example, an applicant whose dependability was 'outstanding' might have a job-performance potential of say, 0.479, whereas one whose dependability was 'very good' might have a score of say, 0.275.

All evaluation criteria could likewise be broken down into ratings, not necessarily always in terms of 'outstanding' versus 'very good'. For example, the education criterion could be divided into the 'doctorate', 'masters', 'bachelors', and 'high school' categories, and then the strength of candidates who hold each of these educational levels could be compared in the usual, paired comparisons way. Moreover, the experience criterion could be broken into say, categories of 'over 15 years', '6-15 years', '3-5 years' and '1-2 years' experience and again, scored for importance.

Hence it becomes a simple matter to score any applicant for desirability. One simply assigns each applicant to a set of bottom level nodes. More exactly, each job applicant would take up one line of the spreadsheet, and each number in each column would give that applicant's rating for dependability, education, experience and so forth. A formula in the right most column would then incorporate all of the *Expert Choice* derived weights, and it would instantly and automatically calculate the total score for as many job applicants as there were on the spreadsheet.

Also, when it comes to complex optimization *Expert Choice* employs a similar tactic. It will not find the optimal strategy itself, but it is used in conjunction with some spreadsheet-based optimization program to actually boost the performance of the latter. *Expert Choice*'s user manual outlines an example. It concerns the choice of magazines in which to advertise one's product. Each magazine has a different sort of readership profile, a different circulation level and different advertising charges.

Now, spreadsheet-based optimization programs indicate in which magazines one ought to place advertisements so that potential 'new sales per dollar spent on advertising' is maximized, and they require several inputs. Such inputs include the total amount that the company is willing to spend on advertising, the readership of each magazine, its cost per advertisement and its potential for catching the eye of typical company customers. Notice how such inputs are simply numbers to be found by research, except for the last one – estimates of each magazine's 'eye-catching potential'. The latter can usually only be arrived at through a mixture of quantitative and qualitative judgements.

Enter *Expert Choice*. It is applied to each magazine. Its 'overall goal' is something like 'eye catching potential' or 'probability of reading the magazine', and its second layer nodes list customer attributes such as income, all of which are scored for importance. It then assesses the magazine-buying potential of various ratings for the second-layer nodes. For instance, levels for the 'income' attribute might be expressed as percentages of that magazine's readership who have incomes greater than $30,000 per annum, percentages of readers who earn greater than $40,000 and so on. Different scores for magazine-reading potential can then be assigned to such income ratings according to how likely it is that people with such an income rating will be attracted by a company advertisement.

Hence by noting the statistics on how its readership is spread across the income groups, *Expert Choice* can estimate a magazine's aggregated, eye-catching potential. Such information can then be fed to the spreadsheet-based, optimization software.

7.4. Summary

The measurement methods within *Expert Choice* have been considerably scrutinized in the literature, some of which will be covered in Chapter 9 below. In the meantime we should briefly note the package's strengths. It certainly does seem to be superior to both *CyberQuest* and *STRAD* at boiling down complex problems into a number of alternative policies and then assisting the user to choose rigorously between them. It cuts straight to the bone of the policymaking process – choice of alternatives.

However, *Expert Choice* thereby loses *CyberQuest*'s ability to stimulate lateral thinking and *STRAD*'s ability to raise awareness of problem complexities. Hence it may err a little towards the 'thinking' end of the thinking-feeling continuum of software styles.

Its hallmarks are its consistency-checking mechanism and its extensive sensitivity testing. Yet the latter brings with it the same dangers reported in the discussion of *STRAD* – users are able to get 'any answer they want' provided they are willing to alter some of their ratings. Hence *Expert Choice*'s capacity for self-delusion, or even for group delusion when policymaking is undertaken in a group setting, are as high as *STRAD*'s.

Put differently, it is possible that *Expert Choice*'s sensitivity tests will erode users' confidence in the wisdom of the recommended policy. They might finish up thinking that many alternative policies seem to be 'best', depending on the relative importance levels placed on a plethora of factors that they find very hard to measure anyway. This can breed cynicism and a nihilistic attitude towards the whole policymaking process.

Lesson 51: Count your blessings

Some packages try to help a policymaker address a complex problem by mapping out an unprecedented level of simultaneous, detailed considerations. But in so doing they can erode confidence that one will ever be able to 'get to the bottom' of the complex policymaking problem.

To them it seems that the more complexity the software takes control of, the more new complexity it reveals. This process is like peeling an onion – the more layers of mystery that are stripped off, the more layers of extra mystery one discovers.

For users who are anxious to come to grips with a policymaking problem straight away, this can be very disconcerting. But all that one can reasonably do is persist, and be thankful that at least our understanding of the problem is now much greater than when we started.

Such an attitude, even when justified, is hardly productive if it is important to make an urgent decision, and if it is not important to make a decision then why make policy at all? To make a final decision we need to be confident (some might say deluded) that the scoring mechanism we have used is not 'rubbery' in the sense that any policy we like can be justified as 'best' simply by altering a few parameter scores. *Strategizer* has some potential here, so we will now direct our attention to this package.

Chapter 8

Frontier Software Case IV: *Strategizer*

Like *Expert Choice*, *Strategizer* rates alternative policies, but it does so in a way that the user finds impossible to control. This is because it uses a simulated, neural network (McClelland and Rumelhart 1988; Nelson and Illingworth, 1991). The latter is better at accommodating the non-linearities, discontinuities, inaccuracies and fragmented data (Noorderhaven, 1995) that are associated with policymaking. As such, *Strategizer*'s neural network may constitute a more effective method than traditional, statistical approaches for anticipating people's policy choices. Moreover, it would theoretically get better and better at such anticipation the more it is used – the system would 'self improve', even when confronted with policies that it has not seen before. In short, *Strategizer* is potentially the quintessential software for assisting humans in the 'anticipate' phase of the policymaking process (Harrison and St John, 1994).

More specifically, *Strategizer*'s neural network trains itself to replicate the way in which various groups of past users make policy. It 'learns' how to replicate the patterns of emphasis they place on different evaluation criteria *whatever policymaking problem is being addressed*. Such an extravagant claim is based on a partially-tested assumption that there exists a set of ten, universal, policy-evaluation criteria that are always thought about by everyone, albeit sometimes only sub-consciously, in all instances of policymaking.

In other words, *Strategizer*'s hallmark is its claimed ability to anticipate how different groups of people make policy. Until now, consideration of how the various community groups might rate different policies seems to have been performed only in a vague, 'guestimating' sort of way by human policymakers at workshops. But here is some software with the potential to do it more rigorously.

The author has been developing *Strategizer* for about ten years. It was formerly called the *Intelligent Planning Machine* and it has since passed through several incarnations that were written in various computer programming languages. Earlier versions were similar to *Strad* in the sense that their purpose was to organize and to clarify all of the confusing data that surround human-oriented policymaking. This is why, at one time, *Strategizer* was simply called *PITS* – the Planners' Initial Thought Straightener (Wyatt, 1988).

The package cannot claim to have been applied to a multitude of problems like the previous three, research frontier packages. It is still rather experimental software.

It has only been used seriously, in its latest, self-improving form, by about sixty people drawn from student classes and staff in academic institutions. Nevertheless, the range of problems that such people have addressed, and left in its associated database of past cases, is wide enough to demonstrate the generic applicability of *Strategizer*, as shown in table 8.1.

Table 8.1. Some problems that have been addressed by *Strategizer*.

Antarctica national park? restricted uses? eco tourism?	Asian forests logging ban? economic sanctions? economic aid?
Clean air public transport? better cars? dearer petrol?	Clean river less stormwater? less industry? passive land uses?
Kangaroos culling? sterilization?	Murders executions? rehabilitation? life sentences?
Scallops alternative methods? total ban? licences?	Soil erosion revegetation? land use changes? farming changes?
Soil salinity education? rehabilitation? revegetation?	Species pest reduction? better habitat? land use practices?
Wetlands monitoring? protection? maintenance?	

Moreover, a version of *Strategizer*, known as *StratBuild*, has been used extensively to give advice within the specialized, 'client briefing' area of the architecture and building discipline (Smith, Kenley and Wyatt, 1998). *StratBuild* differs from *Strategizer* in that the explanatory windows used to clarify the ten, universal evaluation criteria have been tailored to give building-design type examples. Apart from this, the two programs are identical. As such, *Strategizer* could perhaps be further modified, in the future, so that any user can be given a choice of help routines according to the discipline in which they are working.

Note that like *CyberQuest*, *Strategizer* handles the problem of over complexity by focusing on just one part of the policymaking process. But it concentrates neither on the generation of ideas like *CyberQuest* does, nor on the recording, scoring or sensitivity testing of possible policies like *STRAD* and *Expert Choice* do; it devotes itself entirely to 'learning' how to rate policies in the way that groups of past users would. This is why other packages are better at tolerating the delicate discussion, the intrigue and the negotiation that always surrounds policymaking. *Strategizer* is much more dour. It is absolutely determined to go straight to the stage where it is able to evaluate policies on behalf of other groups.

This is not to imply that *Strategizer* cannot be used to underpin a detailed workshop in which policymakers discuss, cooperatively, a complicated problem. It is just that once any such workshop group has agreed upon the goal and on the sub- . . . goals to be pursued, *Strategizer* goes straight into evaluation mode from which it is hard to divert it. Users cannot even nominate their own evaluation criteria – the same criteria are used for every problem.

We saw above, when discussing the *CyberQuest* package, that such a specialized focus may or may not be a good thing in policymaking practice. A stubborn intent to get straight to the 'business end' of policymaking – the scoring of alternatives, is good for efficiency but possibly disastrous for encouraging discussion of wide-ranging and innovative ideas. Packages like *CyberQuest* and *Strategizer* might force an outcome to be achieved every time, by driving users hard towards evaluation of concrete policies, but the quality of their recommendations may suffer through their haste to get to the evaluation stage.

Accordingly, the 'front end' of a package like *Strategizer* must always be extensive human discussion. This needs to proceed for as long as it takes to canvass as wide a range of ideas as is possible. Human participants might wish to use a package like *STRAD* in order to help them do this, because the eventual quality of the suggestions made by any software is only as good as the quality of the policies fed to it at the start.

8.1. Constructing a Hierarchy

Because *Strategizer* is keen to 'learn' about people's different policymaking styles, its first priority is to collect data about each of its users so that it can later observe the demographic characteristics of the differently acting sub-groups. Hence it will not let any users start until they have nominated their age, sex, number of children, highest qualification and occupation, as shown by figure 8.1. It also asks for the user's role in the policymaking problem that is being addressed. Hence later on, when *Strategizer* makes some recommendation that it has 'learned' will probably be favoured by some group, it will also be able to supply some data about the characteristics of the people in that group.

Lesson 52: Seek psychological insights

Initial collection of some personal data could function as an 'ice breaking' activity by which people can get to know each other better. Such data will then help people work together more easily.

Yet such information can often fuel people's prejudices about how certain sorts of people think. If members of the policymaking team introduce themselves, and if other members look at such people's physical appearance while this is taking place, the observers might instantly make up their minds as to why such a person is going to say certain things later. Observers are therefore very likely to miss some of the subtlety and depth of this particular person's contribution. Be more perceptive.

Note that *Strategizer* will itself sort, off-line, users into groups. It does not do this on the basis of prejudices as humans often do. It does so entirely on the basis of users' revealed policymaking styles, and in such a way that the contrasts in policymaking style between clusters of people are maximized, and the contrasts between people's styles within groups are minimized. Hence if a cluster of people is dominated by say, elderly females, then this cluster's policymaking style will be concluded to be characteristic of elderly females. As another example, if another cluster's membership is predominantly say, people with children, then that cluster's policymaking style will be deemed symptomatic of people with children.

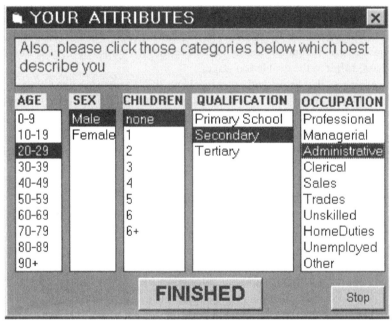

Figure 8.1. *Strategizer* collecting information about the user.

Not only are such assignations of policymaking styles to various types of people likely to be different from people's prejudices on such matters, but finding certain individuals within certain clusters is sometimes likely to be counter intuitive. Hence human type pre-judgements about the way certain people think and go about policymaking will have been neutralized by the package and replaced by more exact analysis of such things. Ultimately, this should result in more accurate, sympathetic and perceptive policymaking.

8.1.1. Identifying the client and options
In keeping with this 'softly, softly' approach designed to encourage users to interact with the computer honestly, *Strategizer* gently guides users through the process of entering their goals and sub-goals. The screen for starting such a process is shown

in figure 8.2, which appears whenever a user clicks 'Begin a new case' on the main menu. The software is asking who the user is planning for. Subsequently it will ask what the overall goal is – the 'aim', and it will ask for up to the three most important sub-goals, which it calls 'options', that help one to achieve this aim.

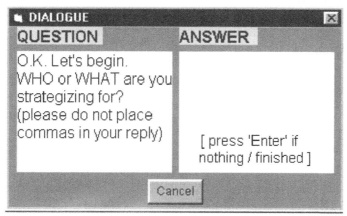

Figure 8.2. *Strategizer* beginning a new case.

Note also that *Strategizer* is straight away forcing the user's thinking into the goals hierarchy mould. That is, as part of its thrust towards evaluation of alternative policies, *Strategizer* encourages users to think of their input options as sub-goals to be pursued in an ordered, hierarchical way. Indeed, simultaneously with the user inputting their aim and options (and possibly sub-options and sub-sub-options), *Strategizer* draws the corresponding goals hierarchy on the other half of the computer screen, and an example of this is shown in figure 8.3.

The policymaking problem shown in this figure involves striving towards an overall aim of 'fewer murders' and the client is 'society'. Moreover, there are three options which might be pursued in order to achieve this aim – 'executions', 'rehabilitation' and 'life sentences' for murderers. As usual, such headlining of options is so that they fit onto the computer screen, but the software actually records everything that users type in when they describe the client, the aim and the options (there is no limit on the number of words allowed). Users can thereafter, at any stage of the policymaking process, get clarification of such things by clicking on 'Clarify', which forces their original descriptions to appear.

Note also that users can delete, rename and add more sub-options. For example, sub-options that contribute towards the achievement of 'rehabilitation' might be 'community integration' and 'public education', whereas sub-options of 'public education' might be 'publicity' and 'school visits'.

Now, the number of sub-options allowed at any part of the goals hierarchy is initially three. Users are then asked whether there is a wild, 'off the wall' option that could possibly be considered. If they answer 'yes' they are asked what it is, and so it is entered as a fourth option. Of course, such a ploy has been inserted to encourage users to 'think outside the circle' in the interests of innovation and greater originality.

Also, users are asked if the 'do nothing' option is a possibility. In its haste to find solutions, policymaking frequently fails to consider the consequences of doing nothing at all. But in some circumstances this may be the best policy. Hence *Strategizer* forces users to think about the 'do nothing' option.

In total therefore, there can be up to five sub-options in any part of the goals hierarchy, and since *Strategizer* allows up to three levels of options, this means that its hierarchy can theoretically handle up to 5 x 5 x 5 = 125 sub- . . . options. In practice, this should not occur because it simply takes too long to score so many sub-options on the ten evaluation criteria. Therefore for very large problems, it is far more practical to use *Strategizer* several times. More specifically, *Strategizer* is first used to compare broad, overall, abstracted strategic directions in which to go.

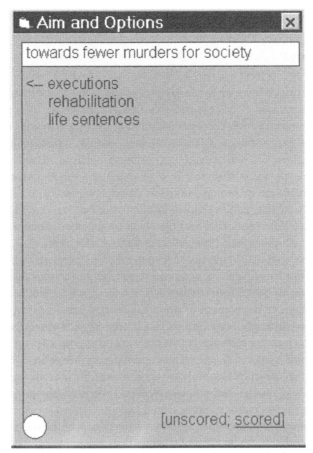

Figure 8.3. *Strategizer* documenting a typical case.

Then, after one such direction has been chosen as the best, *Strategizer* is used again to compare alternative, slightly less abstract and more concrete options for getting us in this direction. After one of the latter has been chosen, the software can be run yet again at a more concrete level still.

8.1.2. Formal versus informal policymaking

Such an approach certainly makes policymaking more manageable, but it begs the question of whether such an hierarchical approach actually constitutes best policymaking practice. On the one hand it seems eminently logical to begin with broad concepts and then, after some overall direction has been chosen, to detail different ways of achieving such a broad policy thrust. But what happens if detailed analyses of the 'nuts and bolts' of the problem situation suggests that some other, non-chosen strategic thrust would have been better? In such circumstances it would obviously have been better to start with all the details and intricacies of the problem situation, in the style of *Strad* and *Expert Choice*, and then build policy gradually, from the bottom up – to adopt a 'feeling' style rather than a 'thinking' style.

But this question will never be resolved. Those who favour bottom up policymaking point out that the top down approach, by failing first to study the details of each strategic direction, has no basis on which to compare the alternative directions anyway. It could therefore make serious errors. Alternatively, the top down policymakers argue that they have enough 'feel' for the relative merits of the broad alternatives in order to judge between them. Moreover, if they went straight to the details of the problem they would risk becoming hopelessly confused by data overload. And data overload can have the serious consequence that one might become sidetracked into certain analyses at the expense of seeing the 'big picture'. Thus one would miss a complete swathe of policy space that harbours the best policy direction. In other words, the bottom up approach might lead to 'local hill climbing' to reach a locally optimal, as distinct from a globally optimal solution.

However, if the top down approach really is too ill informed to make valid judgements, the consequences of taking this approach will probably be even worse. At least the bottom up approach is able to get its teeth into some serious comparative work in order to hone a policy that is a lot better than lots of other policies. But the top down approach, if it takes completely the wrong direction at the start, is likely to lead to utter disaster.

In any event, *Strategizer* opts more for the top down, hierarchical approach. As such, many users will find it difficult to accept that each part of the goals hierarchy insists on containing no more than five sub-options – it seems to be too few. After all, *Expert Choice* allowed up to seven, and even this number sometimes seemed insufficient. But *Strategizer* limits the number of (sub-) options for the sake of (hierarchical) manageability. If one has more options they have to be grouped into five or fewer conceptual approaches. Although this is always possible to do, people who favour the bottom up approach will always resist it – they will be suspicious of the seemingly brutal simplifying assumptions of hierarchy building.

Lesson 53: Top down versus bottom up policymaking

If we know enough about a situation to be able to judge between alternative policy directions, then an abstract, synoptic, 'top down' approach is best. It takes the widest, all inclusive view and so reduces the chances of misplaced effort.

But if the problem setting is truly mysterious, then we really have no choice but to take a detailed, analytical, 'bottom up' approach. Indeed, some professions, such as architecture and to some extent medicine and law, trade on this. Clients simply assume that the all-seeing professionals can, through immersion in the problem's complexities over a long period, craft a solution that is optimal. They will do this by utilizing the resources, intuition and insights to which less experienced people are not privy (Alexander, 1964).

Yet many people see such a stance as a smokescreen for making money. It can actually obscure a tendency for a profession to progress in completely inappropriate ways due to misconceived 'group think'. That is, professionalization can actually lead to inflexible thinking even though it began on a foundation of bottom up, professional expertise.

Nor is policymaking completely immune from this; it sometimes uses case-based reasoning. The latter involves assembling many past cases, in comparable problem settings, where various solutions were tried, with different observed results. One is able to then craft a policy which seems to be the most advisable.

Case based reasoning is in fact endemic throughout business schools, Western medicine and Western law. But all of these professions have been severely criticized for conservatism, lack of imagination and perpetuation of current malpractice.

Hence sincere policymakers should treat policymaking of the case-based kind with caution. They should be wary of all forms of bottom-up approaches that actually evolve into misdirected, top-down stances that are far too myopic.

Yet the hierarchy is not only an efficiency mechanism. It is also an antidote for various problems that plague poor policymaking, for example, 'premature specificity', as explained in Lesson 54. More specifically, *Strategizer* makes users encapsulate their problem into a maximum of five options. This is to parry a human tendency to move prematurely, in terms of possible policies, straight to the details of a problem, rather than taking a more considered, strategic and hence more laterally-thinking stance (Noorderhaven, 1995, p. 26).

Thus a first, conceptual-level running of *Strategizer* is recommended. It will enable policymakers to allocate their precious time better. Then, during the second and subsequent applications of the package they will be able gradually to zero in, always in a lateral thinking sort of way, to the more concrete options. In other words, our use of *Strategizer* demands that any detailed, third-level sub-options that are eventually analysed must first earn their status as serious contenders through a comparative evaluation of their parent goals. By encouraging conceptual goals at the start and comparing them, *Strategizer* is able to cast the net of possible options very widely. In other words, the limiting of sub- . . . options to five at any one time, paradoxically, forces consideration of a much wider range of options than if premature specificity were permitted, as it is in *STRAD* and *Expert Choice*.

Lesson 54: Avoid premature specificity

Consider an urban policymaker aiming at 'quality of life' for a city's inhabitants. Policies for achieving this might include 'buses', 'taxis', 'trains', 'trees', 'parks', 'pollution by-laws', 'local jobs' and 'local democracy'. But deciding straight away on one or some of these would be prematurely specific.

This is because people do not necessarily want buses for their own sake – they want 'mobility'. 'Buses' are only one way of achieving mobility. 'Trains', 'taxis', 'freeways', 'cycling paths' and 'canals' are perhaps better ways. Similarly, people do not always want 'parks' – they want 'amenity'; they may not really want 'jobs' but 'self worth', and so on.

Thus, rather than place 'buses', 'parks' and 'jobs' at the second level of a goals hierarchy, the policymaker needs to insert something like 'mobility', 'amenity' and 'self worth'. This means that maximum abstraction is maintained and no concrete policy; 'taxis' for instance, is rejected prematurely. Indeed, policymakers would be forced to first weigh up the respective merits of 'mobility' versus 'amenity' versus 'self worth' before they do anything else.

Such reasoning can be extended. For example, one might defer the placement of concrete options, like 'buses' and 'trains', under the 'mobility' option. Instead, abstractions like 'public transport' versus 'private transport' could be inserted and decided upon. Yet if policymakers simply specify, prematurely, that it is to be 'buses' versus 'trains', no such thinking can occur. Hence options like 'buses' and 'trains' should not even be mentioned until at least the third level. Moreover, time should only be spent considering such alternatives if one has decided 'mobility', as distinct from 'amenity' and 'self worth', and 'public transport' rather than 'private transport' are worth pursuing.

That is, one should proceed towards the ultimate, concrete policy in a considered and careful, rather than in a premature way. Beware of premature specificity and the narrow and muddled excuse for analytical thinking that it can obscure.

By the same token, multiple applications of *Strategizer* at increasing levels of concreteness will make the exercise as specific as we want; it will get us close to using *Strategizer* for telling us exactly 'what to do tomorrow' – the essence of policymaking. Hence although the name *Strategizer* suggests that it is suitable only for broad policymaking, *Strategizer* can also be useful for more tactical and day-to-day policymaking – provided it is used in a hierarchical fashion. It has an ability to move between the conceptually abstract and the pragmatically concrete.

8.1.3. Accumulating knowledge

Note that throughout the options-entering phase, and indeed throughout all phases of the *Strategizer* program, whenever one clicks on text that is written in a blue colour one will be rewarded with an explanatory window. For instance, the '[unscored; scored]' text of figure 8.3 appears in blue and so when a user clicks this text the explanatory window that is shown in figure 8.4 appears. This figure indicates that two explanation levels can be activated – another explanation can be obtained by clicking on the 'Further Explanation' button.

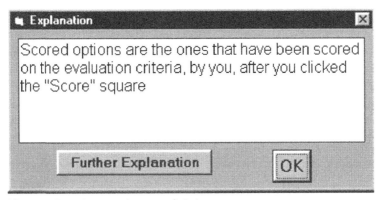

Figure 8.4. *Strategizer* explaining a term.

These two explanations are usually enough for users to understand what they need to know in order to proceed, and it is one reason why *Strategizer* does not have an instructions manual – the explanatory windows seem to suffice on their own. Such a facility fits in with the modern computer practice of providing extensive help routines by enabling users to click on blue text in order to make something else happen, as happens with most web-connected documents. Indeed, much of the power of the World Wide Web stems from such linkages, and this is something that policymaking practice could perhaps take note of.

Such a lesson, prompted simply by a brief observation of the style of *Strategizer*'s help routines and of web pages, seems obvious enough. Indeed, futurist computer scientists have actually taken it one step further, as we saw in Chapter 3. Distributed computing's concept of a 'collective intelligence' is exciting. In it, no one project has a comprehensive perception of how it is contributing overall to the advancement of practice, but taken all together the power of the complete collective of individual policymaking efforts would be awesome.

Lesson 55: Get connected

If policymaking exercises would make linkages to similar projects elsewhere, similarities and contrasts could be highlighted and explored, and so the quality of policymaking would almost certainly increase.

Yet practitioners seldom make such linkages. Looking at what has already happened seems too much like a dreary postmortem. It is far more exciting to plunge straight into one's own, 'unique' policymaking situation. But most policymaking situations are far from unique, and so depriving oneself of the lessons learned by those who have gone before actually limits one's capacity to make policy properly.

We are not recommending that comparisons between policymaking exercises be made in the facile style of much case-based reasoning; we are recommending that incisive comparisons are made with related policymaking efforts. Indeed, such cross checking is probably the only viable way for any discipline to improve its performance over the long term.

University researchers discovered this at least four hundred years ago, and today the world-wide interconnections between researchers underpins virtually all research-based, expanding disciplines. Why not establish connections between policymakers also?

8.2. Scoring the Policies

Strategizer will not be able to evaluate options unless the user clicks 'Score' and then assigns ratings for the options on each of the evaluation criteria. The latter process requires working through ten screens, one for each evaluation criterion in turn, and an example of one such screen is shown in figure 8.5. Note that for this screen an explanation window appears automatically so as to clarify what the current criterion means. This is because it is important that every user has a very accurate understanding of the meaning for each criterion before they proceed further. If they do not, the package's ability to learn criterion importance levels, from successive users, will be impaired because users will have different perceptions of what the different criteria actually measure.

After the user has scored all the policies, by mouse dragging the bars in figure 8.5 to suitable positions, they click the 'Standardize' button. This has the effect of making the (up to) five scores sum to 100.0, and the highest-scoring policy is placed on top, followed by the second and third policies, as shown in figure 8.6. This latter gives users a chance to re-assess their ratings before finally clicking the 'Accept' button. But even after they do this, another button appears in order to ask 'Are you sure?', and so users are given yet another chance to re-consider their ratings. Such caution is advisable because, for the sake of *Strategizer*'s machine-learning routines used later on, it is most important that scoring has been done as accurately as possible.

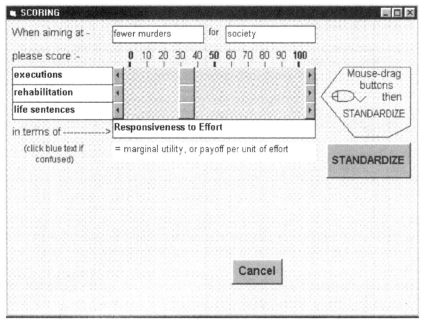

Figure 8.5. *Strategizer* rating policies in terms of the 'responsiveness to effort' criterion.

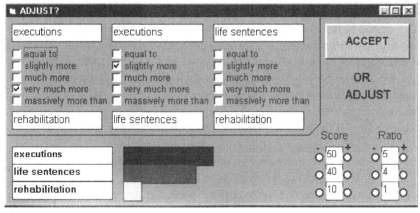

Figure 8.6. *Strategizer* in re-scoring mode.

Notice how in figure 8.6 users are given a choice of the mode in which they can adjust policies' scores. Users can raise or lower the numerical scores by clicking on the plus and minus circles; they can raise or lower their ratios by clicking on the plus and minus circles; or they can rate options in a verbal way. We saw above how *Expert Choice* offers the user a choice of rating methods, because different users feel comfortable with different methods. Yet any procedure that one decides to use will have the same result – it will force a change in the length of the bar for the option concerned, as shown on the bottom left. It will also force changes in the lengths of the bars for all the other policies in order to maintain proportionality.

Hence eventually, scores for all policies on all ten evaluation criteria, will have been entered. The ten 'universal' evaluation criteria are:

➤ *responsiveness to effort* – marginal utility;
➤ *effectiveness* – contribution to achievement of the aim;
➤ *likelihood* – probability of being implemented;
➤ *improvability* – room still left for improvement of this policy;
➤ *permissiveness* – how much it permits pursuit of other policies;
➤ *correctness* – how much it feels like 'the right thing to do';
➤ *speed* – how long it takes to implement;
➤ *ease* – how easy it is to implement;
➤ *autonomy* – non-reliance on other, associated goals;
➤ *safety* – unlikelihood of causing damage.

Strategizer uses these ten because, between them, they seem to cover all the concerns which textbooks say ought to be taken into account whenever one makes policies. But most textbooks on planning and policymaking are about support' disciplines that inhabit the four corners of figure 1.1 above. Hence to find justification for *Strategizer*'s ten criteria, we need to look at literature from each of figure 1.1's four corners.

8.2.1. Scientific criteria

Beginning with the empirical scientists on the top right hand corner of figure 1.1, we see that many psychologists have examined human's policymaking behaviour. Yet although they have reached some consensus that policymaking is actually an attempt to satisfy humans' underlying needs, they have seldom focused on how humans actually decide between such needs. They tend to be more interested in:

The 'concrete' behavioural form of the need itself. (Nuttin, 1984, p. 140)

That is, most behavioural scientists focus on the process of formalizing needs into 'behavioural projects', or policies, rather than examining the initial act of deciding which particular policies should be pursued.

However, there are some exceptions, and such researchers have concluded that choice between motivations depends on each motivations' intensity, or 'valance'. Nuttin (1984) has even suggested some criteria for estimating motivations' valances – 'temporal distance', 'perceived instrumentality', 'reality character' and 'difficulty'. Accordingly, these four policy-evaluation parameters have been adopted by *Strategizer*.

That is, 'difficulty' is actually the obverse of *Strategizer*'s criterion 'ease', and 'temporal distance' is actually the same as *Strategizer*'s criterion of 'speed' – the amount of delay before a motivation will be satisfied. This concept is well known to planners who use critical path and scheduling algorithms – the 'best' plan is the one whose delay sequence, or whose critical path, is the shortest.

Moreover, 'perceived instrumentality' actually means the same as *Strategizer*'s criterion 'effectiveness', and 'reality character' is a quaint way of saying what *Strategizer* refers to as 'likelihood'. Note that, as discussed in Chapter 2, both 'effectiveness' and 'likelihood' are used by policymakers employing the decision trees approach – the 'best' plan is the one whose expected utility, or whose 'effectiveness times likelihood product' is highest.

8.2.2. Operations Research criteria

Moving to the modellers in the top left corner of figure 1.1, some of them conceive policymaking to be a 'simulation' process. They believe that artificially simulating the situation at hand, along with how this situation might alter if it is tampered with, is all one needs for successful policymaking. Such modellers soon become aware of *Strategizer*'s criterion 'autonomy'. This is the concept that recognizes some policies are dependent on the achievement of many other policies for their own attainment, whereas others are more independent.

For instance, a policy such as 'less inflation' is probably dependent on the achievement of other policies such as 'less imports', 'more exports', 'high unemployment' and 'low interest rates', for its own attainment. By contrast, a policy such as 'higher taxes' is more independent. One simply increases taxation rates, and there is little need to achieve related policies. Hence if a policy is overly dependent on a large number of others it is probably less desirable than a more autonomous policy. For this reason autonomy was adopted as *Strategizer*'s fifth policy-evaluation criterion.

Another type of modeller is the optimizer. Such a person sees policymaking as a process of formulating an 'objective function' which has to be maximized or minimized (von Winterfeldt and Edwards, 1986). This involves searching across many alternative combinations of variables in order to test which combination is optimal. For example, when one is planning factory production, one might test a number of combinations of different products to see which of them maximizes company profit. But there is an infinite number of such product mixes within the 'domain of feasible solutions'. Hence the essence of optimization is to jump from one feasible solution to another feasible solution in such a way that each subsequent one found is better than the last one. This is continued until the ultimate, optimal solution is identified.

To achieve such a continuously improving search, any optimizer has to be aware of each product's marginal return or, as *Strategizer* expresses it, its 'responsiveness to effort'. That is, he or she has to be conscious of how much payoff, in terms of improving the objective function, is associated with each extra unit of a variable. This concept is relevant to policymaking – (Burle de Figueiredo and Kaya, 1972), and so 'responsiveness' was adopted as *Strategizer*'s sixth policy-evaluation criterion.

8.2.3. Philosophical criteria

Until now we have considered policy formulation methods that are suitable only for fairly close-ended problems that involve just one, or a few potential policies. Yet human-oriented, wicked problems often involve considering many simultaneous policies. In such situations policymaking is far more problematic. It requires considerable thinking of the type that takes place in the bottom left corner of figure 1.1. But policymaking still gets done, somehow, in such circumstances. Simon (1997) suggested that this is because of 'satisficing' behaviour.

As explained in Chapter 1, satisficing is the process whereby confused policymakers simply accept any policy which yields a satisfactory, as distinct from a best possible solution (Cherniak, 1986). Put another way, within complicated problem domains policymakers do not necessarily optimize – satisfactory achievement of goals is enough. Moreover, satisfactory achievement of goals often means attaining a level of achievement that is an improvement over the current level of satisfaction. Hence in order to identify a satisficing policy, any policymaker needs to have some idea of how well each goal is being satisfied at the moment. It therefore follows that policymakers will often look more favourably on policies that have considerable scope for progress to be made, or 'improvability'. Thus improvability is *Strategizer*'s seventh policy-evaluation criterion.

8.2.4. Workshop criteria

Turning finally to the 'facilitators', at the bottom right of figure 1.1, we see that they are fond of conducting events like policymaking workshops (Bowers and Benford, 1991; Eden, 1992). The latter are discussion groups involving people who have insight into the problem at hand. Such workshops are fuelled by a shared belief that an amicable agreement will eventually be reached about what the best policy is.

But this approach, whilst seemingly better able to clarify the complexities of real-world policymaking, frequently cannot do so. Indeed, workshops often become confused and inconsistent (Russo and Shoemaker, 1989) as well as plagued by over-subjectivity, 'group think', dominance by overbearing individuals and other saboteurs of good policymaking (Janis and Mann, 1977).

Yet despite this, some useful evaluation concepts are usually employed at workshops. One is 'permissiveness', or the propensity of a policy to permit, or at least not to inhibit achievement of other policies. This concept is frequently referred to as 'robustness', and it has a strong pedigree across many types of policymaking. For instance, it is known as 'resilience' in ecological policymaking, as 'flexibility' in budgetary policymaking and as 'hedging' in financial policymaking. Accordingly, 'permissiveness' was adopted as *Strategizer*'s eighth policy-evaluation criterion.

Finally, two other criteria are frequently considered, either implicitly or explicitly, at policymaking workshops. Therefore, these two have also been added to *Strategizer*'s list of 'universal' criteria. The first one is 'correctness', or the extent to which choosing a policy makes one 'feel good'. It may or may not reflect the morality of pursuing a policy. The second is 'safety'.

It should be noted that, true to policymaking software's hierarchical way of thinking, these evaluation criteria are concepts. They are blanket terms that encompass a vast number of potentially more detailed evaluation criteria. For instance, the 'correctness' criterion is an umbrella term that encompasses feelings of righteousness, comfort and morality. Howe (1994) actually conducted a large study of morality amongst strategic planners, and she concluded that morality for some meant 'institutional loyalty', for others it meant 'loyalty to the public' and for still others it meant 'adherence to personal principles'. Moreover, some or all of these might be mixed up to different proportions within the same individual.

Therefore, if we want to predict someone's policymaking behaviour in detail, we do not simply measure the importance they seem to place on say, 'correctness'. We would measure the importance they place on 'institutional loyalty', 'loyalty to the public' and 'loyalty to one's personal principles'. But this would make *Strategizer*, and the whole policymaking process, tedious to the point of impracticality. This is why *Strategizer* settled on ten blanket concepts as the ones that seem to cover, at a broader conceptual level, all the dimensions of people's policymaking behaviour in a manageable way.

Note that our criteria were not arrived at through the use of some multi-variate technique, for example principal component analysis or cluster analysis, or by any empirical attempt to sum up variation in people's policymaking behaviour. This is because we still do not have detailed records of people's policymaking behaviour. Our evaluation criteria were obtained through logical deduction and observation, over several decades, of what policymaking textbooks seem to regard as important.

As such, perhaps it would be better to amalgamate some of our ten criteria, or split some of them, leaving us with eight, or eleven or twelve blanket concepts. But we have persisted with our ten because they appear to work in the sense that they sum up people's different policymaking styles reasonably well. Just how well is a question that can only be answered by further research. In the meantime readers need to remember that our so-called 'universal' policy-evaluation criteria are only universal in the sense that their breadth of coverage is wide. Their depth of detail is not deep enough to cover all things that drive people whenever they make policymaking decisions, but such detail is infinite anyway.

Putting this differently, one could easily dissect each of the ten criteria into several sub-criteria in order to measure policies' worth more accurately. But where would one stop? Such a process would rapidly get out of hand in the sense that users would grow very tired of scoring all of their policies on so many criteria.

8.3. Anticipating Others' Ratings
Once all the ratings for all the policies on all of the evaluation criteria have been entered, a user of *Strategizer* is able to click 'Get strategy'. The result will be a screen like that shown in figure 8.7. The positions of the buttons show the relative,

overall desirability levels of the policy options. For instance, in this example figure 8.7 shows how the 'total' group recommends that the user put more time, money, resources and effort towards implementing the 'executions' policy. This option is marginally more worthwhile than the 'life sentences' policy. In turn, the latter is superior to the 'rehabilitation' policy.

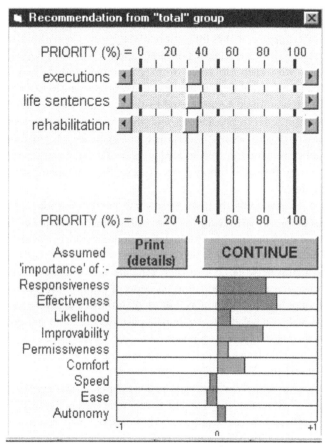

Figure 8.7. *Strategizer* recommending a policy.

8.3.1. Identifying different groups

Note that users of *Strategizer* can employ two 'sensitivity testing' methods. Firstly, they might look carefully at *Strategizer*'s calculated priorities and then see how they change if some criterion scores are changed. Users would then be able to draw conclusions such as:

'if policy 1's rating on the 'safety' criterion was a little higher, then policy 1 would become the highest-scoring policy.'

This would indicate how much one would need to alter certain criteria's scores in order to make policies' priorities come out in the way that the user would have anticipated. But again, as with *Expert Choice*, such sensitivity analysis could be misused. People might manipulate criterion scores to the point where they are not a valid reflection of reality, just to make sure that their favoured policy comes out on top. To get their way they would merely have to convince other participants that their favourite policy's rating on some important criterion should be changed. That is, the software could be used in an intimidatory way.

This is why *Strategizer* makes little effort, of the *Expert Choice* kind, to facilitate sensitivity testing. Instead, it takes a different approach to sensitivity analysis. It simply predicts what each sub-group of its past users would say and leaves it at that. Users can then speculate as to why the different groups will say what they are going to say. Users might be prompted to then discuss ways of reformulating certain policies in order to placate different groups. Yet such direct interference with policies' criterion scores is certainly not encouraged. In other words, *Strategizer* fails to encourage users to explore policies' parameter sensitivities in a manipulative way. Instead it simply gives a feel for the 'community sensitivity' of different policies.

Strategizer achieves this by training separate neural networks for each sub-group of past users – a separate network for males, females, people with children, primary school-educated people, graduates and undergraduates. This is done by assembling only that information which is supplied by, say, females and then training the relevant neural network. Once such separate networks have been trained, *Strategizer* can give a recommendation, in terms of priority levels to be assigned to the different policies, not just on behalf of all past users as shown in figure 8.7, but also separately, on behalf of, say, female past users or other sub-groups. The current user can then compare the females' likely recommendations with the males' likely recommendations, which can in turn be contrasted with old people's likely recommendations and those of other groups besides.

Perhaps more revealingly, we can even do this for groups that have been identified on the basis of cluster analysis. The latter technique uses individuals' respective correlation coefficients between policies' criterion scores and their overall priority score. More specifically, a 'Kohonnen' type of clustering neural network is used, off line, in order to cluster together individuals who have similar patterns of high and low correlations between certain criterion scores and overall policy priority level, that is, individuals who have similar policymaking styles. The Kohonnen method is, again, a neural network type of clustering algorithm, and a case can be made as to why it is superior to traditional, statistical clustering (Kiang *et al.*, 1995; Serrano-Cinca, 1996).

Again, a separate neural network is then 'trained' to mimic each cluster's policymaking style, and such a style is likely to be more consistent than one that characterizes a group based on demographic characteristics. That is, there is no logical reason to suggest that females, or males, or old people have a similar policy-making style, whereas our clusters of people will, by definition, have similar styles.

Thereafter *Strategizer* can offer a number of policy recommendations both on behalf of demographically designated groups of past users and on behalf of similar-person clusters. Participants can then observe how such group-based recommendations vary. They may even change their opinion as to what seems to be the best policy for finding favour with some or most community groups. That is, using *Strategizer* to anticipate community reactions might be useful for constructing a policy that has more community-wide appeal.

The way in which a user of *Strategizer* actually gets a recommendation from any group is to click 'Change advisers' and then select the group he or she wants. This generates a screen like that shown in figure 8.8 which displays the composition of male past users. As we noted above, their ages, numbers of children, educational levels, fields of specialization, problems addressed and so forth were all recorded when they started using *Strategizer*. Such characteristics are arrayed in the grid section on the left of figure 8.8. They can be scrolled through in order to get a 'feel' for the type of people that comprise this group.

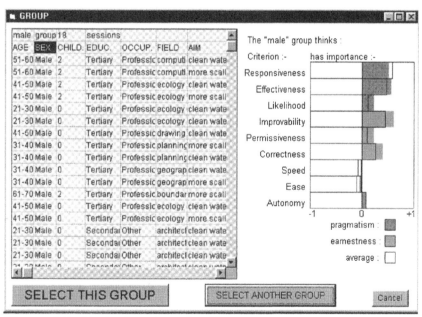

Figure 8.8. *Strategizer* changing the user group.

The right hand side of figure 8.8 is an attempt to pictorialize the attitudes held by the group – its policymaking style. That is, it indicates diagramatically the importance that the group seems to place on each of the ten, universal, policy-evaluation criteria. The widths of the bars are based on simple correlation analysis of policies' evaluation criterion scores and overall policy priority level.

For example, males can be seen to emphasize the 'improvability' criterion the most, followed by 'effectiveness', 'responsiveness' and 'correctness'. Moreover, the author has done some research (Wyatt, 1996c) which suggests that the top three criteria shown in figure 8.8 are symptomatic of a 'pragmatic' approach to policymaking whereas the middle four criteria indicate a more 'alturistic' approach and the remaining ones reflect how 'convenient' any policy is.

Hence the evidence suggests, although the sample numbers are still far too small to be definitive about this, that males are slightly more altruistic in their policymaking style than is the group as a whole. We are able to conclude this because the outlined bars in figure 8.8 correspond to criterion importance levels according to the total group of past users. Males have exceeded such importance levels for the middle three, 'altruistic' criteria. In other words, males can be generally expected to favour policies that are improvable, permissive and correct.

8.3.2. Identifying different policymaking styles

We can test such a hypothesis by clicking 'Select this group' and then clicking on 'Get policy' again. This time we will be given a recommendation based on the

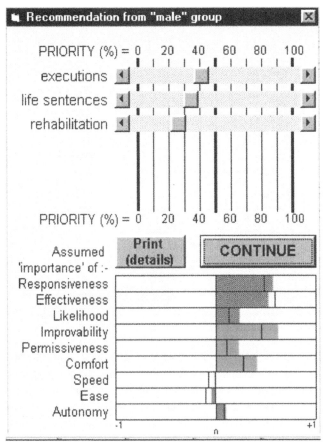

Figure 8.9. *Strategizer* showing the policy recommended by males.

attitudes of just the male past users, not the total past users, and this is shown in figure 8.9. It is evident that, unlike the total group of past users who slightly favoured 'executions' ahead of 'life sentences' in figure 8.7 above, the males put the priority level of 'executions' well ahead of the priority of 'life sentences'. Moreover, the latter are, in turn, further ahead of 'rehabilitation' than hitherto.

This tends to suggest that the group-based recommendations generated by the system, based as they are on 'mysterious' neural networks, are not always predictable. Connections between the apparent policymaking style of a group and its final recommendation is probably much more complicated than we can explain here – hence the use of a neural network to track such inexplicable connections.

Put differently, the fact that males are more in favour of the more pragmatic policy, 'executions', than the general community is, does not seem to reflect their apparent altruism. On the other hand, perhaps executions really are more 'correct' in some sense, not to mention more 'permissive' (of other things), and 'correctness' and 'permissiveness' are fairly strong male priorities according to figure 8.8 (and the bottom part of figure 8.9, which replicates the right part of figure 8.8).

Nevertheless, such thinking surely improves our insight into why certain sorts of people are likely to favour certain kinds of policy. It also forces us to ponder the relative merits of alternative policies. Moreover, one can boost such pondering still further by clicking 'Details/Print'. This will generate, both on the computer screen and on paper if desired, a full list of policies' ratings on each criterion, their overall ratings, and the importance levels assigned to criteria by the group who assigned such policy ratings.

Remember that *Strategizer* can then get recommendations from other groups as well. For example, if we select 'females', their recommendation, based on the same criterion ratings that the current user has entered, are as shown in figure 8.10. This suggests that females favour 'rehabilitation' of murderers and that they do not think 'life sentences' is a good idea. It is also shown in the bottom half of figure 8.10 that the 'effectiveness' criterion is the most important one for them, and since 'rehabilitation' was probably rated as the most 'effective' policy their recommendation is hardly surprising. Moreover, the bottom of figure 8.10 suggests females have a greater aversion than males to 'fast' and 'easy' solutions. This may have caused them to downgrade the 'executions' policy.

Hence by the time recommendations from many groups of past users are extracted from *Strategizer* – males, females, undergraduates, post graduates, professionals, managers and so forth – users should have a good feel for what the different segments of society will probably prefer. In turn, this could alert them to possible compromise policies that are likely to be accepted.

Moreover, users are also able to see what policies various similarly-thinking clusters of people are likely to favour. For instance, the recommendation generated by the Kohonnen clustering-based 'cluster 3' are shown in figure 8.11. This recommendation is different to both the males' and the females' recommendations in that they see 'life sentences' as the best policy.

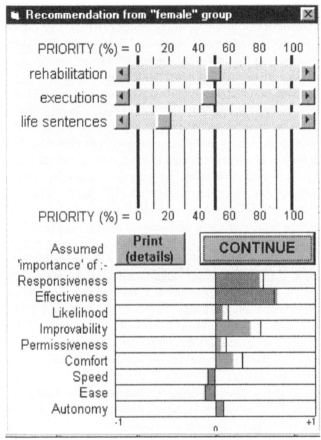

Figure 8.10. *Strategizer* showing the policy recommended by females.

8.3.3. Ensuring the package self-improves

We need to finish by explaining how *Strategizer* gets better and better at anticipating people's policy recommendations the more it is used. After a recommendation has been made, as in figures 8.7, 8.9, 8.10 and 8.11, the user clicks the 'CONTINUE' button to make a window of the type shown in figure 8.12 appear. This window pleads with the user to help *Strategizer* 'learn'. If the user clicks 'No Comment' then the program will not learn anything, but if either 'READY TO ALTER' or 'PRIORITIES ARE VALID' are clicked, learning is about to take place. For example, if 'PRIORITIES ARE VALID' is clicked the user is saying that he or she endorses the policy calculated by *Strategizer*, as shown in the top part of figures 8.7, 8.9, 8.10 and 8.11 – the user is telling the system that it got policies' overall scores 'about right'.

The point to note is that *Strategizer* can actually learn from this. Specifically, it now has two pieces of vital information: the policies' ratings on all of the evaluation criteria, as entered by the user previously, plus policies' overall ratings whose correctness has just been confirmed. Learning can therefore take place. That is, one can deduce and record the interconnections that exist between criterion ratings and overall rating, as replicated by the trained neural network.

Hence if such inputs are repeated across many policymaking problems and across many users, since the ten evaluation criteria used are always the same, *Strategizer* will eventually 'learn' how to predict any policy's rating, based on any pattern of criterion scores, even though it has never been confronted with such a policy before.

However, we have already seen that the neural network approach does not tell us exactly how it documents the connections between each criterion score and overall rating – each connection may be complexly entangled with another. For instance, a high rating on some criterion, say 'effectiveness', might certainly affect

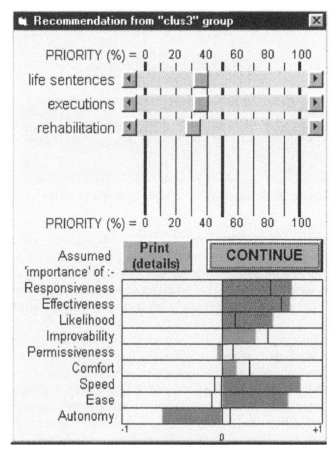

Figure 8.11. *Strategizer* showing the policy recommended by 'cluster 3'.

overall rating, but not until a certain level of some other criterion, say 'safety' has been reached.

Whereas regression type prediction techniques are scarcely able to accommodate such combinatorial, threshold effects, neural networks can. They simply 'soak in' data and, by manipulating their weights on the interconnections between inputs (criterion scores) and output (overall policy score), many hundreds of times, a coherent, trained network will emerge – one that can predict policy choice. The neural network therefore acts like a small child, continually soaking up information, including inaccurate, partial and false information. But eventually, if there exists a coherent connection between all the input scores and their corresponding outputs, it will learn to simulate this connection.

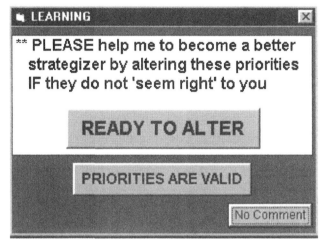

Figure 8.12. *Strategizer* trying to learn from its user.

However, if no such correspondence exists between criterion scores and overall policy rating, the neural network simply will not learn anything – it will remain 'untrained' because there are no coherent relationships to learn. One is able to see whether this happens because, in any neural network software, parameters monitor the accuracy of learning if it takes place – one always knows how well the network is being trained.

With *Strategizer*, learning actually did occur across several types of problem and across several types of user – there really does seem to exist a relationship between inputs (ratings on criteria) and output (policy ratings), no matter who the users are or what problem is being addressed (Wyatt, 1997b). That is, *Strategizer* has strong potential for being a generic policymaking system that self improves (Tesauro, 1995). However, the jury is still out on this until more extensive trials are held across many other policymaking problems, and involving a far greater range and number of users.

Note that if a user decides to help the system learn by clicking 'READY TO ALTER' in figure 8.12, he or she is about to tell *Strategizer* that it did not get the overall policy ratings correct in figure 8.11 – they need altering. Accordingly, a window of the type shown in figure 8.13 appears. The user then 'corrects' overall policy ratings by mouse dragging policies' bars to reflect policy desirability levels according to that user. The program then asks the user if he or she is sure of such opinions, using the same window that was used for scoring policies on criteria, as shown above in figure 8.5. Eventually therefore, the user will indicate that he or she is satisfied with his or her estimates of policies' overall ratings. Hence again, the program now has two sets of vital information from which it can learn: each policy's ratings on all of the evaluation criteria and their (corrected) overall scores. Such information will be added to the system's data bank and fed to the neural network-based learning routines.

The more people that use the system the more data it will have. Hence theoretically, the system will get better and better at 'learning' how to predict

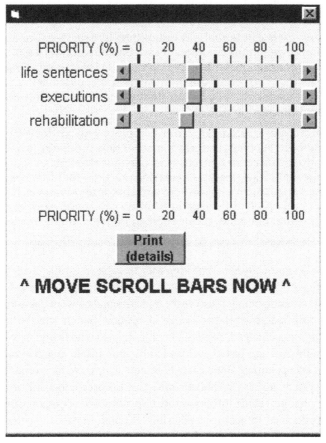

Figure 8.13. *Strategizer* asking the user to correct the policy.

policies' priority levels the more it is used. The neural network might be reluctant to give up its secrets about how it actually learns, but it does present a more 'organic', human-like attempt to generate useful policymaking information for its users. As such, it is possibly one of the better methods yet found for replicating the human learning process.

Lesson 56: Self-improving policymaking

Self-improving neural networks have tremendous potential for boosting policymaking practice. They constitute a computerized system that gets better and better the more it is used. They therefore promise policymaking practice that learns to improve in a cumulative way

But policymaking has long been criticized for not developing in this way. Workshop facilitators might learn a little more about good policymaking from each workshop that they conduct, but the participants usually do not. The latter seem to have more temporary, 'one off' experiences and so they take little, if any, accumulated wisdom to their next policymaking workshop, where they often make the same mistakes.

Strategizer offers a potential way out of this. Its expertise is cumulative; it is self improving in the tradition of case-based reasoning's aspirations, although *Strategizer* does this more rigorously. In other words, *Strategizer* has a chance of furthering the improvement of policymaking practice because it actually accumulates knowledge of best practice in a way used by all scientific disciplines.

Hence although *Strategizer* is not completely scientific – the non-transparency of its neural network mechanisms precludes this – it is a beginning. It is far more rigorous than previous attempts to accumulate knowledge about exemplary policymaking practice – the latter has usually been based on subjective impressions and anecdote. Moreover, it is more rigorous because scientific experimentation can conceivably be carried out using neural networks, albeit at an aggregate and shallow level.

Moreover, scientifically experimenting with *Strategizer*, in order to try to improve our knowledge of policymaking in general, could proceed as follows. One would vary policies' criterion ratings, observe the trained neural network's resulting output, and so build up macro-level knowledge about how output alters when certain criterion scores are changed. We could not look inside the neural network to see exactly why this occurs, just as we can hardly look inside a human brain to see clearly what is happening. But we would be able to observe the overall behaviour of the total system, just as psychologists are able to observe the holistic behaviour of the total person. Hence it follows that a 'psychological' appreciation of how neural networks tend to behave is plausible. Therefore, since our networks are designed to mimic human policymaking, our knowledge of the latter and how to improve it would increase.

8.4. Summary

Strategizer is our best example yet of how software may eventually usurp functions that were previously performed by humans – in this case, the 'learning' of how various community groups will favour certain policies. It is the only package that uses machine learning technology. Moreover, it is unlikely that the user will 'fiddle' its outputs and so become sceptical of their validity. Also, by taking the groups-based, neural network approach one can get interesting, holistic perceptions of the strengths and weaknesses of alternative policies without delving into their detailed aspects and so become hopelessly confused.

Yet such clarity is only achieved using an implicit value judgement about what is important in policymaking. That is, *Strategizer* is predicated on the belief that the most important part of the process is a comparison of policies, and so it is similar to *CyberQuest* in the sense that it simplifies its tasks by concentrating on just one thing. Hence neither of these two packages feel the need to facilitate detailed sensitivity analysis like *STRAD* and *Expert Choice*, nor do they concentrate on the management of uncertainty as *STRAD* does, or the consistency checking for which *Expert Choice* is so well known.

Hence like *CyberQuest*, *Strategizer* errs on the side of over-simplicity when facing the eternal dilemma of 'simplification versus sophistication'. Whether or not this is desirable depends on whether one believes that the things which these two packages have decided to concentrate on, brainstorming and choice anticipation respectively, are really of pivotal importance. We suggest that both are. So perhaps it is best to use of them in combination in order to undertake policymaking in a way that is insightful yet more likely to avoid analysis paralysis which the more complicated *STRAD* and *Expert Choice* packages could induce.

Some readers will strongly disagree with this. They will assert that all knowledge is useful, and so the insights generated by *STRAD* and by *Expert Choice* should never be foregone. What any individual reader thinks about this depends on whether or not they are pragmatic policymakers which, by the way, they can measure using *Strategizer*.

Chapter 9

A United Frontier?

For completeness, our four research frontier packages have been documented in table 9.1, just like we tabulated the software that was described in Chapters 2, 3 and 4. This chapter looks at them all in order to compare and contrast their capabilities and to reach some sort of conclusion about which one is best.

Table 9.1. Research frontier packages for policymaking.

Special skills	Package	Cost	Reference
Generate ideas Package ideas	*CyberQuest*	< $1000	Dickey,1996
Eliminate some ideas Identify policies Manage uncertainty	*STRAD*	< $1000	Friend and Hickling 1997; 1992; Cartwright 1992
Assign scores Reflect	*Expert Choice*	< $1000	Saaty1996,1994; Saaty and Vargas1994
Evaluate policies Learn preferences	*Strategizer*	< $1000	Wyatt 1997*a*, 1997*b*, 1996*c*

But alas, we have decided to risk being accused of fence sitting. We will suggest that exemplary policymaking needs to use all four of our 'research frontier' packages, along with any others if they seem to be particularly useful. In this chapter, therefore, we consider how best to combine our four frontier programs. Each is predicated on a belief that certain actions are absolutely pivotal to best policymaking practice. They therefore concentrate on such supposedly crucial activities. Hence some packages do certain things better than others. It follows that particular packages should be used for particular phases of the policymaking process.

Note that the fact that there are contrasts between our packages is hardly surprising, given that different people from different countries and with different backgrounds have produced them. Everyone sees the world from a unique viewpoint, depending on their own personal experiences. Hence different people build computer software in different ways even though such software has a common purpose – better policymaking. Moreover, different sorts of users have influenced the building of each package, as described above in the Preface.

Nevertheless, we remind readers that our four packages are broadly similar in the sense that they each regard policymaking as being, to some extent, the process of:

➤ think
➤ choose, and
➤ anticipate

Section 9.1 therefore outlines how each package helps policymakers to 'think'. Section 9.2 then compares how the packages assist users to 'choose' the best policy, and section 9.3 indicates how some of them boost our ability to 'anticipate' people's reponses to suggested policies.

9.1 Think

The initial, 'think' part of policymaking involes not only generating ideas that might be useful for solving the problem. It also involves keeping the process manageable by deleting those ideas whose value is low. Moreover, the better ideas need to be packaged into something that is 'marketable' if policymaking is to progress to its next phase in a clear and purposeful manner.

This is all part of initial, 'situational structuring' – a process that has been given increasing prominence by some policymaking software packages. Unless one performs this with some care and precision, the subsequent policymaking is liable to go down some blind-alley type tangent of misplaced inquiry and effort.

Note that although computers can help this process, by recording ideas and tidying up inconsistencies of thought, it is the users rather than the software who have the dominant role in the 'think' phase of policymaking. They alone understand the problem situation, which they interpret with their social awareness. Right now the prospect of having a computer ever do this is inconceivable.

Hence software in this phase of policymaking needs to be 'feeling' in its style in order to replicate and keep track of subtleties within its human users' inputs. Sub-section 9.1.1 looks at the process of generating ideas. Sub-section 9.1.2 then shows how software might help users eliminate some of the unpromising ones, and sub-section 9.1.3 discusses the packaging of some of the better ideas into more palatable suggestions.

9.1.1. Generating ideas

This crucial part of good policymaking, generating bright ideas, is probably best assisted by *CyberQuest*, even though *Expert Choice* also contains a brainstorming module as well. Chapter 5 describes the incredible trouble that *CyberQuest* goes to in order to generate potentially useful suggestions. It also shows how, at several points, *CyberQuest* makes windows appear on the computer screen that invite the user to insert a new idea should one happen to surface while they are doing something else.

Lesson 57: Brainstorm

Much policymaking practice does not begin at the beginning. It begins at the options-evaluation, or 'choose' stage. It is as if the ideas-generation phase is a natural, uniquely human function that is as automatic as breathing. As such, it appears to be an unsuitable subject for purposeful study and certainly not amenable to computer assistance.

Moreover, as the Introduction pointed out, most of us do not study alternative ways of breathing to improve our lives because it hardly seems worth the effort – there are more important things to concentrate on. Likewise, policymaking practice tends to ignore the ideas-generation phase because there are seemingly more important things to get on with, such as simulation modelling and negotiation.

But if initial ideas are poor, so too will be the subsequent policymaking practice. Hence policymaking practice could profit by taking a leaf out of *CyberQuest's* book. The latter shows dogged persistence in trying to wring the last drop of useful creativity out of all participants. Keep brainstorming.

By contrast, *STRAD*, and *Strategizer* simply ask the user to volunteer suggestions. It is as if they have made an assumption that the brainstorming part of policymaking has already been completed. In other words, these two packages' forte is comparison of policies; their generation of options is taken almost as a pre-ordained, *fait accompli*.

Note however, that *STRAD* and *Strategizer* do make some effort to increase users' creativity as well. For example, whenever users of *Strategizer* enter options at one level of the goals hierarchy, they are always asked whether or not there is also a 'long shot' option. This is an attempt to get them to think 'outside the square', and sometimes a very interesting, hitherto unconsidered policy is so generated.

Strategizer also asks, unlike all of the other three packages, whether or not one option might be a pre-requisite for some other option at the same level. If so, the user is encouraged to place the contributor option at a lower level in the hierarchy, along with some comparable lower-level alternatives. This means that the options left on the current level will be at a similar level of abstraction and so, directly comparable. It is impossible to compare the desirability of different options if one is a pre-requisite of the other.

By contrast, the other three packages, *CyberQuest, STRAD* and *Expert Choice*, do not actually separate options from their pre-requisite options. This can, of course, lead to confusion, and to possibly inaccurate conclusions later on in the policymaking process. However, *CyberQuest* and *STRAD* do get over the problem, to some extent, by having 'actions windows'. The latter are for the user to list what should be done now and what should be done later. Presumably, the user should concentrate on the pre-requisite options now and on the dependent options later.

Lesson 58: Horses for courses

If policy needs to be sequential, none of this book's software will be suitable. That is, if the policymaking problem is a matter of identifying the 'critical path' of actions to take – actions which will optimize whatever the policymaker wants to optimize, such as costs, time or pay off – users would be better advised to employ some kind of scheduling software instead.

But more 'free form' software is necessary for addressing wicked and vicious problems. In these, new and different ideas about how to achieve parent goals are always worth considering. Also, proposed actions tend to be alternatives that can be traded off against one another rather than contrived sequences of actions that can be measured directly to determine their payoff.

Note that our packages should not be used to address problems in which some sub-goals are actually 'constraints'. For example, if we have a goal of triggering no more costs than a certain threshold, in the sense that unless such a maximum cost is avoided all policymaking will be ruled out, we are in a constraints-driven, optimization type of problem environment. Hence users would be better off using optimization software.

It is for this reason that *Strategizer* asks the user whether or not any of their suggested 'options' are constraints. If some are, *Strategizer* advises the user to delete them or to consider using optimization software.

Note however that *Expert Choice* actually has some facility for incorporating constraints into its goals hierarchy. It allows users to specify a layer of 'alternative scenarios', like 'low costs' and 'high costs', along with their respective probabilities. Therefore, if the probability of say, 'high costs' is abysmally low, it follows that the high-cost alternatives will all be given relatively low scores, thereby eliminating all of the high-cost alternatives. Thus the costs constraint has been accommodated, albeit only approximately. Similarly, *CyberQuest* and *STRAD* partially overcome the constraints problem by incorporating 'actions' into their policies. Such actions can either alter the constraints themselves, or make it more likely that the constraints are satisfied.

In general however, whenever one's policymaking problem is riddled with limitations that heavily constrain the 'solution space' of possible things to do, optimization software is a better alternative than the packages described here. Our packages address problems whose solution spaces are not usually defined rigorously, and where part of their solution space is even unthought of.

Hence in the initial, ideas-generation phase of policymaking, all four packages have their useful features. But for sheer richness of ideas generated it is hard to go beyond *CyberQuest*. We saw in Chapter 5, for example, how the package could be used to generate a vast array of possible ideas in the vexed problem area of world peace.

9.1.2. Deleting ideas

However, if the process is to remain manageable, some sorting of ideas is necessary. Grouping ideas is one path towards manageability; eliminating poor ideas is another, and all four of our frontier packages ask users to think about deleting some of their options. However, the attempt made by *Strategizer* is a fairly token one. It simply waits to see whether any option scores lower than 10 out of 100 on any evaluation criterion. If it does, there is a possibility that the idea is so 'hopeless', at least in terms of this criterion, that it is not really worth considering as a viable option. Accordingly, users are asked whether they want to remove this low-scoring option from their list of possible policies.

Note that the decision whether to do so is entirely in the hands of the user, not the software. Note also that prompting a user to consider deletion of an option because it has scored lower than 10 is completely arbitrary; it could just as well have been 20 or 5. Yet experience with *Strategizer* suggests that scores seldom drop below 10 and so, whenever they do, it is certainly worth quizzing the user about their viability.

STRAD deletes ideas very effectively. It uses its 'option bar' mechanism whenever there are incompatibilities between options, as explained in Chapter 6. Such option bars are efficient instruments for decimating the number of policymaking 'schemes', the number of which can be overwhelming in large-scale projects. By contrast, *CyberQuest* and *Expert Choice* do not explicitly ask users whether or not they want to delete some of their ideas, although in each case it is very easy to delete options if the user so desires.

Hence the best package for eliminating options is probably *STRAD*. Its option bar mechanism forces users to think very carefully about which ideas are incompatible with which other ideas. Users of the other three packages are able to do this also, but it is *STRAD* that forces policymakers to do it the most explicitly.

9.1.3. Packaging ideas

When it comes to making policymaking ideas more palatable and so more worthy of consideration, there are some significant contrasts between our four frontier packages. The first two, *CyberQuest* and *STRAD*, tend to do this in an aggregative, conceptual way whereas the last two, *Expert Choice* and *Strategizer*, simply treat their ideas as 'options' by scoring, and choosing between them, straight away.

Put differently, *CyberQuest* and *Strad* gradually craft options through their processes of 'idea packaging' and 'scheme formulation' respectively. They demur from directly exploring any single idea on its own, preferring instead first to amalgamate it with other ideas into some sort of consortium of ideas that has more collective potential. By contrast, *Expert Choice* and *Strategizer* assume that such

Lesson 59: Balance your activities

In policymaking, close attention to detail might 'replicate reality' to such a degree that participants become confused, indecisive and prone to 'analysis paralysis'. That is, participants may be so hung up on details that they miss seeing a more considered, laterally thinking policy.

Against this, consideration of pertinent details actually brings some measure of balance on the whole policymaking process. It tends to generate forays into science to resolve difficult questions, into facilitated workshops to tap personal insights, into philosophy to ponder the problem and into modelling, if possible, to optimize policy choice.

Yet a pre-occupation with science, workshopping, philosophizing or modelling can divert policymakers away from practicalities. Hence policymakers need to adopt a balanced, synoptic, considered, 'big picture' approach which is still pragmatic enough to incorporate a fearless confrontation of all issues.

In other words, a balanced approach seems to be the best tactic for current policymakers. It is possible that future research will reveal that an up front, detailed focus on a problem's intricacies is the best way to proceed, but it is likely that such research will find such a recommendation is situation dependent.

amalgamation has already taken place within the minds of participants; that is, ideas already constitute conglomerated, viable options.

This is a fundamental contrast between our first two and our last two packages – explicit crafting of options versus implicit, or assumed pre-crafting of options. *CyberQuest* and *STRAD* appear to be working at a finer level of detail than are *Expert Choice* and *Strategizer*. They help users to assemble options in a more detailed way. Indeed, *STRAD* absolutely epitomizes this. It adopts a 'boots and all' attitude to problem complexity by jumping immediately into a full consideration of all the intricacies that surround possible goals. Whether or not too much confusion is created in the minds of users by such a practice is an open question to which we will return below.

Meanwhile, there is little doubting that *CyberQuest* and *STRAD* are more thorough in their construction of viable policy ideas than are *Expert Choice* and *Strategizer*. The latter are stronger policy choosers than policy suggesters, and it is to the 'choose' phase of policymaking that we now turn.

9.2. Choose

It is one thing to generate, sort and package ideas. They then need to be amalgamated into viable policies. Also, such policies have to be evaluated, or compared against one another, so that the best one(s) can be chosen. How best to do this is a contentious area that turns on the merits or otherwise of different methods of assigning scores to policies. Accordingly, sub-section 9.2.1 deals with identifying policies, sub-section 9.2.2 discusses how to evaluate them and sub-section 9.2.3 describes how to assign scores to them.

9.2.1. Identifying policies

The crux of identifying policies, or 'schemes', is deciding which ideas to incorporate within each policy. Moreover, incorporation of any idea depends on its intrinsic worth, and some packages, simply by the way they list the ideas, can distort users' perception of their desirability.

For instance, *STRAD* has a tendency to suggest to users that the desirability of any idea is related to the number of times it appears within the set of viable 'schemes'. This is because *STRAD* is a very industrious searcher of all the combinatorial, idea possibilities – it automatically counts and displays the number of times that each idea appears within the set of feasible policies. But this can be dangerously hypnotic, as pointed out above.

Chapter 6's village problem was used as an illustration, where the choice between hiring or buying a truck was left open. But buying a truck meant that the old fertilizer kiln would have to be retained. This was because there would not be enough money to buy a new mill as well, and this increased the number of times that the policy 'sell fertilizer only to the citrus industry' appeared as a viable option. Yet if the villagers actually decided to hire a truck, 'buying a truck' would be eliminated, along with all of the schemes it is compatible with, three of which involve 'selling fertilizer only to the citrus industry'. Hence selling fertilizer only to citrus growers would suddenly become a less 'popular' policy, or conversely, 'market expansion' would suddenly appear, based on the numbers, to be a relatively more viable option.

Hence one can imagine someone in a group of *STRAD* users who are passionate about 'market expansion', for example, a government treasury official seeking reduction in the national reliance on fertilizer imports. Such an official would try to force a decision to hire rather than to buy a truck. They might bring in all sorts of arguments such as local truck availability, but all the time their 'hidden agenda' would be to force a decision that will make their preferred alternative, 'market expansion', appear more laudable.

The question therefore arises: which of our packages are more prone to the problem of spurious accuracy and potential deception? Possibly the worst is *Strategizer*, with its recommendations coming from mysterious, 'black box' neural networks – at least with the other three packages one can calculate, with a little persistence, how all numbers were arrived at. Nevertheless, such transparency can be taken too far, as it might be with *CyberQuest, STRAD,* and *Expert Choice*, where one can sometimes manipulate the scores so as to generate any answer one likes in terms of the top-scoring policy. In such situations the software has not produced any recommendation at all – the user has.

Lesson 60: Go slowly

In theory, the policymaking process is supposed to allow all participants to 'see through' the problem to equal extents. But it is a fact of life that some will do this more effectively than others. Hence clever people will be able to use complex details as a diversionary smokescreen in order to achieve their own ends.

It could be countered that such deception happens in real life anyway and that formal policymaking at least gives exploited people a better chance of unmasking unscrupulous team members.

But this will not be the case when software is actually used, by individuals, to bluff and confuse less confident people in the name of 'scientific', quantitative rigour rather than qualitative sensitivity.

This is an old chestnut problem for all procedures that try, for convenience, to 'scientize' policymaking. Hence it is a significant a problem in all software-supported exercises. It can only be parried, albeit partially, by insisting that all decisions are open to the (very patient) scrutiny of everyone.

Note that a practical problem associated with identifying policies is how to limit their number to a size that can be handled. Yet one does not want their number to be slashed too brutally. This is because when efforts have been made to include as many policies within the analysis as possible, such an analysis will be an effective one for wide-ranging policymaking. Alternatively, if fewer policies have been included in the analyses, the package will be a less effective assistant to the policymaker.

This is why *STRAD* tries to handle so many goals. Indeed, many of its so-called Comparison Areas are actually goals, such as the 'balance of trade' Comparison Area in the village example. But did we really need the latter in our list of policies? It could be that balance of trade is a very minor consideration, worthy only of being a factor which rattles around in the back of a user's mind whenever he or she comprehensively evaluates the effectiveness of the policies. But *STRAD* gives all goals equal consideration regardless, and this will mostly constitute uneconomical employment of the user's time.

This is why *Strategizer* takes another approach. It purposely limits the number of goals, on any one level of the goals hierarchy, to five – the most important three plus a 'long shot' goal, if any, plus the 'do nothing' option if appropriate. These (up to) five goals can then be considered synoptically by humans in all their multi-faceted aspects. By contrast, *STRAD* incorporates into its deliberations the 'balance of trade' goal regardless; there is no pre-vetting of the importance of its role in the final decision. This might support the illusion that *STRAD* is a more 'down to earth', practical and relevant way to proceed, but such an approach actually brings with it the considerable risk of distorting users' perception of the true nature of the problem.

Why not, therefore, consider balance of trade as a candidate goal which is allowed to remain in the analysis only if it proves to be a truly important aim to pursue? This is what *Strategizer* does, but in *STRAD* it is given attention no matter what, even when more important considerations might have been left out of the analysis simply because the user got tired before he or she was able to insert them all. One could assume, of course, that users will tend to nominate only the important goals. But this is a dangerous assumption within software that encourages an open-ended list of considerations. *STRAD* has no clearly-stated limit to the number of goals that should be included.

CyberQuest is similar; there seems to be no encouragement of users to think more about the more important ideas. *Expert Choice* is slightly better in that it limits the number of goals on any level of the goals hierarchy to seven in number. This, presumably, tends to encourage the user to insert only the more important ones.

One might counter that *Strategizer*, and *Expert Choice*, go too far in the direction of conciseness – it may simply be impossible to compress a complex problem into just five or seven 'goals' of supreme importance. Yet it is actually possible to sum up any problem using five or even fewer goals simply by going to a higher level of abstraction – to a higher level within the goals hierarchy, as pointed out in the previous chapter.

A further example might reinforce this. In the world peace problem addressed by *CyberQuest* in Chapter 5, we saw that the 'goals' being considered were:

1. United Nations

2. Ecological volunteers

3. No borders

4. Mono culture

5. Mono currency

6. Freely available satellite imagery

7. War crimes publicity

8. Cultural heritage listings

9. Bhuddism

10. War insurance

11. Nation adopting

12. Simulated warfare

13. Technological olympics

We might therefore suggest there are five things being aimed for here, that is, five over-arching, aggregate policies:

1. Political solutions (1, 2)

2. Unifying measures (3 - 5)

3. Publicity (6, 7)

4. Protective mechanisms (8 - 11)

5. War substitutes (12, 13)

In turn, at a higher level of abstraction one might decide that these aggregated goals themselves can be expressed as three, even more aggregated goals:

1. Politics (1, 2)

2. Humanism (3, 4)

3. Substitution (5)

Therefore, if *Strategizer* addressed this problem, a session to evaluate comprehensively the three options of 'Politics', 'Humanism', and 'Substitution', plus possibly a long shot and a do-nothing goal, would first take place. The result would be a recommendation of how much time/money/resources should be put into the pursuit of each policy – their 'priority' level. Then, a separate session could be run to consider alternative ways of achieving the favoured policies. For instance, achieving 'Politics' involves weighing up the relative priorities of 'Political solutions' and 'Unifying measures', and the latter might be summed up by 'No borders', 'Mono culture' and 'Mono currency'.

However, such potential comprehensiveness of the *Strategizer* approach could possibly bring about the very evil that we have already charged *STRAD* of perpetrating. This is a tendency to over-complicate the analysis. Computers are meant to simplify reality in order to make it more manageable rather than reproduce reality in all of its overwhelming complexity. But the hierarchically focussed approach of *Strategizer* at least gives us some control over how much complicatedness is allowed.

Yet it must be remembered that in a way, the focus window of *STRAD*, along with its encouragement of users to recast the problem into chunks of connected Decision Areas, tries to achieve the same thing. Nevertheless, the 'flavour' of *STRAD* is to encourage discussion of lots of considerations simultaneously, and so its potential for having the whole policymaking process degenerate into over-complicated and irresolvable complexity is probably greater.

Hence when it comes to the best package for identifying policies comprehensively but efficiently, it seems to be a line ball decision between *Strad*

Lesson 61: Keep control

Addressing a policymaking problem many times is likely to lead to the consideration of more, rather than fewer policies. This is because during the careful consideration of each option one is likely to think of still more possibilities.

However, most policymaking packages, and projects, simply ask users to list all those multi-level considerations that spring to mind at one, and only one, stage of the process – the beginning. Although new thoughts can always be added later, the chances of this happening in practice are fairly small.

This is because participants tend to have little tolerance for the introduction of still more 'new ideas' once a project has begun to succeed in its aim of encouraging detailed consideration of policies already input.

The solution seems to be better management, with an insistence that it is always permissible to introduce new and vital ideas, at whatever stage, if their quality warrants it. Controlled progress seems more likely to generate lateral inspiration than is some talk fest that appears to be evolving, but which simply rambles.

and *Strategizer*. *CyberQuest* and *Expert Choice* both incorporate 'situation structuring' modules to encourage considerable forethought amongst users about the problem being faced, but they are thereafter dependent on users to formulate policies, fairly subjectively, by themselves. By contrast, *STRAD* and *Strategizer* give more help to the users.

Indeed, *Strategizer* provides considerable help. It keeps users disciplined enough to conceptualize the problem using a limited number of directly comparable alternatives, at each level of the goals hierarchy, while each part of the problem is dealt with in turn. But probably the best policy-identification package is *STRAD*, with its formidable attention to detail along with its option bars and focus windows to assign a semblance of control to such richness.

9.2.2. Evaluating policies

Evaluating policies always involves examining their performances on policy-evaluation criteria. Hence all policymaking software has some method of choosing what the evaluation criteria ought to be. For example, *CyberQuest* insists on only two of them – 'importance' and 'effort', although the user is also asked to consider a huge number of 'possible' evaluation criteria during the 'idea packaging' phase. *STRAD* also uses two compulsory criteria, 'importance' and 'urgency', unless a goal is being addressed which involves the reduction of uncertainty. In the latter case the evaluation criteria used are 'costs', 'gain' and 'problems resulting from delay'. The other evaluation criteria are simply those nominated by the user. *Expert Choice*, likewise, leaves the evaluation criteria to be nominated by the user.

In contrast to these three packages, *Strategizer* insists on there being ten prescribed evaluation criteria for all policies. Hence *Strategizer* is probably the most comprehensive evaluator of the four packages – its ten criteria are claimed to be 'universal' in the sense that they cover everything that anyone would ever think should be taken into account when comparing policies, anywhere.

Nevertheless, all packages cover some of these ten criteria. For instance, 'costs' in *STRAD* correspond to (part of) the 'difficulty' criterion used in *Strategizer*, 'gain' in *STRAD* corresponds to *Strategizer's* 'effectiveness', and *STRAD's* (problems resulting from) 'delay' corresponds partly to *Strategizer's* 'safety'. Note also that *CyberQuest's* 'importance' criterion is actually an amalgamation that reflects some of *Strategizer's* criteria of 'effectiveness', 'likelihood' and 'speed'.

Yet our first three packages almost certainly will not consider all of the evaluation criteria that are always used by *Strategizer*. *CyberQuest* might go the closest. One could argue that it actually gives adequate consideration to:

➤ responsiveness to effort

➤ improvability

➤ ease

➤ speed

➤ permissiveness, and

➤ likelihood.

But it avoids the other four criteria unless, of course, the user nominates them.

Several of *CyberQuest's* criteria are sub-criteria of some criterion that *Strategizer* uses anyway. Hence the full range of the *Strategizer's* coverage will probably remain uncovered by *CyberQuest* as it focuses on the details of only some criteria rather than on all of them.

Thus *Strategizer* differs from our other three packages in that it always uses its ten universal criteria to evaluate alternative policies. By contrast, the other packages ask their human user(s) to nominate suitable judgemental criteria, *Strategizer* assumes that any criterion that people come up with will simply be part of its own, pivotal, key criteria. Thus *Strategizer's* goals-evaluation procedure is actually less complicated, yet ironically, more comprehensive. Therefore, *Strategizer* is almost certainly the best of our research frontier packages when it comes to comprehensiveness of evaluation.

9.2.3. Assigning scores to policies

The other issue that needs considering when it comes to evaluating policies is, of course, the intrinsic validity of the scoring method used. We saw above how the producers of *Expert Choice* claim that the quality of ratings attained by them far exceeds the quality of ratings obtained by any other policymaking package. Indeed, the only scores worth taking any notice of at all are those obtained by *Expert Choice* – the rest have no validity. Such an extreme claim deserves our scrutiny.

As pointed out in Chapter 7, the promoters of *Expert Choice* claim that scores obtained by their package are 'ratio scale' scores, whereas all of the other packages collect 'interval scale' scores. Only ratio scale scores can be added or multiplied together. Interval scale scores, the ones collected by all the packages except *Expert Choice*, cannot. If interval scale scores are in fact added together or multiplied, a nonsense result is obtained. Hence only ratio scale scores will suffice for valid totalling of policies' scores across several criteria. This will not be an easy concept for many readers to grasp, and so it will now be explained using a concrete analogy.

The latter concerns the exercise of evaluating the intrinsic ability levels of say, three different marathon runners. The information we have is their performance in two marathon races. Firstly, there is a 'cold' race that was held in cool, flat conditions where all competitors recorded relatively fast times. Secondly, there is a 'hot' race which was held during a heat wave across mountainous terrain and in which all competitors recorded relatively slow times. That is, we have two criteria for the three runners – their scores for how well they ran in the cool race and in the hot race. Somehow we need to amalgamate these two separate pieces of information in order to rate each runner, overall.

At each race, one could get an idea of how well the three runners performed in two ways – by collecting interval scale scores for each of them and by collecting ratio scales for each of them. To collect interval scores we would stand at the finish line of the cold race and note that runner A finished 15 minutes behind the winner and 15 minutes ahead of runner B. The latter, in turn, finished fifteen minutes ahead of runner C. We would then have interval type scores. We would have noted the (time) intervals between the runners. We could then do the same thing for the hot race and find, say, that runner A finished 30 minutes behind the winner and one hour ahead of runner B. The latter, in turn finished one hour ahead of runner C, as shown in the left hand, example 1 in table 9.2.

Now, we could get an additive score of 45 minutes for runner A – an interval behind the winner of 15 minutes in the cold race plus 30 minutes in the hot race. The corresponding score would be 90 for runner B – 30 minutes behind the winner in the cold race plus 60 minutes in the hot race, and 135 for runner C – 45 minutes in the cold race and 90 minutes in the hot race. But this would NOT mean that runner A is twice as good as runner B (90/45 = 2). Nor would it mean that runner A is three times as good as runner C (135/45 = 3), or that runner B is one and a half times as good as runner C (135/90 = 1.5), or anything.

To make valid overall assessments we need nothing less than ratio scores. In this instance they can be obtained by looking not at the intervals between runners at the finish, but at the total time they took to run both races. These might be, say, for the cold race, 150 minutes for runner A, 165 minutes for runner B and 180 minutes for runner C, and for the hot race 180 minutes for runner A, 210 minutes for runner B and 240 minutes for runner C. Hence their total scores would be 330 for runner A (a time of 150 minutes in the cold race plus 180 in the hot race), 375 for runner B (165 plus 210) and 420 for runner C (180 plus 240). Hence if we wanted to define quality in this way we could actually reach conclusions such as runner A is 1.13 better than runner B (375/330 = 1.13) and runner B is 1.12 times better than runner C (420/375 = 1.12).

Table 9.2. When interval data are used, conclusions change. When ratio data are used, conclusions do not change.

	EXAMPLE 1				EXAMPLE 2			
	Time taken by :				Time taken by :			
	Winner	A	B	C	Winner	A	B	C
cold race	135	150	165	180	126	150	165	180
hot race	150	180	210	240	130	180	210	240
	Interval scoring :				**Interval scoring :**			
	(minutes behind the winner)				(minutes behind the winner)			
	A	B		C	A	B		C
cold race	15	30		45	24	39		54
hot race	30	60		90	50	80		110
ADDED	45	90		135	74	119		164
	i.e. A seems **twice** as good as B because 90/45 = 2				i.e. A now seems **1.6** better than B because 119/74 = 1.6			
	Ratio scoring :				**Ratio scoring :**			
	(total time)				(total time)			
	A	B		C	A	B		C
cold race	150	165		180	150	165		180
hot race	180	210		240	180	210		240
ADDED	330	375		420	330	375		420
	i.e. A is **1.13** times as good as B because 375/330 = 1.13				i.e. A is **1.13** times as good as B because 375/330 = 1.13			

The reason we can say such things is that ratio scores incorporate an absolute zero, in this case the best time possible for the race, zero seconds. This acts as a measuring stick for absolute quality. No runner can run better than zero time, and so if all runners are measured against this ideal of absolute zero, we can calculate the percentage differences between them. By contrast, we can do no such thing with interval data. The zero point for interval data is always arbitrary; it is an accident that depends upon whatever we happen to choose as our zero point on that particular occasion.

For instance, in our example we chose the winner of the race's time, 135 minutes in the cold race and 150 minutes in the hot race, as our zero point. But what if some other person was later found to have run in the cold race and finished in a world record time of 125 minutes? Also, what if another runner who was used to hot and hilly conditions was found to have run the hot race in the excellent time of 130 minutes? This is shown as Example 2 in table 9.2. Notice how the relative, interval type scores for runners A, B and C have now changed to 74, 119 and 164 respectively. Hence runner A no longer seems twice as good as runner B (90/45 = 2) but only 1.6 times as good (119/74 = 1.6).

In other words, we have used exactly the same data but we have reached a very different result. The only thing that has changed has been the arbitrary zero point; its location always depends on who happened to win the race that particular day. This should not alter our perception of the relative gaps between runners A, B and C, but it does – if we use interval data. Put differently, results based on interval data are always accidental. By contrast, a result based on ratio data never changes. In interval scaling the zero score is arbitrary, so our conclusions change. But with ratio scoring the zero point stays constant and so, therefore, our conclusions also stay the same, as shown in the bottom third of table 9.2.

In both methods however, we have given equal importance to results of the cold and the hot race. This is probably not as it should be. Marathon races are not usually run in heatwaves and across mountains, and so anyone who does well in the hot race might not necessarily be a good marathon racer. Hence the weight given to the scores obtained from the hot race might have to be scaled down to some extent. That is, we need to score the two races, or criteria, for their relative importances as an indicator of overall running ability. We should then factor such importances into the calculations in table 9.2. But again, we can estimate the relative importances of criteria in two ways, by interval scoring and by ratio scoring.

Now, the *Expert Choice* package estimates both scores on criteria, and importance levels of criteria using a ratio scale. It does this by taking the smallest score as the zero point, and then comparing the relative magnitude of each other score to this smallest score using 'paired comparisons'. Hence we finish up with ratio data, for each policy on each criterion, which show how the magnitude of the smallest score compares with each of the others' ratio scores. We also finish with scores for the importance of each criterion showing how the smallest, least important criterion compares to each of the others' ratio scores again. Thus we are able to multiply policies' criterion scores by the importances of the criteria and so come up with a valid, unchanging, ratio type rating for each policy.

But alas, the other three packages do not come up with valid, unchanging ratings for alternative policies. This is because they only use interval data. For example, *STRAD* has users 'mouse pull' a dot along a bar to represent each policy's score on the criterion being dealt with. This is a little like observing which policy finishes ahead of which other policies and by how much – interval scores. Moreover, users are asked to do exactly the same thing to rate criteria's importance levels.

Also, in *Strategizer* policies are rated on any criterion by having the user pull squares along scroll bars in a very similar way to that adopted by *STRAD* users. However, the scoring of criterion importances is probably a little more satisfactory since the neural network 'learns' such criterion importances, presumably in more of a ratio scale sort of manner rather than have the user nominate them as interval scores.

Finally, in *CyberQuest* the user is asked to nominate ideas' scores on any criterion as a number out of ten, which is a method that does incorporate some notion of an absolute zero – the minimum imaginable score acts as the absolute zero. However, the results will probably be more like interval data. This is because users naturally think about the gaps between the alternatives rather than think much about what sort of alternative would have a zero score – the focus is on intervals and so the result will be interval type scores rather than ratio scores. Moreover, as we have seen, *CyberQuest* makes judgements about the importance levels of criteria in a very arbitrary, non-ratio scale fashion.

Hence the assertion by the writers of *Expert Choice* appears, at first sight, to be justified. Their package uses ratio data at all times and the other packages use interval data, either completely or to a dominant extent. Therefore, the only valid policy scores are obtainable using *Expert Choice*, not the other packages.

Yet *Expert Choice's* superiority may not be as clear cut as it seems, and we say this for at least three reasons. Firstly, the paired comparisons method that *Expert Choice* uses to collect its ratio data is extremely tedious. Users can therefore become so tired that they begin to input inaccurate responses to questions. By contrast, the comparison of policies is much quicker using packages that ask users to move dots along bars. Hence in large scale policymaking exercises the input data from packages other than *Expert Choice*, even if it is interval rather than ratio, is probably more accurate. *Expert Choice* loses some of its advantage if the data input is less accurate anyway.

Secondly, the *Strategizer* package always standardizes users' scores to numbers adding to 100. It then asks users whether they are willing to accept such scores. This is a little like saying that the user has 100 casino chips to spend on the alternative policies, and so chips are allocated according to intrinsic worth. That is, a woeful policy might get hardly any, or even no chips at all, and a clearly superior policy might get most of the chips. Such a procedure, therefore, does introduce some notion of absolute zero – useless policies will score close to such a zero, so *Strategizer's* scores might be less interval and more ratio in nature than it first seems.

Thirdly, and this is the most important observation, *Expert Choice* itself does not seem to collect genuine ratio scale scores either. True ratio scores are those that are set against an absolute zero that never changes; *Expert Choice* uses the smallest-scoring alternative as its absolute zero; but this surely changes over time. That is, the smallest-scoring policy one day might be displaced by a differently-scoring policy another day, because of a slight reformulation of the available alternative policies.

Hence the absolute zero point moves. This is the cardinal sin that the interval scoring-based packages are accused of. It is true that the zero, as measured by *Expert Choice*, may not move as much as do the arbitrary zero points used by the interval scale packages, but move it does. Hence although *Expert Choice* might give the most accurate policy ratings on any one day, in the fullness of time and within the total scheme of things, it too will be prone to inconsistent results.

It is therefore possible that some people will conclude that all this fuss over ratio versus interval scoring is a storm in a teacup. In practice, it possibly makes little difference what package we use. After all, packages are only supposed to indicate, in the most general of terms, what seem to be the better policies. The ultimate decision is always left to human users. Inexactness in human oriented policymaking, and the lack of precise, invariant data tend to make the analytical gymnastics performed by *Expert Choice* smack of overkill.

This seems to be especially the case when one considers what actually has happened in the market place. If *Expert Choice* was so utterly superior it would be applied exclusively – no other policymaking package would ever be used. But this has not happened. Users seem to be of the opinion that policymaking is such an inexact activity that greater accuracy in one particular package might be of minimal significance.

In other words, most policymaking software is good enough to serve its rather inexact purpose. *Expert Choice* might show clearly and consistently what seems to be the better policies, but so too, to a closer extent than *Expert Choice* producers might admit, do at least some of the other packages. *Expert Choice* might score policies more accurately than some other packages do in the short term, but it basically reflects only the current project's transitory inputs and feelings – just like most of the other packages.

This is, of course, not the last word on rating policies. There is actually a large literature dedicated to describing the many possible ways of scoring alternatives (see for example Smith, 1982*a*; 1982*b*). To laypersons this literature can be bewildering in its opacity. Yet it stands to reason that if one is really sincere about undertaking the best possible policymaking one needs to select the best possible scoring method.

Hence we can conclude that how to score policies the best way is a complicated and difficult question whose surface we have only managed to scratch. We therefore leave it to the mathematicians and philosophers to debate. Meanwhile, of course, we should definitely conclude that *Expert Choice* is the best of our four research frontier packages at assigning valid scores to alternative policies.

9.3. Anticipate

We have already defined 'anticipate' as predicting how people will respond once policymaking has been completed – at least completed in the sense of finishing the first cycle of the circular, never ending policymaking process. Accordingly, we here consider three components of anticipation. Firstly, sub-section 9.3.1 considers how to anticipate whether or not people will approve of the policymaking process that has been undertaken enough to accept its recommendations. Secondly, sub-section 9.3.2 looks at how to confront, and to try to reduce uncertainty that always plagues policymaking. Thirdly, sub-section 9.3.3 discusses how to anticipate people's favoured policies.

9.3.1. Reflecting

One of the most important parts of reflecting on people's responses to policymaking is having knowledge of what they expect from the process. For instance, it is probably true that people want software to suggest which concrete, 'flesh and blood' policies ought to be pursued now. They do not want evaluations, no matter how valid, of the alternative, vague, conceptual 'areas of thrust' that some say should be selected at the outset. That is, some would argue strongly that policymaking is mostly about scheduling and so any approach that ignores sequence, by concentrating only on·evaluating the relative merits of different policy directions, is too abstracted from reality to be of much use in the real world.

On the other hand, it could be argued that expecting a recommendation of exactly what ought to be done, right now, demonstrates an over-idealistic faith in the ability of any policymaking exercise to do this accurately. Only people who are empathetic with the problem situation can properly decide what ought to be done now. Hence having a policymaking project that is pretentious enough to suggest such things could be dangerously misleading. It could result in a situation where those affected are worse off than they would have been without any policymaking at all.

As a specific example, note that *Strad's* recommendations as to which 'goals' ought to be pursued immediately come mostly from their ratings for 'importance' and 'urgency'. Yet such ratings depend, implicitly, on what additional goals are also being aimed for. That is, if some goals are selected for attention simultaneously, the urgency and importance of the goal in question might go up or down accordingly. But the related goals were selected for attention partly on the basis of whether or not the present goals have already been chosen for attention due to their scores for urgency and importance. Such scores depend, in turn, partly upon the presence or absence of the·related goals themselves.

Such an impossible, 'catch 22' situation makes it very dangerous to select one goal at the expense of another inter-connected goal. The final recommendation for action obviously depends upon which other action was selected first. Computers (and non-empathetic policymakers) are entirely unable to handle such circularity. Only involved humans can, because they have some chance of properly dealing with the 'chicken and egg' problem. They can step back from it and consider alternative policies in more abstract terms so as to assess their overall merit, 'all things considered', before making a decision to pursue them. In this way they avoid premature straight jacketing of what other policies should also be aimed for.

This is how *Strategizer* works; it puts more onus on the overall conceptual wisdom and the synoptic, evaluating power of human beings than do most other policymaking packages. This could be a wiser way of proceeding. That is, *Strategizer* encourages users to look very carefully at what generalized alternatives are available, to evaluate them and to choose, with the aid of past users of the software and the machine-learning routines if necessary, which ones have more intrinsic merit.

The user can then re-run the software at some other time in order to use the same approach for deciding what more detailed things ought to be done. In other words, users can run *Strategizer* to decide between overall, long-term policy directions to take; run it again to decide which middle-term policy directions to take, and so on. Users can run the program to decide which pressing options should be aimed at right now, because the longer-term policy decisions have already been taken. Such an approach seems safer than *CyberQuest* and *STRAD's* approach of mixing considerations across the abstraction and time dimensions by throwing all considerations in together, long-, middle- and short-term, and then trying somehow to overcome circularity on the spot.

But in fairness it should be remembered that *STRAD* does allow the user to sort each focus of concerns in terms of their urgency. One can then consider the most urgent issues first, the second most urgent second and so on. This goes some of the way towards guarding against the rejection of some actions simply because incompatible actions have been preselected. But the problem never goes away completely.

Lesson 62: Policymaking can be ideological

Policymaking can sometimes err towards what some people regard as misdirected, participatory waffle. Alternatively, policymaking can be pushed towards what others would regard as dangerously cryptic conciseness. Deciding which bias to risk is certainly a dilemma of practice. Yet this question of emphasis will never be resolved by each side putting forward rational arguments. Their conflict is ideological.

Participatory policymaking is currently enjoying considerable popularity within the Western world's literature as it continues to work through its disillusionment with the technocratic approach adopted during the 1960s and 1970s. Yet on the other hand, some countries are achieving considerable economic success through precise policymaking that uses less participatory techniques.

Many Westerners argue that the participatory approach, at long last, represents a more 'feminine' method of consensus building, and so it deserves a chance because many 'masculine' policymaking methods have failed us in the past. But quite apart from the fact that little, if any rigorous research has been completed to support the efficacy of such gender-based typecasting, such a classification of emphases only appears plausible on anecdotal and intuitive grounds.

Indeed, some would argue the opposite. They would insist that the 'new wave' approaches will be more disastrous than the old methods ever were, because they lack focus and verification. But alas, ideological differences between policymakers will probably always be with us. Human-oriented policymaking is nothing if it is not an introspective discipline.

Note that we can theoretically overcome such circularity by using *STRAD* in a flexible way. This will enable later insertion of decisions that were previously unthought of, and the whole process can be started again. But it is possible to imagine circumstances in which such a tactic would lead to so much complexity that participants would be overwhelmed, and so it might be preferable to opt for programs more like *Strategizer* and *Expert Choice*. To some people these packages might appear to be cryptic, arbitrary and overly abstracted from reality, but they are at least able to help humans sum up ultra-complex situations to the point where they can probably make coherent recommendations.

This, in fact, is the fundamental difference between *STRAD* and *CyberQuest* versus *Expert Choice* and *Strategizer*. The first two encourage a detailed, dialogue-soaked and participatory approach to policymaking which, at its worst, can degenerate to a non-productive 'talk fest'. By contrast, *Expert Choice* and *Startegizer* encourage a distilled, focused and manageable approach to policymaking which, at its worst can lead to suppression of the problem's richness.

The choice basically comes down to whether or not you believe that complicated, 'workshop'-stimulating, 'feeling' software, of the *CyberQuest* and *STRAD* variety, is liable to produce better policy than will the software designed for the concise, machine learning-assisted perceptiveness displayed by *Expert Choice* and *Strategizer's* more 'thinking' style. It comes down to what one feels most comfortable with. We cannot decide on behalf of any reader.

The ideal, of course, would be to use all packages. Yet even to do this with aplomb requires that one is aware of some of the more subtle differences between them. For example, many policymakers simply believe that as a matter of faith policymaking should invariably be 'feeling' in style. They are so obsessed with learning about and eventually understanding the beliefs and desires of participants, they do not even think about the alternative approach of formulating a more consistent and defensible policy. The result is policymaking that aims at being, and usually is empathetic with its human participants; it no doubt makes its perpetrators feel smugly satisfied; but is it the best form of policymaking?

Many would argue that it is not. This is because the people that the empathetic policymakers have gone to so much trouble to study are invariably moody and capricious. It is simply human nature that people's attitudes one day are often different to the attitudes they had on another day. Hence to choose a policy on one particular day, no matter how it seems to fit with participants desires, could actually be a disaster in terms of people's continuing satisfaction. What is therefore needed is some sort of more prescribed and rigorous procedure that gets closer to identifying people's underlying, less changeable core beliefs. It is only knowledge of these that will ensure satisfaction with policymaking over the long haul.

Hence it is difficult to say which package is able best to reflect on people's choices. All packages have their own idiosyncrasies, some of which are effective for predicting people's responses and some of which are not. Probably the best of our packages is *Expert Choice*. This is because one of its trademark features, extensive sensitivity testing of policies, encourages the user to think in great detail about how people place different emphases on different policy-evaluation criteria and different policies.

Lesson 63: Regulate participation

Policymaking that is all too eager to interpret people's feelings, at one particular point in time only, can be unreliable. That is, the sort of policymaking that wears its 'participation' badge with pride can often, paradoxically, not gain much participatory insight at all.

This is because such an approach often incorporates 'feel good' procedures, and the latter can produce woolly thinking along with lack of scrutiny and rigour. Hence even though they appear to be doing a sterling job at getting inside people's heads, by relating to participants meaningfully, workshop-based policymakers can frequently misinterpret people's true values.

There is little doubt that policymakers will always find participatory methods to be vital, but they need to be implemented with a degree of moderation and care.

9.3.2. Managing uncertainty

One of the biggest barriers to anticipation of people's responses is the presence of uncertainty. If this can be understood and reduced, then policymaking can proceed far more confidently. But *STRAD* is the only one of our four frontier packages that does this in an explicit way (Cartwright, 1992). Indeed, as already noted in Chapter 6, *STRAD's* 'strategic choice' approach is sometimes actually referred to as the 'management of uncertainty'.

By contrast, our other packages simply assume that uncertainty is not within the user's control. They assume that uncertainty can simply be discounted if we make an 'on balance' or an 'all things being equal' sort of assumption. But uncertainty will not go away, and all things will probably not be equal. Why should they be? Uncertainty is almost guaranteed to persist.

STRAD therefore constitutes our most practical and 'down to earth' software in a policy-implementation sense. This is epitomized by its assignment of an 'urgency' score to each Decision Area. That is, *STRAD* actually sees policymaking as, partly, a scheduling problem. Hence it is no accident that *STRAD's* final recommendation table is divided into two: one part suggests what should be done now and another part describes what should be done in the future – a scheduling part and a strategic part. By contrast, *Strategizer* refuses to deal with scheduling issues because it wants to retain its 'strategic purity'. It deals with only the strategic part of policymaking.

9.3.3. Learning people's preferences

Finally, if one really wants to anticipate how people will respond to policymaking, it would be a great help to be able to predict which actual policies they are likely to prefer. If software does not know this, then perhaps it can 'learn'. But of our four frontier packages, the only one that incorporates a learning capability is *Strategizer*. The first three are purely reflective in the sense that they take in only, and simply reflect back, the views of the current users. By contrast, *Strategizer* actually tries to learn from its past users so that it becomes better and better at recommending policy the more it is used. Hence it is the only one of the four that claims to become gradually proficient at predicting the likely preferences of different sorts of people for different policies.

It is important to realize that *Strategizer* can only make such an extravagant claim because it assumes that all policymaking, everywhere and in every problem area, uses its ten 'universal' evaluation criteria. It is only by looking at policies' scores on such criteria, and relating these scores to the overall score, that *Strategizer* has any chance of learning to anticipate overall score across all problem domains. By contrast, the other packages cannot undertake similar learning because none of them use ever-present evaluation criteria. They all work on the assumption that evaluation criteria should be selected according to the problem being addressed.

In other words, *Strategizer's* learning mechanism is predicated on an assumption that certain types of people will emphasize certain types of evaluation criteria no matter what the problem area is. This is similar to certain psychological theories of the type that suggest some individuals have an innate propensity for risk taking whereas others are inherently conservative. That is, *Strategizer* is predicated on an assumption that people have core policymaking values.

Moreover, it is assumed that such core values, or propensities to place a relatively large importance on certain policy-evaluation criteria, shine through even when the problem addressed influences policymaking behaviour. For example, although policymakers might put less store on the 'probability' of success when they are undertaking policymaking using someone else's money as distinct from their own money, in general, attitudes towards the importance of probability should persist regardless. All software needs to do is learn about such differences, which is the function of *Strategizer's* neural networks.

But this grand assumption that people's emphases on different evaluation criteria will remain relatively constant across different problem areas and across time, requires further research to confirm or confound. Initial results seem promising (Wyatt, 1997*b*), but the assumption has by no means been proven.

Note, however, that one does not have to be convinced of the truth of this underlying theory in order simply to 'try out' the software in search of possibly valuable insights into policymaking. That is, even if the predictions of *Strategizer* are unfounded, the very act of considering the possible preferences of certain community groups could lead to much more community sensitivity on the part of the policymaker. Hence *Strategizer* can probably be used to gain insight into people's policy preferences by both sceptics and true believers.

9.4. Combining Packages

It is time to recap. Basically, we have found that *CyberQuest* and *STRAD* are 'feeling' in their style whereas *Expert Choice* and *Strategizer* are more 'thinking' in their approach. Moreover, one would tend to use them in the order in which they have been presented – *CyberQuest* and *STRAD* to help us 'think', *Expert Choice* to help us 'choose' and *Strategizer* to help us 'anticipate'. Also, we should note the contrast between the first and last packages – *CyberQuest* and *Strategizer*, and the middle two – *STRAD* and *Expert Choice*. *CyberQuest* and *Strategizer* are specialized and focused whereas *STRAD* and *Expert Choice* are less specialized and willing to cover more of the total policymaking process.

With these contrasts in mind, we can now recommend how the four packages should be combined. This is shown in figure 9.1. Specifically, *CyberQuest* should be used at the beginning of all serious policymaking projects. It stimulates the user's imagination and prompts him or her to generate innovative ideas. Hence in the interests of 'casting the net widely' to obtain a plethora of initial, policy-relevant ideas and so avoid premature specificity, one would be well advised to use *CyberQuest* first up.

| PHASE | TASK | PERFORMED BY? | | | |
		CyberQuest	*STRAD*	*Expert Choice*	*Strategizer*
Think	Generate ideas	**yes**	yes	yes	yes
	Eliminate some	yes	**yes**	yes	yes
	Package ideas	**yes**	yes	yes	yes
Choose	Identify policies	yes	**yes**	yes	yes
	Evaluate policies	yes	yes	yes	**yes**
	Assign scores	yes	yes	**yes**	yes
Anticipate	Reflect	yes	yes	**yes**	yes
	Manage uncertainty	no	**yes**	no	no
	Learn preferences	no	no	no	**yes**

Figure 9.1. Using each of the four research frontier packages at different stages of the policymaking process.

Then, since *STRAD* is very effective at eliminating unfeasible combinations of plans/ideas/options using its 'option bar' mechanism, it makes sense to go from *CyberQuest* to *STRAD*, as shown, when it gets to the idea-elimination stage. But when it comes to amalgamating notional ideas into more coherent 'packaged' ideas, *CyberQuest* is probably best again.

Pressing on, when it comes to choosing a bundle of ideas, or policy, *Strad* is probably the best package for actually identifying them, but once identified, they are probably best evaluated using *Strategizer* because of the thoroughness of its evaluation criteria. Moreover, the actual assignment of scores is almost certainly best done using *Expert Choice* because of its ability to achieve almost ratio scale scores.

Finally, in terms of reflecting on the total policymaking exercise, *Expert Choice* is probably the best due to its concentration on sensitivity testing. We have also seen that *STRAD* is the only package fully to address uncertainty and *Strategizer* is the only one that tries to learn people's policy preferences.

In summary therefore, it seems that policymakers are best advised to use *CyberQuest*, *Expert Choice* and *Strategizer* for two phases of policymaking each and *Strad* for three phases. If one's budget is limited it might, therefore, be worthwhile purchasing only *STRAD*, or perhaps a combination of *STRAD* and either *Strategizer* or *Expert Choice*. Yet it is of little use activating such packages if one has not got the initial task right – generation of innovative ideas, and *CyberQuest* is necessary to do this optimally. Therefore, if one is serious about finding a high-quality policy, it is difficult to argue against purchasing all four packages.

If all four are purchased, there is, of course, an alternative procedure for combining them – use each package in turn to address the whole problem. Should certain policies emerge as best according to several packages, then they are probably more worthwhile than policies recommended as 'best' by only one or two of the packages. Yet since all packages are relatively deficient in at least some parts of the policymaking process, by far the best way to proceed still seems to be activation of all four packages in the sequence shown by figure 9.1.

9.4. Summary

This chapter explained how our four packages have their respective strengths and weaknesses. Therefore they need to be used, all together, in a judicious fashion that utilizes the strengths and avoids the weaknesses of each one. This reflects policymaking practice itself, where practitioners should always be mindful of their own strengths and weaknesses, as well as those of all other participants in the process.

Chapter 10

Conclusions

We finally come to the end of this rather opinionated book. Despite its pretensions of rigour, its lessons-extraction process has hardly been objective. Hence the discussion of some packages has simply served as a launching pad from which the author could parade his prejudices. In the process some readers will have been offended by his dogmatism, by his lack of knowledge or by both.

Nevertheless, we hope that the whole exercise has managed to extract some useful lessons for improved practical policymaking. This concluding chapter now gives coherence to such lessons, which number 63, by amalgamating them into six overall recommendations. The recommendations have often been inspired by our four packages that are at the so-called research frontier, but other packages have also provided valuable insights.

Specifically, section 10.1 details the six recommendations and explains how they fit into what we have argued is the quintessential sequence of activities that policymaking practitioners adopt. Section 10.2 then outlines how the use of software can both help and hinder implementation of this sequence, and it derives one last, final lesson for practitioners.

10.1. Recommendations

At the risk of oversimplifying what is obviously a very subtle and delicate process, we have been at pains to point out above how most policymaking passes, or should pass, through three phases – 'think', 'choose' and 'anticipate (consequences)'. Now, it just so happens that our six recommendations fit neatly into this sequence. That is, two of them help policymakers to think about which options to pursue; two of them improve our ability to choose between options, and the remaining two enhance policymakers' ability to anticipate the consequences of implementing the different options.

This is set out in figure 10.1, where the arrows convey the sequential nature of the 'think-choose-anticipate' process.

Recommendation 1 – Think laterally

Obviously, lateral thinking is a vital part of all exemplary policymaking. But in the real world, most policymaking exercises seldom become known for their originality. They may start out with the best of intentions in terms of the range of issues that they will persist in considering, but sooner or later they get swamped under an irresistible tide of vested interests, politics, lack of skills, shortage of time and paucity of resources. This forces the policymaking exercise to focus on

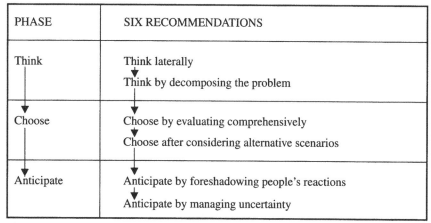

PHASE	SIX RECOMMENDATIONS
Think	Think laterally ↓ Think by decomposing the problem
Choose	Choose by evaluating comprehensively ↓ Choose after considering alternative scenarios
Anticipate	Anticipate by foreshadowing people's reactions ↓ Anticipate by managing uncertainty

Figure 10.1. Improved policymaking.

only certain options and to exclude many other useful ones altogether. Sometimes cultural forces are the root cause of this. For instance, in many societies a social elite performs policymaking exclusively, which can be very bad news for the range and the depth of the policy ideas that are ultimately considered. Each of our six recommendations will now be detailed in turn.

Moreover, even within some advanced nations, policymaking professionals have never heard of brainstorming and other creativity-boosting procedures. Hence reading books like this one may give budding policymakers from such countries an initial, and ultimately fruitful insight into many of the consciousness-expanding techniques outlined above. Many of these techniques are quick, cheap and easy to apply, as epitomized by *CyberQuest* and by several of the packages discussed above under the headings of groupware, gameware and business-oriented software.

Adoption of these methods seems to be policymaking's only hope for tapping into the vast reservoir of human insight that is sitting, largely unexploited, within the general community. Such grassroots wisdom should never be underestimated. Indeed, the former Soviet world chess champion, Boris Spasky, once played six correspondence games with readers of the *Ural Workers' Daily* in which the readership's most popular suggestion was always taken as the counter move to Spasky's move. Yet far from the world champion having it all his own way by winning all six games, Spasky won two, lost two and drew two.

In short, there is a huge amount of eminently useful wisdom out there within the proletariat, and such a reservoir of expertise has huge potential for improving the laterality of policymaking. The sooner that current policymaking practice taps into this, the sooner it will begin to improve. The good news is that the chances of this happening appear to be increasing. As we have pointed out above, greater use of the Internet and the resulting popularization of education and other things, including policymaking, is accelerating. Policymaking, therefore, should 'seize the day'.

Recommendation 2 – Think by decomposing the problem

It needs to be remembered that improving the 'think' phase of policymaking by swamping participants with a brilliant plethora of ingenious policy options is a double-edged sword. If it is performed with sufficient enthusiasm to maximize the laterality of one's thinking, then it will almost certainly swamp policymakers into a state of indecisive confusion. To counter this, all serious policymaking needs to structure itself in some way. And the structuring method recommended by most of this book's software is decomposition of the grand problem into smaller and more manageable problems, usually by means of a goals hierarchy.

Yet many policymaking practitioners, and even the theoreticians who advise them, frequently reject the goals hierarchy. For example, some social scientists have pointed out that hierarchies can oversimplify our perceptions and so lead us to unrealistically glib thinking. Also, computer scientists are fond of demonstrating how redundancy within hierarchical data structures makes them inferior to relational database structures (Burrough and MacDonnell, 1998). Moreover, the fickle dictates of academic fashion, as well as many workshop facilitators' mania for more intuitive, 'feel good' processes, cause many commentators to simply reject the structured approach to policymaking out of hand.

Such rejection is, of course, based on the most laudable of intentions – more perceptive policymaking. But it is dangerous. It is actually a result of the analytical tradition or the design tradition, as described in the Introduction to this book, filtering too close to the 'business end' of policymaking. As we have seen, this can lead to analysis paralysis on the one hand and to perilous leaps of faith on the other. It is far better to try to decompose the policymaking problem, so that it can be given greater clarity and manageability, before blazing ahead into fully blown analysis or frenetic design.

Besides, we have noted that ordinary people, with a little coaching, can perfectly understand the concept of the goals hierarchy. It is a natural notion and it is used in so many fields of endeavour. As such, policymaking practitioners and theoreticians should be humble enough to accept its benefits with good grace. Without decomposing the problem into less difficult parts, it is difficult to see how human-oriented policymaking can be performed with any sustainable level of viability. Policymaking must always be in control of itself.

Recommendation 3 – Choose by evaluating options comprehensively

So much for improved thinking. When it comes to better choice of options, it is obvious that this can only be achieved when the criteria, on which choices are based, cover all of the considerations that are important. Put differently, policymakers will find it of little use thinking laterally and carefully if they then evaluate all their clever options in a non-exhaustive way. Like the options themselves, choice criteria need to be maximally wide ranging. Yet the history of policymaking is littered with examples of inappropriate policies being chosen simply because so many aspects of the environment, as implicit within the evaluation criteria, were not even considered.

Several programs described above, particularly some of the business-oriented packages and *CyberQuest* and *Strategizer*, went to considerable trouble to correct this tendency. *Strategizer* even claims to be using universal evaluation criteria that are applicable to policymaking problems anywhere at any time. Policymaking practice ought, therefore, at least to consider using all of this program's ten criteria.

Nevertheless, one could argue that *Strategizer's* ten criteria are too general and insufficiently focused to achieve incisive policymaking, and in a way they are. Yet they actually need to be abstract in nature. This is because they act as an umbrella for all of the concerns that policymakers might come up with. Hence, so long as all such concerns are addressed, we should be getting closer to comprehensive evaluation, at least in a generalist sense.

An alternative is, of course, taken by some software packages – saturate the policymaker with as many evaluation criteria as can be thought of, more than any individual policymaking project will ever need, in the hope that all the important ones are eventually used. Or, one could take a more common approach, echoed in much software, of letting participants themselves nominate the evaluation criteria that seem to be most suitable to the problem at hand.

Yet both of these alternatives tempt the policymaker to become too specialized and focused on just some of the issues of the moment. This almost always leads to omission of other important considerations that have been temporarily forgotten about, and the result is a lack of true comprehensiveness in policy evaluation. In other words, policymakers have a natural tendency to consider only those criteria that seem particularly, but temporarily poignant.

Put differently, policymakers find it tempting to dive straight into discussions of the factors with which they have most recently been preoccupied. The latter are usually non-abstract considerations, and the result is a lack of breadth, premature specificity and hence myopic choices. To counter this, policymaking needs to remain cognisant of the 'big picture', always. Context is everything.

Recommendation 4 – Choose after considering alternative scenarios

It is important to remember that, even when the big picture is kept constantly in sight, choosing between options is always done in partial ignorance. By definition, policy choice will always be moulded by our view of the future, and we will always be in the dark about what the future holds in store because it has not yet happened.

Nevertheless, much practical policymaking is arrogant enough to sweep this ignorance under the carpet. It is as if it has put so much effort in decision support activities that it is then reluctant to scrutinize properly what one is being told by the simulation models. It simply assumes, because it is less troublesome to do so, that the models' forecasts are to be accepted as gospel. This is despite current simulation modelling, especially within the human-oriented arena of vicious problems, being simply too unsophisticated to give us much of an idea about the true nature of the future. Poor policymaking inevitably follows.

One possible solution to this is to incorporate consideration of several alternative scenarios into all policymaking exercises, as is competently done by the *Expert Choice* software. Simply assuming that one particular state of the world will pertain in the future is not good enough for exemplary policymaking. Policymakers need to accept that a number of future states are eminently possible and the sooner that we become aware of, and partly prepared for their possible repercussions the better it will be for the ultimate success of policymaking practice.

More specifically, a good way to proceed is to consider various alternative, future states, along with as much data about their respective levels of likelihood that one is able to find. The latter does not necessarily have to be hard, statistical data, for we have seen that it can also include information extracted from people's heads. Yet only after it has been collected and digested will any policymaking exercise be confident that it is actually recursing towards the best known option given the *range* of future possibilities.

Moreover, such iteration needs to be done not only thoroughly, but also with the maximum involvement of those who will actually be affected by the considered policies. This is because the planned-for often have a good feel for what the future holds since, after all, it is they who will have the most influence in moulding their future.

In short, policymaking that is based on a less than complete canvassing of future possible changes to the environment will always be suspect. Exemplary policymaking needs to be more 'streetwise' than this. It needs to be open minded about the future.

Recommendation 5 – Anticipate by foreshadowing people's reactions

Alas, policymaking can sometimes be a complete failure even when both the 'think' and the 'choose' phase have been performed in an exemplary manner. That is, there are circumstances in which a chosen policy will be entirely unsuitable even though it has been selected only after considerable lateral thinking, careful problem decomposition, comprehensive evaluation of alternatives and versatile forecasting of future states. Such circumstances pertain when some powerful social groups, or all groups, reject a chosen policy. Whenever a policy is unacceptable to those in the community who do, or should count, then it will not be a worthwhile policy.

Therefore, we need some way of foreshadowing people's reactions to alternative policies, and the Game Theory-based, *NAIADE* package that was described above in Chapter 3 has some promise here. It predicts which coalitions of vested interest groups are likely to form as a response to different policies being adopted. Moreover, the *Strategizer* package anticipates various sorts of people's likely response to each policy option, and it even claims to get better and better at doing this the more it is used.

Practical policymaking needs to follow this lead. It should 'scientize' to the point of being able to find incisive parallels within different policymakers' knowledge of community reactions to different policies, in different places, at different times – policy science. We have seen that competitive, modern conditions might be working against this ever happening on a large scale. But we have also seen that other aspects of modern technology are making inter-exercise comparisons more feasible.

Whichever force wins out, there is still little doubt that much current policymaking practice has suffered considerable damage through being unable, or unwilling to foreshadow community reactions to its prescriptions. This needs to change if it is to improve its performance. Policymaking needs to be more prognostic.

Recommendation 6: Anticipate by managing uncertainty

A final improvement to modern policymaking practice would occur if it incorporated more techniques that are designed to identify, and to take precautions in view of uncertainty. Chapter 6 pointed out that almost all current policymaking practice, and the software that assists it, simply assumes uncertainty away. It undertakes its deliberations on the basis of 'all things being equal'. This means that one does not know what will happen in many areas, and so one simply assumes that a balance of forces will neutralize the effect of all the different kinds of uncertainty.

But there is actually no evidence that such a balance of uncertain forces is any more likely than an imbalance. Moreover, we are unlikely to ever know the answer to such a riddle. As the 'soft systems methodologists' point out, uncertainty in policymaking is not the sort of uncertainty that can be measured using statistics and probability – it is the kind of uncertainty that people feel.

Thus policymakers have no alternative other than to confront uncertainty head on, like the *STRAD* software encourages them to do. Policymakers need to document as much as is known about uncertainty, categorize it, and think deeply about how to decrease it. It is little use making policy, no matter how expertly, if sheer environmental uncertainty is going to wipe away its validity within a short time.

In a nutshell, policymaking needs to cushion itself against uncertainty by adopting a cautious approach. Indeed, one should even adopt a 'safety first' stance whenever the uncertain consequences of not doing so could be catastrophic.

10.2. Now What?

By way of summary, we have now reached the stage of recommending that exemplary policymaking practice should be laterally thinking, in control of itself, contextually aware, futuristically open minded, prognostic and cautious. But what will using software do to the chances of policymaking practice being all of these things?

To answer, we end this book in a similar way to that in which we began it. That is, at the start of Chapter 1 we let some computer packages 'speak for themselves', and so we now let a human talk about what happened when they used a package.

The following narrative originally took the form of a column written by Stephen Manes, for *PC Magazine*, on January 28, 1986. It is reproduced with the publisher's kind permission:

Well, Bud Jr. certainly got my money's worth out of his college education. What he does mostly is spout sixty-dollar words he picked up from those silk-tie friends of his and tell me how I should modernize the farm like his'n. 'Modernize myself right into bankruptcy like your high-roller pals' is what I always say to that, which shuts him up awhile.

Me, I'm getting on, but I keep my end up just fine. Can't say the same for old Flossie. She's not as young as she used to be, and she just can't pull the plow the way she could back when. Used to was she could start off half an hour after the rooster crowed and go till noon without stopping, and then put on the feedbag and then go on past sunset without hardly a whimper. But lately it got so I had to think about putting the old girl out to pasture.

Me and Flossie been together a lot of years, so at first it like to broke my heart to think about it, and we just kept on keeping on. But every chance he got, Bud Jr. kept whining I ought to at least get into the 19th century even if I didn't believe in the 20th, and the least I could do if I didn't want to buy one of them newflanged computers to count the cornstalks was get me a air-conditioned tractor like his'n. Me, what I always say is, if you have to have an air-conditioned tractor, then the next thing you know you'll want a colored TV.

But Bud Jr. takes after his pop in a couple of ways, and I guess I mentioned this and that problem with Flossie once too often because the next thing I know, he traipses in the front door with this little suitcase. He says I been shilly-shallying long enough (except he used some sixty-five dollar word) and with the help of this here computer I'll make my decision once and for all. He plugs her in and fires her up and plunks me down in front of this little green Martian TV.

This isn't even Greek to me, but Bud Jr. learnt all about this stuff in some school or someplace. He says this is called Light Year, which only reminds me of the drought of '37. 'It is a decision-making system,' says he.

'Something like a coin with heads on one side and tails on the other,' says I.

'Watch the screen,' says my unamused offspring. I believe I forgot to mention I am Bud Sr.

The first thing that shows up is a little box that says ALTERNATIVES at the top. Then he types in Flossie at the top and Tractor right underneath. Those are my alternatives, no two ways about it.

He fiddles with the keys and the next thing I know there's a screen with the word CRITERIA on the top of it. I would of guessed that was either a town in Kansas or a disease, but Bud Jr. looks at me very patientlike and tells me what it means.

Then he says to tell him what is important in making this decision. 'Give me a for example,' says I.

'Well, take Initial Cost,' Bud Jr. says. 'You've already got Flossie, so she's free. A tractor will cost you, say, ten thousand.'

'Not if I don't get one of them fancy dudes with the factory air, it won't.'

'We don't need to worry about the price till later,' says he. And he types Initial Cost on top. Then he moves down a line, and types in Upkeep.

'How about Resale Value?' says I.

Bud Jr. looks at me as if he's about to bust a gut with pride. 'You're starting to get the hang of this, Pop.' Pop is what he calls me when his defenses are down.

'I'm just playing along,' says I. 'What about how much work you can do in a day?'

'Very important. We'll call that Output.' I ask him why not just call it how much work you can do in a day, and he says that won't fit into the little box. Maybe all them seventy-dollar words come into the world on account of the easy way to say it don't fit into little boxes on green TVs.

Anyway, we type in Dependability, and Loyalty, and Sentimental Value, and Attitude. Then I think of something else.

'Put Aggravation in there,' I say. 'Flossie has been aggravating me something fierce lately.' Bud Jr. gives me a look, but he pecks it in.

So then he says it's time to give these things weights. 'I haven't put Flossie on the scales in a long time,' I say, 'but she don't weigh as much as no tractor.' Bud Jr. gives me a dirty look and says he don't mean that kind of weight. What I'm supposed to do is pick a number from 1 to 100 to tell the machine how important each category is. One hundred is real important, but 30 is not-so-very. I give 80 to Output, and 70 to Upkeep all the way down to 20 for Sentimental Value. You can't plow with no sentiment.

Next Bud Jr. says we have to pick a mode for each one. Pie à la is the only mode I ever heard about, but Bud Jr. says we got to figure out whether we want to compare numbers, or words, or pitchers. I don't have the foggiest, so I tell him to try a little of each flavor.

Then the next thing we have to do is fill in the blanks like on one of them contests nobody ever wins. First we have to do the ones with the numbers, but before you can do that, you have to decide what's most desirable and what's least desirable. You would think a thinking machine that's supposed to help you decide could decide for itself that when something costs you ten thousand smackers it's less desirable than if it costs you zip, but Bud Jr. says no, you got to tell it, which we do.

We work out all the numbers for Cost and Upkeep and Resale Value, and then it's time for Output and Dependability. These come with lines on them that go from Most Desirable to Least Desirable, and you move an X from one end to the other or somewhere in the middle.

The thinking machine can't figure out that the work a tractor can do is closer to Most Desirable and the way Flossie is going she's nearly off the other end, so I let it know. And as for Loyalty, a tractor isn't going to run off on you and disappear for a while because it's taken a shine to some other tractor, so the Xs on that one come out pretty much the same way.

Then we get to the Verbal ones. You get to pick from a list of words like Maximum, Extreme, High, Moderate, Low, Minimum, and Absent. I figure any machine would probably give me Moderate Aggravation, but the way Flossie's been carrying on lately, Extreme is the only score I could give her on that one. For Attitude I could pick from Fantastic, Good, Fair, Bad, and Terrible. I figure a tractor will have an OK attitude, but by now I bet you can guess how Flossie come out. When it come to Sentimental Value I give her Maximum at first, but the more I think about it she ends up down at Moderate. That still beats out the tractor.

According to Bud Jr., MBA, as it says on that business card of his with the writing you can feel, it's time for RULES. Me, I don't know any that apply here except maybe the golden one of do unto other people before they do unto you. But Mr. Educated says the only kinds of rules you can apply is simple ones like if Aggravation is too high, the machine can knock somebody out of the running. I say Flossie would lose right away if we made up a rule like that, which doesn't seem fair, and the long and short of it is we skip the rules part.

Then the next thing Bud Jr. says is 'Watch this!' He moves the little light over the word EVALUATE, and the next thing I know, up there on the screen is two long bars, one for Flossie and one for the Tractor. The one for Flossie is a trifle longer. It says out of a possible 360 points, Flossie got 183 and Tractor got 169.

Cut off my nose and fry me for a catfish! I suddenly get this oystery feeling in the back of my gullet. 'Well, if your machine don't lie, 'I say kind of glumlike, 'I guess I'm stuck with Flossie.'

'Not so fast,' says Bud Jr., who looks kind of upset but not half as much as me. 'This is where the computer really comes in handy.' He presses a key and up come some more little bars, one for each thing we rated Flossie on. 'See, Pop, now the computer will let you play what-if.'

'What if I just kick you and it out of here right now?'

Bud Jr. gives me one of those 'I'm trying to be patient' looks of his. 'Dad, this is scientific. Now, look here. Maybe you want to change the weights of some of these factors.'

He uses his finger to point to a couple of the little bars, and then I get the gag and go along. 'Poor Flossie did pretty bad on Output. You know, I guess that's more important than your old man thought. And that Sentimental Value mush? Well, we shouldn't let sentiment stand in the way of making these here scientific decisions, should we?' We make a couple more changes and Bud Jr. types 'em in and presses more buttons, and guess what?

It's Tractor over Flossie 177 to 165. 'You know, that recount was slicker than the way Mayor Delp stole the election.'

But I got to admit the machine done its job. The minute I saw Flossie win, I felt terrible. I would of done anything to change the score, and that's what I did. Still, it's like I said at the beginning: You can do the same if you just flip a coin. When you start rooting for heads, you know what you really want to do.

Well, to make this story short, Bud Jr. went home and printed everything up on some gizmo of his, and that very day I booted Flossie out the gate and found myself a nice tractor with good rubber on the tires and a seat that rattles your kidneys like it ought to and good old country air instead of the factory kind. I told Bud Jr. thanks for helping me cheat, but he said I actually done right anyway on account of the computer got fooled in the Aggravation department and gave more points for Extreme than for Low, and when he fixed it Flossie came out on the bottom even before we played 'what-if.'

Well, the computer was right. I been a happier man than anytime in my 49 years of married life since I divorced the old girl and bought the tractor and I don't have to buy no golden anniversary present neither.

You'd think Bud Jr. would be tickled pink, which he was at first. But now he says I should of kept Flossie after all, because the computer didn't add up no alimony payments and lawyer bills, which would of tipped the scales the other way.

Personally, I think the old girl's what's got him tickled. She moved in with him now that he needs her rent to make the payments on that air-conditioned tractor, and for the life of me I don't know why, but she's running around now with a smile on her face and about 20 years off her age and some lunk in a funeral suit from uptown, which Bud Jr. thinks is no way for the mother of a MBA to behave.

I tell you, the old girl and Bud Jr. would never admit it, but me, I wonder if Flossie just might of 'what-iffed' that computing machine in the first place.

We need to summarize what occurred here in order to learn from it. Bud and Bud Junior used a 1986 policymaking package that we mentioned above, *Light Year*, to help them choose between Flossie and a tractor. They evaluated their two alternatives using criteria which they nominated themselves:

➤ Initial Cost,
➤ Upkeep,
➤ Resale Value,
➤ Output,
➤ Dependability,
➤ Loyalty,
➤ Sentimental Value,
➤ Attitude, and
➤ Aggravation.

When the software chose Flossie, they altered the weight placed on the Output criterion in order to make it more important, and they decreased the weight on Sentimental Value to make it less important. This, of course, made the software choose the tractor, and later on, Bud Junior even reassured his father that the software's first decision had been incorrect anyway. This was because they had given a large amount of points for an extreme value on the Aggravation criterion, whereas they should have given high aggravation a small amount of points. Hence Flossie would have lost anyway, even if they had not tampered with the original weights.

In short, the two Buds showed great enthusiasm for using *Light Year* to 'legitimate' the decision that they wanted to make in the first place. They were besotted with the prospect of buying a shiny new tractor. They were therefore willing to increase the importance of Output, and to down play the importance of Sentimental Value, or do whatever else it took to make the software tell them what they thought they wanted to hear.

Yet they obviously made the wrong decision. Bud Senior became overburdened with payments for both his new tractor and for the alimony and divorce costs that he had not anticipated. Worse, Bud Junior used the software to justify his own purchase of his 'top of the range' tractor. This forced him to take in Flossie as a boarder in order to raise revenue for payments on his tractor, which brought him into contact with his mother's annoying, new boyfriend. The only person to come out on top seemed to be Flossie. She eventually found herself being cared for properly, by her new beau, rather than being treated like a beast of burden on the farm.

Why did such outcomes occur? Before answering, remember that in order to perform policymaking properly the two Buds needed three capabilities: consciousness, emotions and free will (unpredictability). These are precisely the three capabilities that our packages, who 'talked' to us in Chapter 1, said people believe computers do not possess but which actually can be simulated through computation. Such capabilities have therefore been added to figure 10.1, above, in order to produce figure 10.2.

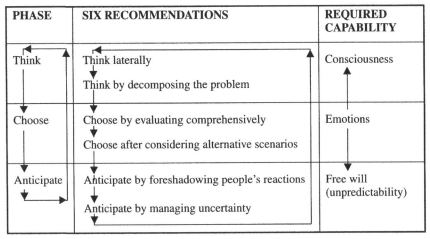

PHASE	SIX RECOMMENDATIONS	REQUIRED CAPABILITY
Think	Think laterally Think by decomposing the problem	Consciousness
Choose	Choose by evaluating comprehensively Choose after considering alternative scenarios	Emotions
Anticipate	Anticipate by foreshadowing people's reactions Anticipate by managing uncertainty	Free will (unpredictability)

Figure 10.2. Improved, computer-assisted policymaking.

Looking at figure 10.2, we see that Bud and Bud Junior came to grief at all three stages of the policymaking process. Firstly, they were at a disadvantage performing the first, consciousness-based, 'think' phase of policymaking because *CyberQuest* and other sophisticated brainstorming software were not generally available in 1986. But if they had used them, Bud Senior and his son would certainly have thought more laterally about other possible alternatives and so not necessarily have settled on just their two options. For instance, they might have also considered increasing their revenue by changing their crops, or by selling the farm, or by fertilizing more, or by accommodating paying guests on their property, or whatever.

Moreover, Bud and his son may have had more success if they had decomposed their total problem a little more enthusiastically. That is, setting up a goals hierarchy may have made them realize that increased farm revenue is simply a means to some end rather than an end in itself. That is, their overall end might have been designated as something like 'have a satisfying and fulfilling lifestyle', and things additional to farm revenue are important for achieving this, such as good health, harmonious family relationships and leisure time. Mere consideration of such things might have made them decide to keep Flossie as an important part of their family, which they did not, and which they now regret.

In short, the software that they used was somewhat dated. More sophisticated software that puts more emphasis either on brainstorming, or on building a contextual goals hierarchy, or both, has been developed since 1986. Such software may have led them to a more satisfactory policy.

Similar comments apply to the emotions-based, 'choose' part of the policymaking process. Our two main characters used only the evaluation criteria that they thought of themselves. Hence by no stretch of the imagination did they evaluate comprehensively. By contrast, if they had considered just a few of *Strategizer's* compulsory criteria, such as Correctness, Speed and Autonomy, then their zeal to make the decision they thought they wanted to make would have been revealed for what it really was – partially informed.

Moreover, they certainly did not make their decision after considering a number of possible scenarios. In fact, the prospect of future financial difficulties, alimony, divorce and jealousy did not even enter their heads. Use of *Expert Choice*, which encourages policymakers to think about alternative scenarios, may not have made them think of such possibilities either, but at least it would have made this more likely than did the simpler software that they were stuck with back in 1986. The cryptic nature of the latter made them simplify their perception of their own emotions – to their ultimate regret.

Finally, it hardly needs to be reiterated how the two Buds were demonstrably inadequate in the 'anticipate' phase of the policymaking process. It never occurred to them that Flossie, after they had sent her out the gate, might soothe her aggravation in the arms of someone willing to treat her better than a horse. But we have seen above how some software has been written since 1986 that does make an attempt to foreshadow how different individuals will react to different policy alternatives. Bud Junior and his father could certainly have profited by using these packages.

Also, the latest version of the *STRAD* software, with its emphasis on the management of uncertainty, was not available in 1986 either. If it had been, our two farmers would have been able to prepare themselves for responding less painfully to uncertain repercussions of jettisoning Flossie from the farm. At the very least, they could have prepared themselves to better adjust to her running around with 'some lunk in a funeral suit from uptown'.

Overall, there is little doubt that anticipation of such possible and uncertain consequences would have forced them to at least rethink their whole policymaking problem. Hence one thing that using the latest policymaking software certainly does is to force us to think of the recursive, never ending nature of exemplary policymaking. For this reason we have added the feedback loop to figure 10.2. It is always tempting to think of policymaking as a one-directional, sequential process, as shown in figure 10.1 above. Using software soon makes us realize that it is not; it needs considerable and continued soul searching if it is to be performed satisfactorily.

Indeed, this is probably the principal message to come out of figure 10.2 and the one on which we shall finish this book. It is fairly obvious that computerization in policymaking has made the most progress in terms of helping the first and the last of the 'required capabilities'. Software is now available that can document, suggest, and remember elements of the situation to the point of raising one's level of consciousness. There is also software that is now coming into the main stream which helps one to anticipate policy consequences in the uncertainty-plagued, 'anticipate' phase of the policymaking process.

But it is in the middle, 'choose' phase where computer assistance has made the least progress. This is more of a human preserve, based as it is on humans' emotions. Software can help in an oblique way by alerting humans to additional judgemental criteria, by reminding them of inconsistencies in their choices so far, and by impressing upon them the nature of various future possible environments. Indeed even the *Light Year* software recognized the importance of this phase by encouraging users to reassess their emotions by altering criteria weights in a 'what if' manner.

Yet performance of this core policymaking activity – decision making – depends on how humans intrinsically *feel* about their emotions. It does not depend on what the computer reports to them in terms of the equilibrium of their current circumstances and the psuedo legitimacy of their judgements. And, as we have noted, computer-based meddling in this core, emotion-based process can actually have the effect of deluding users into believing that temporary considerations, like buying a new tractor, are more important than the permanent ones, like family breakdown.

Hence in our story, the only person not to use software, Flossie, was probably the best policymaker. She felt dissatisfied enough with her exploitation to aggravate her family about it, and it is possible that her 'taking a shine' to someone else prompted the two farmers to begin their policymaking exercise in the first place. She finally got what she wanted because she was in touch with her emotions. By contrast, the two males were not in touch with their true emotions; they used software as a substitute for them and they did not get what they wanted. This is possibly what prompted Bud Senior's wry comment about how Flossie had probably 'what-iffed' Bud Junior's software in the first place.

Hence we can extract, from this abortive attempt by two farmers to use software to make a better policy decision, a final recommendation for policymaking practice – *know yourself.* At present it is possible only for humans to know themselves and software assistance can actually cloud one's self understanding. That is, self knowledge needs to come from within the human being, and it is such knowledge that is likely to drive future progress in computer-assisted policymaking, as indicated by the arrows outwards from 'emotions' in figure 10.2.

Remember, however, that rather than contribute only peripherally as at present, it is possible that software will one day help us to know ourselves better – at a more intimate level. Such progress possibly depends on advances being made in the human 'gene mapping' project. It will be interesting to see what transpires in years to come.

References

Ackoff, R. L. (1978) *The Art of Problem Solving*. New York: Wiley.

Ackoff, R. L. (1979) Resurrecting the future of Operations Research. *Journal of the Operational Research Society*, **30**, pp. 189-199.

Ackoff, R. L. (1981) *Creating the Corporate Future*. New York: Wiley.

Aiken, M., Govindarajulu, C. D. and Horgan, D. (1995) Using a group decision support system for school-based decision making. *Education*, **115**(3), pp. 420-426.

Alexander, C. (1964) *Notes on the Synthesis of Form*. Harvard: Harvard University Press.

Alexander, C. (1972) A city is not a tree in Bell, G. and Tyrwhitt, J. (eds.) *Human Identity in the Urban Environment*. London: Penguin.

Aoki, Y., Osaragi, T. and Nagai, A. (1996) Use of the area dividing method to minimise expected error in land-use forecasts. *Environment and Planning B*, **23**(6), pp. 655-666.

Badiru, A. B., Pulat, P. S. and Kang, M. (1993) DDM: Decision support system for hierarchical dynamic decision making. *Decision Support Systems*, **10**(1), pp. 1-18.

Barr, A. and Feigenbaum, E. A. (1981) (eds.) *The Handbook of Artificial Intelligence*, Volume 1. London: Pitman.

Belton, V. and Elder, M.D. (1994) Decision support systems: learning from visual interactive modelling. *Decision Support Systems*, **12**(5), pp. 355-364

Best, J. B. (1992) *Cognitive Psychology*, 3rd ed. St Paul, Min: West.

Bolan, R. (1967) Emerging views of planning. *Journal of the American Institute of Planners*, **33**(3), pp. 233-245.

Bolan, R. (1974) Mapping the planning theory terrain, in Godschalk, D. R. (ed.) *Planning in America: Learning from Turbulence*. Chicago: American Institute of Planners.

Bond, A. H. and Gasser, L. (eds.) (1988) *Readings in Distributed Artificial Intelligence*. Los Altos, CA: Morgan Kaufmann.

Boritz, J. E. (1983) *Planning for the Internal Audit Function*. Altamonte Springs, FL: Institute of Internal Auditors Research Foundation.

Bowers, J. M. and Benford S. D. (eds.) (1991) *Studies in Computer Supported Cooperative Work*. Amsterdam: North Holland.

Brans, J. and Mareschal, B. (1994) The PROMCALC and GAIA decision support system for multicriteria decision aid. *Decision Support Systems*, **12**(4), pp. 297-310.

Buffa, F., Marzano, G. and Norese, M. (1996) MACRAME: a modelling methodology in multifactor contexts. *Decision Support Systems* **17**(4), pp. 331-343.

Bui, T. (1992) Building DSS for negotiators: a three-step design process. *IEEE*, pp. 164-173.

Burle de Figueiredo, J. and Kaya, Y. (1972) Effort satisfaction analysis. *Futures*, **4** (4), pp. 314-324.

Burrough, P. A. and McDonnell, R. A. (1998) *Principles of Geographical Information Systems*. Oxford: Oxford University Press.

Cacez-Kecmanovic, D. (1994) Organizational activity support systems. *Decision Support Systems*, **12**(5), pp. 365-379.

Campbell, J. (1989) *The Improbable Machine*. New York: Simon and Schuster.

Carbonell, J. G. (ed.) (1990) *Machine Learning: Paradigms and Methods*. Cambridge, Mass: MIT Press.

Carter, G. M., Murray, M. P., Walker, R. G. and Walker, W. E. (1992) Building *Organizational Decision Support Systems*. Boston: Academic Press.

Cartwright, T. (1973) Problems, solutions, strategies. *Journal of the American Institute of Planners*, **39**(3), pp. 179-187.

Cartwright, T. J. (1992) STRAD: a new role for computers in planning. *Computers, Environment and Urban Systems*, **16**, pp. 77-82.

Chambers, I. and Taylor, M. (1996) Planning with GENIE: a model for forecasting and decisionmaking. *Environment and Planning B*, **23**(6), pp. 697-710.

Checkland, P (1984) Rethinking a Systems Approach in Tomlinson, I (ed.) *Rethinking the Process of Operational Research and Systems Analysis*. Oxford: Pergamon.

Checkland, P. (1989) Soft systems methodology, in Rosenhead, J. (ed.) *Rational Analysis for a Problematic World*. Chichester: Wiley, pp. 71-100.

Chidambaram, L., Bostrom, R. P. and Wynne, B. F. (1991) The impact of GDSS on group development. *Journal of Management Information Systems*, **7**(3), pp. 7-27.

Cherniak, C. (1986) *Minimal Rationality*. Cambridge, Mass: Bradford/MIT Press.

Christensen, K. S. (1985) Coping with uncertainty in planning. *American Planning Association Journal*, Winter, pp. 63-73.

Churchman, C. W. (1968) *The Systems Approach*. New York: Delaconte Press.

Claxton, K. T. (1970) *Wilhelm Roentgen*. Geneva: Heron Books

Coffee, P. (1994) Software smartens up: neural network and genetic algorithm tools can help companies struggling to keep track of data. *PC Week*, **11**(25), pp. 122.

Coffee, P. and Moser, K. D. (1990) Sygenex Inc. Criterium 1.0. *PC Week*, **7**(25), pp. 120-122.

Collins, H. (1992) Will machines ever think? *New Scientist*, June 30, pp. 36-40.

Colson, G. and Mareschal, B. (1994) JUDGES: a descriptive group decision support system for the ranking of items. *Decision Support Systems*, **12**(5), pp. 391-404.

Cope, R. G. (1989) *High Involvement Strategic Planning: When People and their Ideas Matter*. Oxford: Basil Blackwell.

Coursey, D. (1992) Groupware speeds decision making. *InfoWorld*, **14**(27), p. 43.

Csaki, P., Rapcsak, T., Turchanyi, P. and Vermes, M. (1995) R and D for group decision aid in Hungary by WINGDSS, a Microsoft Windows based, group decision support system. *Decision Support Systems*, **14**(3), pp. 205-217.

Cunningham, I. (1994) *The Wisdom of Strategic Learning: The Self-Managed Learning Solution*. London: McGraw-Hill.

Curley, B. (1997) Decision-support package stands to boost selling at National City. *Bank Systems and Technology*, **34**(6), p. 54.

Dale, B. and Cooper, C. (1992) *Total Quality and Human Resources*. Cambridge, Mass: Blackwell.

Daly, N. R. (1996) Reaching board decisions online. *Association Management*, **48**(1), pp. 43-48.

David, F. R. (1997) *Concepts of Strategic Management*. Upper Saddle River, NJ: Prentice Hall.

Davidson, C. (1997) Trust me, Iím an expert. *New Scientist*, **156**(2111), pp. 26-30.

Dickey, J. W. (1995) *CyberQuest: Background Theory and Experiences*. Norwood, NJ: Ablex.

Doran, J. (1992) Distrbuted AI and its applications, in Marik, V., Stepankova, O. and Trappl, R. (eds.) *Advanced Topics in Artificial Intelligence*. Berlin: Springer-Verlag, pp. 368-372.

Eden, C. (1989) Using cognitive mapping for strategic options development and analysis (SODA), in Rosenhead, J. (ed.) *Rational Analysis for a Problematic World*. Chichester: John Wiley, pp. 21-42.

Eden, C. (1992) Strategy development as a social process. *Journal of Management Studies*, **29**(6), pp. 799-811.

Edwards, J.S. and Finlay, P.N. (1997) *Decision Making with Computers: the Spreadsheet and Beyond*. London: Pitman.

Ekenberg, L., Danielson, M. and Boman, M. (1997) Imposing security constraints on agent-based decision support. *Decision Support Systems*, **20**(1), pp. 3-15.

Epinasse, B. (1994) A cognitivist model for decision support: COGNITA project, a problem formulation assistant. *Decision Support Systems*, **12**(4), pp. 277-286.

Experience in Software Inc. (1998a) *Project KickStart*. Berkeley (company brochure).

Experience in Software Inc. (1998b) *The Idea Generator*. Berkeley (company brochure).

Experience in Software Inc. (1998c) *The Art of Negotiating* Berkeley (company brochure).

Experience in Software Inc. (1998d) *The Digital MBA* Berkeley (company brochure).

Fersko-Weiss, H. (1989) High-end project managers make the plans. *PC Magazine*, **8**(9), pp. 155-177.

Fersko-Weiss, H. (1990) Easy planning with *Project Outlook*. *PC Magazine* **9**(15), p. 354.

Fetzer, J. H. (1990) *Artificial Intelligence: Its Scope and Limits*. Dordrecht: Kluwer.

Feuche, M. (1990) AT&T employs CASE strategy for competitive edge. *MIS Week* **11**(6), 17

Fraser, N.M. & Hipel K.W. (1988) Negotiation support systems for conflict analysis. *Management Decision Support Systems*, 13-21

Frentzen, J. (1990) Software tools support decision making. *PC Week*, **7**(25), pp. 119-122.

Forrester, J. W. (1969) *Urban Dynamics*. Cambridge, Mass: MIT Press.

Forrester, J. W. (1973) *World Dynamics*. Cambridge, Mass: Wright-Allen Press.

French, S. (1986) *Decision Theory: An Introduction to the Mathematics of Rationality*. Chichester: Ellis Horwood.

French, S. E. (1989) *Readings in Decision Analysis*. London: Chapman and Hall.

Friend, J. K. (1983) Reflections on rationality in strategic choice. *Environment and Planning B*, **10**(1), pp. 63-69.

Friend, J. K. (1989) The strategic choice approach, in Rosenhead, J. (ed.) *Rational Analysis for a Problematic World*. Chichester: John Wiley, pp. 121-157.

Friend, J. K. (1992) New directions in software for strategic choice. *European Journal of Operational Research*, **61**, pp. 154-164.

Friend, J. K. and Hickling, A. (1997) *Planning under Pressure*, 2nd ed. New York: Pergamon.

Friend, J. K. and Jessop, W. N. (1969) *Local Government and Strategic Choice*. London: Tavistock.

Gibbons, R. (1992) *A Primer in Game Theory*. New York: Harvester/Wheatsheaf.

Goodstein, L. D., Nolan, T. M. and Pfeiffer, J. W. (1993) *Applied Strategic Planning*. New York: McGraw-Hill.

Gottesman, B. Z. (1995) QuestMap: lines of communications. *PC Magazine*, **14**(20), p. 218.

Haefele, J.W. (1962) *Creativity and Innovation*. London: Reinhold

Hampden-Turner, C. (1970) *Radical Man*. Cambridge, Mass: Schankman.

Harrison, J. S. and St John, C. H. (1994) *Strategic Management of Organizations and Stakeholders*. Minneapolis/St Paul: West.

Hayes, K. E. and Fotheringham, A. S. (1984) *Gravity and Spatial Interaction Models*. Beverley Hills, CA: Sage.

Henig, M. I. (1996) Solving MCDM problems: process concepts. *Journal of Multi-criteria Decision Analysis*, **5**, pp. 3-21.

Hill, M. (1972) A goals-achievement matrix for evaluating alternative plans, in Robinson, I. M. (ed.) *Decision-making in Urban Planning*. Beverly Hills, CA: Sage.

Hodge, G. L., Canada, J. R. and Masri, W. R. (1992) Low cost micro computer software for multi-attribute decision analysis. *Engineering Economist*, **37**(2), pp. 184-192.

Hoos, I. R. (1972) *Systems Analysis in Public Policy: a Critique*. Los Angeles, CA: University of California Press.

Hoos, I. R. (1974) Can systems analysis solve social problems? *Datamation*, June, pp. 82-92.

Hornby, R. E. and Golder, P. A. (1994) SDP: A strategic DSS. *Decision Support Systems*, **11**(1), pp. 45-51.

Howard, N. (1989) The manager as politician and general: the metagame approach to analysing cooperation and conflict, in Rosenhead, J. (ed.) *Rational Analysis for a Problematic World*. Chichester: John Wiley, pp. 239-261.

Howe, E. (1994) *Acting on Ethics in City Planning*. New Brunswick, NJ: Center for Urban Policy Research.

http://www.gryphonsystems.com

http://www.checkmateplan.com

http://www.fbs.hw.ac.uk

http://www.palisade.com

http://www.planmagic.com

http://www.strategic-dynamics.com

Humphry, S. (1992) Tools help objectify decision making: managers can quantify risks. *PC Week*, **9**(10), pp. 113-116.

Hussey, D. E. (1995) *Rethinking Strategic Management*. Chichester: John Wiley.

Janis, I. L. and Mann, L. (1977) *Decision-making: A Psychological Analysis of Conflict, Choice and Commitment*. New York: Macmillan.

Jarke, M., Jelassi, A. and Shakun, M. (1987) MEDIATOR : towards a negotiation support system. *European Journal of Operational Research*, **31**, pp. 314-334.

Kelly, S. (1994) *Data Warehousing: The Route to Mass Customisation*. Chichester: John Wiley.

Kepner, C. H. (1981) *The New Rational Manager*. Princeton, NJ: Princeton Research Press.

Kepner-Tregoe Inc. (1986) *DECISION AIDE II Manual*. Princeton, NJ: Kepner-Tregoe Inc.

Kersten, C. (1985) NEGO: group decision support system. *Information and Management*, **8**, pp. 237-246.

Kiang, M. Y., Kulkarni, U. R. and Tam, K. Y. (1995) Self-organizing map network as an interactive clustering tool – an application to group technology. *Decision Support Systems*, **15**(4), pp. 351-374.

Kitano, H. (1996) Nausicaa and the Sirens: A tale of two intelligent autonomous agents. *IEEE Expert*, **11**(6), pp. 60-62.

Kiss, L. N. M., J. and Nadeau, R. (1994) ELECCALC – an interactive software for modelling the decision maker's preferences. *Decision Support Systems*, **12**(5), pp. 31-326.

Klosterman, R. E. (1997) The What If? Collaborative planning support system, in *Proceedings of the Fifth International Conference on Computers in Urban Planning and Urban Management*, Mumbai, 1997. New Delhi: Narosa Publishing House, Volume 2, pp. 692-702.

Knack, R. (1994) Brainstorming by byte. *Planning*, **60**(1), pp. 19-23.

Landsbergen, D. (1997) Decision quality, confidence and commitment with expert systems. *Journal of Public Administration Research and Theory*, **7**(1), pp. 131-158.

Larson, M. (1997) Manage your project before it manages you. *Quality*, **36**(9), pp. 64-67.

Levin, C. (1993) Patient, heal thyself. *PC Magazine*, **12**(5), p. 32.

Lim, L. and Benbasat, I. (1993) A theoretical perspective of negotiation support systems. *Journal of Management Information Systems*, **9**(3), pp. 27-44.

Matwin, S., Szpakowicz, S., Koperczac, Z., Kersten, G. E. and Michalowski, W. (1989) Negoplan: an expert system shell for negotiation support. *IEEE Expert*, **4**(4), pp. 50-62.

Management Software Association (1994) The strategist's software directory. *The Journal of Business Strategy*, **15**(1), pp. 48 *et seq.*

McClelland, J. L. and Rumelhart, D. E. (1988) *Explorations in Parallel Distributed Processing*. Cambridge, Mass: MIT Press.

Menegolo, L. (1996) *NAIADE* ISPRA Site. Joint Research Centre for the European Commission.

Miley, M. (1993) Agent technology. *MacWEEK*, **7**(16), pp. 41-46.

Miller, G. A. (1956) The magical number seven plus or minus two: some limits to our capacity for processing information. *The Psychological Review*, **63**, pp. 81-97.

Mintzberg, H. (1994) *The Rise and Fall of Strategic Planning*. London: Prentice-Hall.

Mochlman, T., Lesser, V. and Buteau, B. (1992) Decentralized negotiation: An approach to the distributed planning problem. *Group Decision and Negotiation*, **2**, pp. 16-191.

Mockler, R. (1991) A catalogue of commercially available software for strategic planning. *Planning Review*, **19**(3), pp. 28-35.

Moormann and Lochte-Holtgreven (1993) An approach for an integrated DSS for strategic planning. *Decision Support Systems*, **10**(4), pp. 401-411.

Myers, P. R. and Briggs, I. (1993) *Gifts Differing: Understanding Personality Type*. Palo Alto, CA: CPP Books.

Noorderhaven, N. G. (1995) *Strategic Decision Making*. Wokingham, Berks: Addison-Wesley.

Nelson, R. R. (1974) Intellectualizing about the moon-ghetto metaphor: a study of the current malaise of rational analysis of social problems. *Policy Sciences*, **5**, pp. 375-414.

Nelson, M. M. and Illingworth, W. T. (1991) *A Practical Guide to Neural Nets*. Reading, Mass: Addison-Wesley.

Nuttin, J. (1984) *Motivation, Planning and Action*. Hillsdale, NJ: Leuven University Press/ Lawrence Erlbaum.

Openshaw, S. (1997*a*) *Artificial Intelligence in Geography*. Chichester: John Wiley.

Openshaw, S. (1997*b*) Building fuzzy spatial interaction models, in Fischer, M.

and Getis, A. (eds.) *Recent Developments in Spatial Analysis*. Berlin: Springer, pp. 360-383.

Patterson, J. (1976) The Changing Nature of Planning: from Philosopher King to Municipal Dogcatcher. *Proceedings of the 14th Biennial Congress of the Royal Australian Planning Institute*. Adelaide: RAPI.

Peschel, J.(1996) *DecideRight* relieves anxiety of passing judgement. *InfoWorld* **18**(34), p. 86.

Pinker, J. (1994) *The Language Instinct*. London: Penguin.

Pinson, S. D., Louca, J. A. and Moraitis, P. A (1997) Distributed decision support system for strategic planning. *Decision Support Systems*, **20**(1), pp. 35-51.

Quah, T., Tan, C., Raman, K. S. and Srinivasan, B. (1996) Towards integrating rule-based expert systems and neural networks. *Decision Support Systems*, **17**(2), pp. 99-118.

Radding, A. (1995) Support decision makers with a data warehouse. *Datamation*, **41**(5), pp. 53-57.

Raiffa, H. (1970) *Decision Analysis: Introductory Lectures on Choices under Uncertainty*, 2nd ed. Menlo Park, CA: Addison-Wesley,

Rangaswamy, A. and Lilien, G. L. (1997) Software tools for new product development. *Journal of Marketing Research*, **34**(1), pp. 177-184.

Rawlinson, J. G. (1994) *Creative Thinking and Brainstorming*. Aldershot: Gower.

Rickards, T. (1988) *Creativity at Work*. Brookfield, Vermont: Gower.

Riesbeck, C. K. and Schank, R. C. (1989) *Inside Case-based Reasoning*. Hillsdale, NJ: Lawrence Erlbaum.

Rittel, W. J. and Webber, M. M. (1973) Dilemmas in a general theory of planning. *Journal of Policy Sciences*, **3**, pp. 155-169.

Rittel, W. J. and Webber, M. M. (1974) Wicked problems, in Cross, N., Elliott, D. and Roy, P. (eds.) *Man-made Futures*. London: Hutchinson, pp. 272-280.

Rooney, P. (1997) Milagro K.net ActiveX controls ease group-decision making. *PC Week*, **14**(2), p. 41.

Rosenhead, J. (ed.) (1989*a*) *Rational Analysis for a Problematic World*. Chichester: John Wiley.

Rosenhead, J. (1989*b*) Introduction: old and new paradigms of analysis, in Rosenhead, J. (ed.) *Rational Analysis for a Problematic World*. Chichester: John Wiley, pp. 1-20.

Rosenhead, J. (1989*c*) Robustness analysis: keeping your options open, in Rosenhead, J. (ed.) *Rational Analysis for a Problematic World*. Chichester: John Wiley, pp. 193-218.

Rothfeder, J. (1985) *Minds over Matter*. New York: Simon and Schuster.

Rubenking, N. J. (1990) *BestChoice3*: low-cost decision support for complex problems. *PC Magazine*, **9**(4), p. 46.

Russo, J. E. and Shoemaker J. H. (1989) *Decision Traps: Ten Barriers to Brilliant Decision Making and How to Overcome Them*. New York: Doubleday.

Saaty, T. L. (1994) *Fundamentals of Decision Making and Priority Theory.* Pittsburgh: RWS Publications.

Saaty, T. L. (1996) *Decision Making with Dependence and Feedback: the Analytic Network Process.* Pittsburgh: RWS Publications.

Saaty, T. L. and Vargas, L. G. (1994) *Decision Making in Economic, Political, Social and Technological Environments with the Analytic Hierarchy Process.* Pittsburgh: RWS Publications.

Sacerdoti, E. D. (1977) *A Structure for Plans and Behaviour.* New York: Elsevier.

Samarasan, D. K. (1993) Analysis, modelling and the management of international negotiations. *Theory and Decision*, **34**, pp. 275-291.

Schank, R. (1984) *The Cognitive Computer.* Reading, Mass: Addison-Wesley.

Seiter, C. (1998) Affordable decision-making tool for managers. *PC World*, **16**(2), pp.118-119.

Seligman, D. (1996) Decisions, decisions. *Fortune*, **33**(5), pp. 137-137.

Serrano-Cinca, C. (1996) Self-organizing neural networks for financial diagnosis. *Decision Support Systems*, **17**(3), pp. 227-238.

Shaw, M. L. G. (1980) *On Becoming a Personal Scientist.* London and New York: Academic Press.

Sillince, J. (1986) *A Theory of Planning.* Aldershot, Hants: Gower.

Simon, H. A. (1981) *The Science of the Artificial*, 2nd ed. Cambridge Mass.: MIT Press.

Simon, H. A. (1997) *Administrative Behaviour*, 4th ed. New York: The Free Press.

Simons, G. (1983) *Are Computers Alive?: Evolution and Life Forms.* Brighton, Sussex: Harvester Press.

Small, C. H. (1992) Innovative software stimulates engineering creativity. *EDN*, **37** (3), pp. 59-64.

Smith, P. N. (1982a) Multidomensional environmental evaluation: aspects of current research. *Queensland Planning Papers* (Department of Regional and Town Planning). Brisbane: University of Queensland, pp. 7-15.

Smith, P. N. (1982b) Fuzzy multiobjective plan evaluation with multiple interest groups. *Queensland Planning Papers* (Department of Regional and Town Planning). Brisbane: University of Queensland, pp. 16-32.

Smith, J., Kenley, R. and Wyatt, R. (1998) Evaluating the client briefing problem: an exploratory study. *Engineering, Construction and Architectural Management*, **5** (4), 387-399.

Solzhenitsyn, A. (1971) *Stories and Prose Poems.* London: Penguin.

Starr, P. (1994) Seductions of Sim. *The American Prospect,* Spring (17), pp. 19-30.

Stewart, T. J. (1992) A critical survey of the status of multiple criteria decision making theory and practice. *OMEGA,* **20** (5/6), pp. 569-586.

Stein, S. M. and Harper T. L. (1996) Planning theory for environmentally sustainable planning. *Geography Research Forum,* **16**, pp. 80-100.

Stove, D. C. (1982) *Popper and After: Four Modern Irrationalists.* New York: Pergamon.

Sycara, K. P. (1993) Machine learning for intelligent support of conflict resolution. *Decision Support Systems*, **10**, pp.121-136.

Sycara, K., Pannu, A., Williamson, M., Zeng, D. and Decker, K. (1996) Distributed intelligent agents *IEEE Expert* , **11** (6), pp. 36-47.

Tesauro, G. (1995) TD-GAMMON: a self-teaching backgammon program in Murray, A. F. (ed.) *Applications of Neural Networks.* Dordrecht, Netherlands: Kluwer, pp. 267-285.

Thierauf, R. J. (1988) *User-oriented Decision Support Systems: Accent on Problem Finding.* Englewood Cliffs, New Jersey: Prentice Hall.

Thierauf, R. J. (1993) *Creative Computer Software for Strategic Thinking and Decision Making.* Wesport, Connecticut: Quorum Books.

Turkle, S. (1984) *The Second Self: Computers and the Human Spirit.* New York: Simon and Schuster.

Von Bertalanfy, L. (1968) *General Systems Theory: Foundations, Development, Applications.* New York: Braziller.

Von Winterfeldt, D. and Edwards, W. (1986) *Decision Analysis and Behavioural Research.* Cambridge: Cambridge University Press.

Van Grundy, A. B. (1985) *Techniques of Structured Problem Solving,* 2nd ed. New York: Van Nostrand Reinhold.

Velox Systems Corporation (1998) *SMARTLINK 2000.* Wyomissing PA, (company brochure).

Waddington, C. H. (1977) *Tools for Thought.* New York: Basic Books.

Watson, S. R. and Buede, D. M. (1987) *Decision Synthesis: The Princples and Practice of Decision Analysis.* Cambridge: Cambridge University Press.

Webber, M. M. (1983) The myth of rationality: development planning revisited. *Environment and Planning B,* **10** (1), pp. 89-99.

Weizenbaum, J. (1976) *Computer Power and Human Reason.* San Francisco: W.H. Freeman.

Westland, J. C. (1995) Bayesian alternatives to neural computing. *IEEE Transactions on Systems, Man and Cybernetics,* **25** (10), pp. 59-68.

Whittington, R. (1993) *What is Strategy? – and does it matter?* London: Routledge.

Wierzbicki, A. D., Krus, L. and Makowski, M. (1993) The role of multi-objective optimization in negotiation and mediation support. *Theory and Decision,* **34**, pp. 201-214.

Wilkenfeld, J., Kraus, S., Holley, K. M. and Harris, M. A. (1995) GENIE: A decision support system for crisis negotiations. *Decision Support Systems,* **14**(4), pp. 369-391.

Wilson, G. (1993) *Problem Solving and Decision Making.* London: Kogan Page.

Winograd, T. and Flores, F. (1986) *Understanding Computers and Cognition: New Foundations for Design.* Norwood, New Jersey: Ablex.

Wright, G. (1984) *Behavioural Decision Theory.* London: Penguin.

Wyatt, R. G. (1978) The death and life of great Australian planners. *Polis,* **5**(2), pp. 33-37.

Wyatt, R. (1980) Complexity: policymakers' divider and possible conqueror. *Environment and Planning B,* **7**, pp. 265-272.

Wyatt, R.G. (1988) Removing emotional distortion from expert systems. *Proceedings of the IEEE Conference on Systems, Man and Cybernetics,* Beijing, pp. 820-823.

Wyatt, R. (1989) *Intelligent Planning.* London: Unwin Hyman.

Wyatt, R. (1996a) Transcending the retreat from rationality. *Environment and Planning B,* **23** (6), pp. 639-654.

Wyatt, R. G. (1996b) Evaluating strategies using a simulated neural network. *Environment and Planning B,* **23**(6), pp. 685-696.

Wyatt, R. G. (1996c) Strategic planning using neural network-based, Delphi workshop software. Presented to American Collegiate Schools of Planning Conference, Toronto, Canada and System Dynamics '96, Boston, USA, July.

Wyatt, R. (1997a) Reversing decision support systems to reveal differences in human strategizing behaviour, in Timmermans, H. (ed.) *Decision Support Systems in Urban Planning.* London: E & FN Spon, pp. 87-106.

Wyatt, R. (1997b) Consistency of planning style. *Proceedings of the Fifth International Conference on Computers in Urban Planning and Urban Management* Mumbai, 1997, New Delhi: Narcosa Publishing House, Volume 1, pp. 181-192.

Yocum, K. R. (1990) Business Plan Toolkit. *PC-Computing,* **3**(3), pp. 161-162.

Zadeh, L. A. (1986) Is probability theory sufficient for dealing with uncertainty in AI?: A negative view in Kanal, L. N. and Lemmer, J. F. (eds.) *Uncertainty in Artificial Inteligence.* Amsterdam: North-Holland, pp. 103-116.

Index

ACA package 42
acceptability of policies 145
actors in the *Expert Choice* package 145
Advia Danprod package 41
Advia Decide and Manage package 65
Advia Strategic Activity Costing package
    61
Alacrity Strategy package 65
alternatives 138, 222
analysis paralysis xvi, xviii
analysis-based policymaking xvi
analytic hierarchy 43
anti technology xx, 70
anticipate 20, 28, 208, 217, 228
    contrast with simulate 44
anticipating policy choices 181
applied outcomes of theories xii
arbitrariness
    when scoring 106, 196
    within policymaking 46
artefacts' effect on human behaviour 3
artificial intelligence 82
@RISK package 46
Automan 2.0 package 34

Benchmarking Software package 62
Best Alternative package 34
BestChoice3 package 34
boosterism 76
boredom in policymaking xviii
Braincel package 88
brainstorming 14, 32
    electronic versus human 41
    memory-based 100
    online 55
    software for 41
    need for 194
    underlying assumption of 100
breakthroughs 11
BUNDOPT package 42
Business Development Expert package 61
Business Insight package 65
Business Policy Toolkit package 63
Business Wits package 34

CART package 60
CESA package 83
CHECKMATE package 65
chess xi

choices 31
choose 20, 28, 43, 197, 217, 227, 228
clarity of methods 57
client identification within the *CyberQuest*
    package 94
client identification within the *Strategizer*
    package 169
clustering 98
    neural 182
    of decision areas 118
    of ideas 98, 99
    of users of a package 168
COGNITA package 40, 81
cognitive mapping 39
cognitive science 79
combining policymaking packages 214
Commander Prism package 63
community wisdom 217
Competitive Advantage package 63
complexity 7
    handling of 164
    of modern civilization xv
    of policymaking 59
computer mediated communication 56
computer programs 2
CONAN package 59
Confidence Factor package 35
conflict management 58
    within the *STRAD* package 117
consciousness 1, 226
Consensus Builder package 34
control of destiny xv
COPE package 39
creativity 7
    computer-aided amplification of ,
    143
    enhancement 194
credentialism 62
CRISP package 66
criteria 28, 33, 34, 110, 202, 213, 222, 225
    from operations research 178
    from workshops 179
    philosophical 179
    scientific 177
    used within the *Strategizer* package
    177
Criteria Rank package 34
Criterium package 33
critical path analysis 38

Crosstarget package 62
Crystal Ball package 64
CyberQuest package 92-113, 192-215,
    217, 219, 226
    applications of 93
    history of 92
    sequence of steps within 95

dangers of popularity 124
Data Desk package 61
data mining 60
DATA package 37
data warehousing 59
DDM package 43
DecideRight package 33
Decision Aide II package 29
Decision Analysis package 33
decision making 5, 228
Decision Pad package 34
decision science xvii
decision support 5
    over-ambitious systems 51
    planning support systems 5
    software 48
decision tree analysis 37
DecisionMaker package 68
Decisions?/Decisions! package 33
Definitive Scenario package 52
DENEGOT package 68
descriptor pairs 99
design-based policymaking xvi
detrimental effect of modelling 52
Diagnostic Audit package 41
distributed computing 53, 88, 174
dominance 35
DPL package 61
DSDSS package 53
dynamic systems analysis 45

economic rationalism xxi, 76
ELECCALC package 44
Eliza program 56
emotions 1, 226, 228
Enlisted Force Management System
    package 48
equilibrium 1
evaluation xvii, 36, 167, 218, 224, 227
    literature 208
    of policies 202
    of schemes 123
    overload 106
Evolver package 86
Execustat package 61
expected utility 37, 144, 146

non-correspondence with human
    behaviour 147
Expert Choice package 137-164, 192-215,
    220, 227
    applications of 137
    'distributive' mode of scoring in 151
    handling inconsistency in 152
    handling large problems with 162
    history of 137
    'ideal' mode of scoring in 151
    multiplication of scores in 147
    optimizing with 162
    rescoring in 156
    sensitivity testing in 156
expert systems 65, 82
    research into the benefits of 83
Extend package 62

facilitators 13,
flexibility in policymaking 153
focusing 3, 6
    within the *STRAD* package 119
4cast2 package 63
Forecast Pro package 63
Forest package 60
free will 1, 226
fuzzy logic 87

GAIA package 44, 57
game theory 56
gameware 56
genetic algorithms 85
    applications of 87
    for stockmarket prediction 86
GENIE package 69, 86
goals 16, 118
    amalgamating 200
goals hierarchy 24, 26, 141, 218, 226
    components of 27
    correct terminology to use with 28
    timelessness of 32
    within the *Expert Choice* package
    141
    within the *Strategizer* package 167
GOALWARE package 29,
group attitudes 183
group think 179
GroupSystemsV package 55
groupware 55
GroupWorks package 55

hidden agendas 117
human interaction 11
human interest xxi

human personality 17
    dimension of 18
    types of 17
humanism xx
IdeaFisher package 42, 92
ideas 98
    clustering of 98, 99
    generation of 193
    packaging of 109, 196
    ruling out 196
    screening of 105
if-then rules 34, 82
impact of decision areas on comparison
    areas 125
inaccuracy 124
inconsistency 152
influence diagrams 61
intelligence 1
intelligent agents 88
intransitive scores (see inconsistency)
ISES package 68
IThink package 45

K.net package 55
Key words 98
    matching against a data base 92, 100
KnowledgeSeeker package 61

Lateral thinking 101, 171, 216
learning 182, 213
Life long learning 78
Lightyear package 34, 222, 225, 228
locked policies 133
Lotus Notes package 55

MACRAME package 39
ManagePro package 63
MAPS package 64
Market Dynamics package 64
Marketing Manager package 41
MARKSTAT package 63
MATCH package 68
MATS package 35
MCBARG package 68
MDS package 35
MEDIATOR package 68
meetings 96
messes 7, 30
*Micr-Mulcre Interactive Decision Support
    System* package 35
Mindlink package 41
MindLink Problem Solver package 42
mindware 56
MktSim package 64

modellers 13
*Models for Strategic Management
    Software* package 29
Monte Carlo simulation 64
morality 180
multi agent systems 90
    problems with 91
multi-criteria decision making xvii
multi-criteria software 33
musts 30

NAIADE package 35, 44, 220
NamePro package 41
needs 30
NEGO package 68
NEGOPOLICY package 68
negotiation support systems 67
NEGOTIATOR package 68
Negotiator Pro package 69
NEULONET package 84
neural networks 83, 185
    applications of 87
    disadvantage of 85
    used for clustering people 182
    used within the *Strategizer* package
    182, 188
new product development 41
numbers 146
    dangers in policymaking 146
    interval scale 204
    ratio scale 150, 204
    the *Expert Choice* package's use of
    204

OASS package 55
Open Policy package 38
operations research 72
    contrasts with soft systems
    methodology 73
optimization 162, 178
    using spreadsheets for 53
options 5
    combining 123
    identifying 138
    identifying within the *Strategizer*
    package 169

P/G% package 35
pair-wise comparisons 34, 43
    tedium of 207
    within the *Expert Choice* package
    149
paradigm shifts 70
path-finding algorithms 37

patience 140
PC Prism package 63
personal responsibility xxi
PERSUADER package 68
philosophers 13
planning 4
    application-oriented 25
    as a sport 5
    core meaning of 4
    human-oriented 11
    identifying styles of 184
    overlap with simulation 5, 36
    participatory 40, 210, 212
    prescriptive 6
    styles of 16
    types of 4
Policy Magic Analysis package 65,
policymaking 10,
    'top-down' versus 'bottom-up', 171
    abstract versus practical xx
    academic attitudes towards xx
    automatic xv
    balanced 12, 20
    bringing clarity to 95
    circularity within 45, 209
    computer-aided versus human 81
    deception in 198, 199
    decisive 80
    dedication within 42
    detailed versus 'big picture', 197
    different emphases xii
    discipline in xix
    excitement of xix
    fashion in 77
    fuzzy 88
    generic techniques of i
    gurus in xi, xvii,
    human-oriented 2
    inaccuracy in 124
    increasing the originality of 106
    learning lessons from programs
    about ix
    luxury of 31
    management of 202
    maximizing the effectiveness of xix
    modes of 14, 108
    naturalness of xix
    need for improvement in xv
    novelty in 75
    phases of 28, 193,
    pivotal act of xviii
    preparedness for 77
    principles of xvii
    projects 30

    reflection as part of 209
    saleable 110
    sequence within 209
    styles of 12
    subjective xvii
    Thierauf's requirements for 66
    traditional approaches towards xvi
    underlying methods of xvi
    unsolvability of 8
Policymaking Computer Model software
    29
Portfolio Plus package 65
PREFCAL package 68
prejudice 167
premature specificity 172
Premium Solver! package 86
problem decomposition 24, 31, 218, 226
    within the *Expert Choice* package
    141
    within the *STRAD* package 120
    within the *Strategizer* package 167
problems 6,
    close-ended 7
    dimensions 97
    dissolving 8
    fuzzy 7, 9
    insight 7, 8
    open-ended 7
    strategic 7
    tactical 7
    tame 7
    vicious 7, 9
    wicked 7, 8
Profiler 2000 package 60
Project Outlook package 38
Project package 38
PROMCALC method 44

Q+E package 60
Q1000 package 62
quality control 62
QuestMap package 55
QuickKeys package 90

rating of alternatives within the *Expert
    Choice* package 146
rating of options within the *STRAD*
    package 125, 127
rational comprehensive approach 24, 26,
    70, 218
    relationship with operations research
    73
    stages of 72
    steps within 89

recording issues 116
research frontier software xii
research frontier technology 89
Resource Allocation package 63
risk analysis 46
risks 32
robustness analysis 75
role playing 32
ruling out ideas 196
ruling out inappropriate methods 195
ruling out inappropriate policies 122

SAM package 68
scenarios 219, 227
        accommodation by the *Expert
        Choice* package 144
scheduling 37
        software for 47
science 175
scientists 13
        secrecy amongst 84
scoring 203, 223
        'distributive' mode of 151
        'ideal' mode of 151
        need for consciousness when 160
        need for varied methods of 156, 176
        of alternatives within the *Expert
        Choice* package 146
        of options within the *STRAD*
        package 125
        of options within the *Strategizer*
        package 175
        of schemes within the *STRAD*
        package 129
        reviewing 154
SDMS package 56
SDP package 66
SDSS package 51
self improving packages 186, 190
selfconscious societies xvi
sensitivity testing 156
        dynamic 156
        gradient 159
sensitivity testing using spreadsheets 53
Seriatim package 34
short versus long responses 94
significance 127
SimCity package 54
simulation 1
        true nature of 54
situation structuring 31, 138
Smart Forecasts I package 64
SMARTLINK 2000 package 66
social programs 9

SODA method 39
Soft Pac Solutions package 35
soft systems analysis 16
soft systems methodology 72
        problems with 74
software 2
        business 61
        classification of 22
        credibility of commercial 64
        dedicated 38
        definitions of 9
        didactic power of ix
        domain-specific 60
        feeling-based 26, 30, 51, 66, 193,
        211
        flight simulator 46
        for business forecasting 63
        for exploring data 61
        for marketing 41
        for project management 38
        poor performance of 107
        role in policymaking of xi
        styles of 19, 38
        substituting for humans xi
        thinking-based 27, 30, 33, 51, 66,
        193, 211
        typical evolution of xi
        unique characteristics of 4
stake holder analysis 55, 67
STRAD package 114-136, 192-215, 221,
        227
        applications of 115
        comparison areas in 117
        decision areas in 115
        elimination of schemes in 129
        history of 114
        option bars in 121
        progress reporting in 135
        schemes in 123, 128
        uncertainty areas in 117
Strat-Analyst package 29,
strategic planning
        difference to policymaking 10
        different styles of 10
        effectiveness of ixi
        essence of 10
        formalization of 10
        textbooks about xi
strategies 9,
Strategizer package 165-191, 192-215,
        219, 220
        anticipation of others' policy choices
        in 181, 185
        applications of 166

ensuring self improvement in 186
evaluation criteria used in 177
history of 165
learning mechanism in 182
scoring in 175
Strategy Analyst package 29
Strategy Roundtable Enterprise package 65
Stratplan package 54
sub-goals 5, 141
    amalgamating 200
    different names for 27
    limiting the number of 199
    types of 199
SUPERTREE package 29
synthesizing 9

taking refuge in research 34
TeamFocus package 55
TeamKit/VM package 55
Tempo II Plus package 90
text understanding 82
The Art of Negotiating package 69
The Digital MBA package 54
The Idea Generator package 42
theory compared to practice 15
theory generation by computer 87
think 20, 28, 38, 193, 217, 226

Toprank package 52
Trees package 60
Turbo Spring-stat package 61
turbulence 78, 134

uncertainty 73, 117
    managing 131, 212, 221, 227
    margins of 128,
    prominence of 131,
    tractability of 132,
unselfconscious societies xvi

valance of evaluation criteria 177
Value Index package 34
Viewpoint package 38
VisionQuest package 55
visualizaton 79

wants 30
weights 225
    of comparison areas within the
    STRAD package 126,
'what-if' analysis 33, 224, 228
WhatIf? package 48
What's Best package 86
WINGDSS package 29
wisdom in software xi
workshops 179, 211